$3 Chicken Meals

Delicious, Low-Cost Dishes for Your Family

Ellen Brown

LYONS PRESS
Guilford, Connecticut

An imprint of Globe Pequot Press

To Suzanne Cavedon, Janet Morrell, and Kate Hamilton Pardee, my Nantucket "chick" friends, with whom I've shared countless great chicken meals as well as evenings sharing thoughts.

To buy books in quantity for corporate use
or incentives, call **(800) 962–0973**
or e-mail **premiums@GlobePequot.com**.

Lyons Press is an imprint of Globe Pequot Press.

Project editor: Jessica Haberman
Layout artist: Kevin Mak
Design: Sheryl P. Kober

Library of Congress Cataloging-in-Publication Data

Brown, Ellen.
 $3 chicken meals : delicious, low-cost dishes for your family / Ellen Brown.
   p. cm.
 Includes index.
 ISBN 978-1-59921-889-2
 1. Cookery (Chicken) 2. Low budget cookery. I. Title. II. Title: Three dollar chicken meals.
 TX750.5.C45B757 2010
 641.6'65—dc22

                                                          2009039432

Printed in the United States of America

10 9 8 7 6 5 4 3 2 1

Contents

Chapter 1: Saving Money at the Supermarket   **1**

This chapter is your recipe for eating better for less money. Here are all the tips you need to stretch your food budget via strategies for using coupons, shopping sales, and shopping your own pantry.

Chapter 2: Chicken 101   **16**

With any activity—including cooking chicken—you start with the basics, and those are what you'll find in this chapter. These include how to cut up your own chickens, how to make chicken stock, and many simple ways to flavor chickens—from instant spice rubs to long brines.

Chapter 3: $1 Nibbles and Noshes: Snacks, Hors d'Oeuvres, and Appetizers   **35**

The "little dishes" in this chapter aren't your main meal, although a few of them together could become one. These are the treats you take on a picnic, and the nibbles you put out for guests.

Chapter 4: Meals in a Bowl: Entree Soups from the World's Cauldrons   **69**

In the dictionary they should have chicken soup as part of the definition of "comfort food." And it's not just Americans who think so. The recipes in this chapter are for soups around the world—all of which are comforting as well as exciting.

Chapter 5: Slowly Does It: Dishes Made with Whole and Cut-Up Chickens   **96**

That large roast chicken you bake on a Sunday can serve as the basis for a few meals, but not all recipes for whole birds or their component parts take a lot of time. These dishes run the gamut of flavors and forms.

Chapter 6: The Daily Grind: Dishes Based on Ground Turkey and Chicken 124

Ground turkey is becoming the ground beef of the twenty-first century with good reason. It's as versatile as ground beef, and it contains less saturated fat at a lower cost. From meatloaf to chili and shepherd's pie, these hearty dishes will bring smiles.

Chapter 7: Redefining Fast Food: Dishes Made with Boneless, Skinless Chicken Breasts 156

There's nothing like the speed with which a meal made from boneless, skinless chicken can come to the table, and many recipes in this chapter are stir-fries that finish in merely minutes.

Chapter 8: Everything Tastes Better Outdoors: Grilled Chicken and Chicken Parts 174

Time to fire up the barbie! Whether grilling is a seasonal treat or a year-round option, grilled chicken is a delight. You'll find a range of ways to prepare it in this chapter, including many recipes for whole chickens.

Chapter 9: The Second Time Around: Dishes Made with Precooked Chicken 197

These dishes are not like television reruns; these are exciting premieres united by the fact that you're starting with the chicken already cooked—which means these recipes are on the table fast!

Chapter 10: Salad Daze: Entree Salads with Cold Veggies and Sometimes Hot Chicken 224

The ubiquitous chef's salad has a lot of competition these days, from many salads made from precooked chicken with vibrant dressings to a dazzling array of healthful dishes combining freshly cooked grilled chicken with crunchy vegetables.

Preface

If you're like most Americans, it's a safe bet that roughly three nights a week you're having some form of chicken for dinner. Maybe it's a big roaster filling the house with a luscious aroma on a Sunday afternoon. Or perhaps it's a quick stir-fry that will be ready in less time than the rice that goes with it on a weeknight. It could be a steamy bowl of soup with pieces of chicken joined by vegetables and other flavors to warm you in the winter; or maybe it's a salad topped with chicken for a crunchy, healthful meal on a warm summer night.

Even if you're not eating lots of chicken now, chances are that, if all the economic forecasts prove true, chicken will become a big part of your diet for many years to come. The era of "cheap food" in America is gone forever; even if the price of a gallon of gasoline remains less than the cost of a gallon of milk, food prices will probably not return to the bargain basement we knew and loved.

The causes for this increase in food costs are many and varied, and the reasons are global and not just national or local. For example, if corn farmers in Iowa are selling their crop to ethanol producers, then the cost of the remaining corn—which is used to feed chickens and pigs—escalates proportionally, and that leads to increases in the cost of the animals that ate the corn. If people in India's growing middle class finally have enough money to include more meats in their meals, then the cost of meat will rise in all countries; it's the simple equation of supply and demand. So the chicken—which is raised according to practices that maximize its value—is now our best buddy for a bargain.

But how times have changed! In the seventeenth century, King Henry IV of France's Prime Minister Sully used "a chicken in every pot" as a metaphor for the prosperity he wished for his citizens. In the 1600s, chickens then were associated with luxury rather than with fast food.

The equation of chicken with high living continued for some 300 years. It's ironic that the campaign promise of "a chicken in every pot and a car in every garage" was made by Herbert Hoover in 1928—a year before the start of the twentieth century's Great Depression. At that point, American per capita chicken consumption—less than 1 pound per person per year—could have literally fit in one pot!

Only around 1910 did Americans begin to raise chickens for egg production rather than for exhibition, so showpieces became dinner table centerpieces. The sea change occurred after World War II with the adoption of industrial farming practices, and by 1945 Americans were eating about 5 pounds per year. Chicken was still more expensive than lobster, shrimp, or steak, so chicken was reserved for Sunday dinner, holidays, or a special event.

As we all know, the chickens of today are frequently less expensive than the potatoes with which they're served. Chicken is the food that dominates the center of Americans' plates, with per capita consumption now topping 90 pounds. That figure has more than doubled since 1970, and beef consumption has declined as a result.

Why has the little bird eclipsed the big cow? There are many reasons. In addition to being inexpensive, chickens cook quickly compared to other forms of protein of the same weight; that's important in an era when time is almost as precious a commodity as money. And chicken is also healthier than red meats, discounting the saturated fat in the skin, or how those nutritional benefits are reduced or eliminated by deep-frying.

Chickens are not just in pots anymore; they're also cooking on the grill, topping salads, and floating in soups. We're always looking for new ways to serve chicken because we're doing so more often, and that's where *$3 Chicken Meals* comes in.

In this book you'll not only find more than 250 new ways to serve chicken (and some ways for ground turkey, too), you'll be learning how to save money when serving chicken; that's a skill you can then transfer to your current arsenal of chicken recipes, too.

Chicken is now sold most often as its component parts, with the leg and thigh quarters the least expensive option—although if you buy thighs and legs it's more expensive. There's no question that the coveted boneless, skinless breasts fetch the highest price by far. And how are all these pieces gathered? Obviously, by someone cutting up whole chickens.

With my help, that's what you're going to learn how to do, and you'll be saving lots of money once you've started doing it. Cutting up chickens into pieces hardly requires the delicacy of brain surgery. All it takes is a sharp knife, a good pair of shears, and about 5 minutes of your time—once you've done it a few times. Suddenly, all your per-piece chicken is priced the same!

Cutting up your own chicken will give you the wings to serve as a snack, the boneless breasts to sauté or stir-fry, the legs and thighs to bake, livers to transform into pâté, and miscellaneous trimmings like the wing tips to make chicken stock. *Nothing* goes to waste; it's the way a professional kitchen is run, and you'll see such savings you'll feel like the winner in this cost-conscious sweepstakes.

There are also many options in this book for ways to roast whole chickens, and then you'll have leftovers that you can "stretch" to feed your family on another night. There are many recipes that feed six people with just a few cups of diced cooked chicken.

What differentiates recipes in *$3 Chicken Meals*, and other books in the $3 Meals series, is that they are only made with *real* ingredients. There are no cans of "cream of something soup" or other convenience products that are high in price, loaded with chemicals, and low on nutrition.

$3 Chicken Meals will show you that you can prepare dishes that hide the fact that you made them on a strict budget. So not only are you feeding your family more economically, you're also feeling good that you're creating delicious dishes that pamper your taste buds as they pinch pennies to keep them in your pocket.

Happy Cooking!

—Ellen Brown
Providence, Rhode Island

Acknowledgments

While writing a book is a solitary endeavor, its publication is a team effort. My thanks go to:

Mary Norris, editorial director at Globe Pequot Press, for so willingly picking up the mantle to serve as editor for this series.

Jess Haberman and Julie Marsh, project editors at Globe Pequot Press, for their guidance and help all through the production process, and Jessie Shiers for her eagle-eyed copy editing.

Diana Nuhn, senior designer at Globe Pequot Press, for her inspired covers, and proofreader Jennifer Renk for her excellent work.

Ed Claflin, my agent, for his constant support and great sense of humor.

My many friends who shared their palates at tastings, their favorite chicken recipes, and their tips for saving money. Special thanks to Fox Wetle, Suzanne Cavedon, Kenn Speiser, Jim Reynolds, Vicki Veh, and my dear sister Nancy Dubler.

Tigger and Patches, my furry companions, whose time romping in my office always cheers up my day.

Introduction

Famed nineteenth-century French gastronome Jean Anthelme Brillat-Savarin once wrote that "poultry is for the cook what canvas is for the painter." Its inherently mild flavor takes to myriad methods of seasoning, and it is relatively quick to cook, too. And it's now the centerpiece of the American diet; each one of us eats more than 90 pounds per year. Today, chickens are also big business. Almost one-fifth of the world's 3.8 billion chickens reside in the United States.

Our increased consumption probably has more to do with economics than culinary choices. The bottom line truth is that chicken is cheaper than almost any cut of red meat—especially if you eat the whole bird and not just its boneless, skinless breast. Food costs have increased at a greater rate from 2007 until now than at any time in American history, so we have to become creative and stretch our limited food budgets. That's where this book, and others in the $3 Meals series, comes to the rescue.

The goal of the $3 Meals series is an ambitious one; this small amount of money—less than the cost of a large fast food burger or a slice of gourmet pizza—is for your *whole meal!* That includes the greens for your tossed salad and the dressing with which it's tossed. It includes the pasta or rice you cook to enjoy all the gravy from a stew. And it includes a sweet treat for dessert. So unlike many books that promise cost-conscious cooking, this book means it!

By using this book, you're cooking to combat what I term the "Three C's" of modern living—Cost, Convenience, and Chemicals. You pay more money for convenience foods that are loaded with chemicals. It's as simple as that. The "Three C's" are an evil trio, and cooking these recipes you'll learn how to avoid bumping into them.

And chemicals don't necessarily mean that convenience foods are immune from potential problems with food safety. An estimated 15,000 Americans were sickened with salmonella in 2007 from eating Banquet frozen turkey pot pies. Major food manufacturers, including ConAgra Foods, owner of Banquet, Swanson, and Hungry-Man, have conceded that they cannot assure the safety of items, and have shifted the burden of safe cooking to you—the consumer.

But you have no fears when cooking the pot pies, or any other recipe, in *$3 Chicken Meals*. In addition to fresh, minimally processed chicken, these dishes are made with real ingredients that once grew from the land. These recipes do specify canned beans and tomatoes, plus some inexpensive frozen vegetables that do not diminish the quality of a dish, and add the benefit of speeding its preparation.

Those are still natural foods, and represent a good value, too. Canned tomatoes, for example, also have better flavor than fresh ones bought for a lot more money out of season, and frozen spinach delivers the same nutritional value as fresh, and can be prepared in a fraction of the amount of time.

What takes chicken from the bargain department and turns it into a high-priced meal is how you buy it, and what you cook it with. You'll learn in *$3 Chicken Meals* how to save countless dollars a year by cutting up your own chickens into their component parts; that way nothing goes to waste and the edible meat is the least expensive per pound.

As a general rule it is safe to say that the more a food is processed, the more expensive it becomes. Carrot sticks are more expensive than whole carrots that need peeling and cutting; preseasoned rice or stuffing mix is more expensive than adding seasonings to the base ingredient. And buying chicken wings—the part of the chicken with the least edible meat—at a premium price falls into the same category.

But it makes little sense to spend mere pennies on your chicken meat, and then use a recipe calling for artichoke hearts or fresh asparagus that are three times the cost of the protein! The more than 250 easy recipes in *$3 Chicken Meals*, comprising American favorites and dishes drawn from many popular foreign cuisines—from Asian and Hispanic to classic French and the sunny foods of the Mediterranean and Caribbean—all tempt your taste buds, but remain within your budget.

The foundation of the $3 Meals series is all the tricks I've learned in professional kitchens—including my own catering kitchen. Professional cooks learn to minimize waste; wasted food translates to lower profit. That means that the onion peels and celery leaves that you might be throwing into your compost bin or garbage can now become an asset because you'll have them frozen to make stocks. And you'll know you have succeeded in waste-free cooking when, at the end of the week, there's nothing in the refrigerator to throw away!

There are a few ingredient compromises taken to trim costs for this series; however, these shortcuts trim preparation time, too. These are the first books in the more than 2 dozen I've written for which I use bottled lemon and lime juice in recipe development rather than juice freshly squeezed from the fruits themselves; I discovered it took a bit more juice to achieve the flavor I was after, but with the escalated cost of citrus fruits this was a sacrifice that I chose to make. The same is true with vegetables; many of these recipes call for cost-effective frozen vegetables rather than fresh. For vegetables such as the chopped spinach added to a soup or casserole, or the peas added to many dishes, it really doesn't matter.

I've also limited the range of herbs and spices specified to a core group of less than a dozen. There's no need to purchase an expensive dried herb that you may never use again.

On the other hand, there are standards I will never bend. I truly believe that unsalted butter is so far superior to margarine that any minimal cost savings from using margarine was not worth the tradedown in flavor. Good quality Parmesan cheese, freshly grated when you need it, is another ingredient well worth the splurge. You use very little of it, because once grated it takes up far more volume than in a block, and its innate flavor is far superior.

The same is true for using fresh parsley, cilantro, and dill. While most herbs deliver flavor in their dried form, these leafy herbs do not. Luckily, they are used so often that they are inexpensive to buy and don't go to waste—especially with the tricks I'll teach you on how to freeze them.

There's a feeling of empowerment that comes from feeding your family delicious meals that are healthy, and along the way you've been eating like royalty on a peon's budget.

Chapter 1:
Saving Money at the Supermarket

Stretching your food budget begins with advance planning. Think of plotting and planning your supermarket trips as if you were planning for a vacation. Your first step is to decide on your destination—what supermarket you'll use. After that you buy some guidebooks (in this case the Sunday newspaper) and do other research online (like print out coupons) and then you start looking for the good deals to get you to where you want to go.

In this case, where you want to go is to treat yourself to a vacation, and the way you're going to afford it in these challenging economic times is by savvy shopping. At any given moment there are *billions* of dollars of grocery coupons in the world waiting to be redeemed—assuming they are for products you already use or would like to use if you could afford them. In addition to coupons, there are rebates; if you spend a few cents on a stamp, it could reap many dollars coming back from manufacturers.

In fact, in one week of following the tips in this chapter you will have more than made up for the cost of this book—and then you'll have all the cost-conscious recipes to pamper your palate for years to come.

Next to housing and auto expenses, food is our major annual expense, as it is around the world. The fact that Americans spend about a 15 percent chunk of disposable income on food still remains the envy of most people living in the industrialized world. Just across the border in Canada the figure is 18 percent, while in Mexico it is more than 25 percent. To put this into context, from January 1 to the end of February, all the money you make goes to your yearly food budget.

Most of the tips are specific to food shopping; this *is* a cookbook. But there are also hints for saving money in other segments of your budget. It's all coming out of the same wallet. I wish I could promise you a clear and uncluttered path. But every rule has an exception, as you'll see below.

PLAN *BEFORE* YOU SHOP

The most important step to cost-effective cooking is to decide logically and intelligently what you're going to cook for the week. That may sound simple, but if you're in the habit of deciding when you're leaving work at the end of the day, chances are you've ended up with a lot of high-calorie frozen pizza or greasy Chinese carry-out.

The first step is to "shop" in a place you know well; it's your own kitchen. Look and see what's still in the refrigerator, and how that food—which you've already purchased and perhaps also cooked—can be utilized. That's where many recipes in this book come into play. Some leftover cooked carrots? Sounds like there's a soup in your future.

Now look and see what foods you have in the freezer. Part of savvy shopping is stocking up on foods when they're on sale; in fact, sales of free-standing freezers have grown by more than 10 percent during the past few years, while sales of all other major appliances have gone down. And with good reason—a free-standing freezer allows you to take advantage of sales. Especially foods like boneless, skinless chicken breasts—the time-crunched cook's best friend—which go on sale frequently and are almost prohibitive in price when they're not on sale. You should always have a cache of them ready to cook, for the recipes in this book as well as recipes that are more indulgent.

But preparing food for the freezer to insure quality is important. Never freeze meats, poultry, or seafood in the supermarket wrapping alone. To guard against freezer burn, double wrap food in freezer paper or place it in heavy resealable plastic bags.

Mark the purchase date on raw food, and the date when frozen on cooked items, and use them within three months. The recipes in this book use less meat, fish, and poultry than many in other cookbooks; these high-priced foods are also higher in calories. Therefore, it's important to repackage meats into smaller packages than those you buy, too. Scan recipes and look at the amount of the particular meat specified; that's what size your packages destined for the freezer should be.

Keep a list taped to the front of your freezer. It should list contents and date when they were frozen. Mark off foods as you take them out and add foods as you put them in.

Also, part of your strategy as a cook is to do it only a few nights a week; that means when you're making recipes that can be doubled—like a pasta sauce or stew—you make larger batches and freeze a portion.

Those meals are "dinner insurance" for nights you don't want to cook. Those are the nights that you previously would have brought in the bucket of chicken or the pizza, and spent more money for more calories by far.

The other factor that enters into the initial planning is looking at your depletion list, and seeing what foods and other products need to be purchased. A jar of peanut butter or a bottle of dishwashing liquid might not factor into meal plans, but they do cost money—so they have to be factored into your budget. Some weeks you might not need many supplies, but it always seems to me that all of the cleaning supplies seem to deplete the same week.

Now you've got the "raw data" to look at the weekly sales circulars from your newspaper or delivered with your mail. Those sales should form the core for your menu planning.

PUSHING THAT CART WITH PURPOSE

So it's a new you entering the supermarket. First of all, you have a list, and it's for more than a few days. And you're going to buy what's on your list. Here's the first rule: stick to that list. Never go shopping when you're hungry; that's when nonessential treats wind up in your basket. Always go shopping alone; unwanted items end up in the cart to keep peace in the family. And—here's an idea that might seem counterintuitive—go shopping when you're in a hurry. It's those occasions when you have the time to dawdle that the shortcakes end up coming home when all you really wanted were the strawberries.

But as promised, here are some exceptions to the rule of keeping to your list. You've got to be flexible enough to take advantage of some unexpected great sales. Next to frugality, flexibility is the key to saving money on groceries.

It's easy if the sale is a markdown on meat; you see the $2 off coupon and put it in the cart, with the intention of either cooking it that night or freezing it. All supermarkets mark down meat on the day before the expiration sticker. The meat is still perfectly fine, and should it turn out not to be, you can take it back for a refund. So go ahead and take advantage of the markdown.

Then you notice a small oval sticker with the word "Save." Is turkey breast at $1.09 a real bargain? You'll know it is if you keep track of prices, and know that a few weeks ago it was $3.99 per pound.

You now have two options. Buy the off-list bargains and freeze them, or use them this week. In place of what? And what effect will that have on the rest of your list?

That's why I suggest freezing bargains, assuming you can absorb the extra cost on this week's grocery bill. If not, then look at what produce, shelf-stable, and dairy items on the list were tied to a protein you're now crossing off, and delete them, too.

But meat isn't the only department of the supermarket that has "remainder bins." Look in produce, bakery, and grocery. I've gotten some perfectly ripe bananas with black spots—just the way they should be—for pennies a pound, while the ones that are bright yellow (and still tasteless) are five times the cost.

Supermarkets are almost all designed to funnel traffic first into the produce section; that is the last place you want to shop. Begin with the proteins, since many items in other sections of your list relate to the entrees of the dinners you have planned. Once they are gathered, go through and get the shelf-stable items, then the dairy products (so they will not be in the cart for too long) and end with the produce. Using this method, the fragile produce is on the top of the basket, not crushed by the gallons of milk.

The last step is packing the groceries. If you live in an area where you have the option of packing them yourself, place items stored together in the same bag. That way all of your produce can go directly into the refrigerator, and canned goods destined for the basement will be stored in one trip.

COUPON CLIPPING 101

It's part art, it's part science, and it all leads to more money in your wallet. Consider this portion of the chapter your Guerilla Guide to Coupons. There's more to it than just clipping them. Of course, unless you clip them or glean them from other channels (see some ideas below) then you can't save money. So that's where you're going to start—but, trust me, it's just the beginning.

Forget that image you have of the lady wearing the hairnet and the "sensible shoes" in line at the supermarket digging through what seems to be a bottomless pit of tiny pieces of paper looking for the right coupon for this or that. Clipping coupons—in case you haven't heard—is *cool*. And it should be. At any given moment there are *billions of dollars*

of coupons floating around out there, according to the folks at www
.grocerycouponguide.com, one of the growing list of similar sites dedicated to helping you save money.

And not only is it becoming easier to access these savings, you're
a Neanderthal if you don't. The fact that you're reading this book—and
will be cooking from it—shows that you care about trimming the size of
your grocery bill. So it's time to get with the program.

Even the Sunday newspaper (as long as they still exist) is a treasure
trove of coupons. I found a $5 off coupon for a premium cat food my
finicky cats liked in a local paper, which cost 50 cents. It was worth it to
buy four copies of the paper; I spent $2 but I then netted an $18 savings
on the cat food.

The first decision you have to make is how you're going to orga-
nize your coupons. There are myriad ways and each has its fans. It's up
to you to decide which is right for you, your family, and the way you
shop:

- **Arrange the coupons by aisle in the supermarket** if you only
  shop in one store consistently.

- **Arrange them by category** of product (like cereals, cleaning supplies, dairy products, etc.) if you shop in many stores.

- **Arrange them alphabetically** if you have coupons that you use in
  various types of stores beyond the grocery store.

- **Arrange them by expiration date.** Coupons are only valid for a
  certain time period; it can be a few weeks or a few months. And
  part of the strategy of coupon clipping is to maximize the value,
  which frequently comes close to the expiration date. Some of
  the best coupons are those for "buy one, get one free." However,
  when the coupon first appears the item is at full price. But what
  about two weeks later when the item is on sale at your store?
  Then the "buy one, get one free" can mean you're actually getting four cans for the price of one at the original retail price.

Storage systems for arranging coupons are as varied as methods of
organizing them. I personally use envelopes, and keep the stack held

together with a low-tech paper clip. I've also seen people with whole wallets and tiny accordion binders dedicated to coupons. If you don't have a small child riding on the top of the cart, another alternative is to get a loose-leaf notebook with clear envelopes instead of pages.

LEARN THE LINGO

Coupons are printed on very small pieces of paper, and even with 20-20 eyesight or reading glasses many people—including me—need to use a magnifying glass to read all the fine print. There are many legal phrases that have to be part of every coupon, too.

In the same way that baseball fans know that RBI means "runs batted in," coupon collectors know that WSL means "while supplies last." Here's a list of many abbreviations found on coupons:

- **AR.** After Rebate.

- **B1G1 or BOGO.** Buy one, get one free.

- **CRT.** Cash Register Receipt.

- **DC.** Double coupon, which is a coupon the store—not the manufacturer—doubles in value.

- **DCRT.** Dated Cash Register Receipt, which proves you purchased the item during the right time period.

- **FAR.** Free After Rebate.

- **IP.** Internet Printed Coupons.

- **ISO.** In-Store Only.

- **IVC.** Instant Value Coupon, which are the pull-offs found on products in the supermarket that are redeemed as you pay.

- **MIR.** Mail In Rebate.

- **NED.** No Expiration Date.

- **OAS.** On Any Size, which means the coupon is good for any size package of that particular product.

- **OYNSO.** On Your Next Shopping Order, which means that you must return to the same store; the coupon will not be good at another store.

- **POP.** Proof of Purchase, and these are the little panels found on packages that you have to cut off and send in to receive a rebate.

- **WSL.** While Supply Lasts, which means you can't demand a "rain check" to use the coupon at a later date once the product is again in stock.

> While you might just be becoming more aware of them, coupons are nothing new. They began in the late 1800s when Coca-Cola and Grape Nuts offered coupons to consumers. Currently more than 3,000 companies use coupons as part of their marketing plans, and shoppers save more than $5 billion a year by redeeming the coupons.

BARGAIN SHOPPING 2.0

Every grocery store has weekly sales, and those foods are the place to start your planning for new purchases; that's how you're saving money beyond using coupons. And almost every town has competing supermarket chains that offer different products on sale. It's worth your time to shop in a few venues, because it will generate the most savings. That way you can also determine which chain offers the best store brands, and purchase them while you're there for the weekly bargains. Here are other ways to save:

- **"Junk mail" may contain more than junk.** Don't toss those Valpak and other coupon envelopes that arrive in the mail. Look through them carefully, and you'll find not only coupons for food products, but for many services, too.

- **Spend a stamp to get a rebate.** Many large manufacturers are now sending out coupon books or cash vouchers usable in many stores to customers who mail in receipts demonstrating that they have purchased about $50 of products. For example, Procter & Gamble, the country's largest advertiser and the company for which the term "soap opera" was invented, is switching millions of dollars from the airwaves to these sorts of promotions.

- **Find bargains online.** It's difficult for me to list specific Web sites because they may be defunct by the time you're reading this book, but there are hundreds of dollars worth of savings to be culled by printing coupons from Web sites, and for high end organic products, it's the only way to access coupons. Ones I use frequently are www.couponmom.com and www.coupons.com, and I also look for the coupon offers on such culinary sites as www .epicurious.com and www.foodnetwork.com. You will find coupons there, some tied to actual recipes. Also visit manufacturers' Web sites, which offer both coupons and redemption savings.

- **Find coupons in the store.** Look for those little machines projecting out from the shelves; they usually contain coupons that can be used instantly when you check out. Also, don't throw out your receipt until you've looked at it carefully. There are frequently coupons printed on the back. The cashier may also hand you other small slips of paper with your cash register receipt; most of them are coupons for future purchases of items you just bought. They may be from the same brand or they may be from a competing brand. Either way, they offer savings.

- **Stock up on cans.** Even if you live in a small apartment without a basement storage unit, it makes sense to stock up on canned goods when they're on sale. The answer is to use every spare inch of space. The same plastic containers that fit under your bed to hold out of season clothing can also become a pantry for canned goods.

- **Shuffle those cards.** Even if I can't convince you to clip coupons, the least you can do for yourself to save money is take the 5 minutes required to sign up for store loyalty cards; many national brands as well as store brands are on sale only when using the card. While the current system has you hand the card to the cashier at the checkout, that will be changing in the near future. Shopping carts will be equipped with card readers that will generate instant coupons according to your purchasing habits. I keep my stack of loyalty cards in the glove box of my car; that way they don't clutter my purse but I always have them when shopping.

- **Look for blanket discounts.** While it does take time to cull coupons, many supermarket chains send flyers in the mail that offer a set amount off the total, for example $10 off a total of $50. These are the easiest way to save money, and many national drug store chains, such as CVS, do the same. Just remember to have a loyalty card for those stores to take advantage of the savings.

- **Get a bargain buddy.** There's no question that supermarkets try to lure customers with "buy one, get one free" promotions, and sometimes one is all you really want. And those massive cases of paper towels at the warehouse clubs are also a good deal—if you have unlimited storage space. The answer? Find a bargain buddy with whom you can split large purchases. My friends and I also swap coupons we won't use but the other person will. Going back to my example of the cat food savings, there were dog food coupons on the same page, so I turned them over to a canine-owning friend.

LEARNING THE ROPES

The well-informed shopper is the shopper who is saving money, and the information you need to make the best purchasing decision is right there on the supermarket shelves. It's the shelf tag that gives you the cost per unit of measurement. The units can be quarts for salad dressing, ounces for dry cereal, or pounds for canned goods. All you have to do is look carefully.

But you do have to make sure you're comparing apples to apples and oranges to oranges—or in this example, stocks to stocks. Some can be priced by the quart, while others are by the pound.

- **Check out store brands.** Store brands and generics have been improving in quality during the past few years, and according to *Consumer Reports*, buying them can save anywhere from 15 percent to 50 percent. Moving from a national brand to a store brand is a personal decision, and sometimes money is not the only factor. For example, I have used many store brands of chlorine bleach, and have returned to Clorox time and again. But I find no difference between generic corn flakes and those from the market leaders. Store brands can also be less expensive than national brands on sale—and with coupons.

- **Compare prices within the store.** Many foods—such as cold cuts and cheeses—are sold in multiple areas of the store, so check out those alternate locations. Sliced ham may be less expensive in a cellophane package shelved with the refrigerated foods than at the deli counter.

- **Look high and low.** Manufacturers pay a premium price to shelve products at eye level, and you're paying for that placement when you're paying their prices. Look at the top and bottom shelves in aisles like cereal and canned goods. That's where you'll find the lower prices.

- **Buy the basics.** When is a bargain not a bargain? When you're paying for water or you're paying for a little labor. That's why even though a 15-ounce can of beans is less expensive than the same quantity of dried beans (approximately a pound), you're still better off buying the dried beans. One pound of dried beans makes the equivalent of four or five cans of beans. In the same way, a bar of Monterey Jack cheese is much less expensive per pound than a bag of grated Monterey Jack cheese. In addition to saving money, the freshly grated cheese will have more flavor because cheese loses flavor rapidly when grated. And pre-cut and pre-washed vegetables are truly exorbitant.

- **Watch the scanner.** I know it's tempting to catch up on pop culture by leafing through the tabloids at the checkout, but that's the last thing you should be doing. Watching the clerk scan your order usually saves you money. For example, make sure all the instant savings coupons are peeled off; this includes marked-down meats and coupons on boxes and bags. Then, make sure sale items are ringing up at the right price.

WASTE NOT, WANT NOT

We're now going to start listing exceptions to all the rules you just read, because a bargain isn't a bargain if you end up throwing some of it away. Remember that the goal is to waste nothing. Start by annotating your shopping list with quantities for the recipes you'll be cooking. That way you can begin to gauge when a bargain is a bargain. Here are other ways to buy only what you need:

- **Don't overbuy.** Sure, the large can of diced tomatoes is less per pound than the smaller can. But what will you do with the remainder of the can if all you need is a small amount? The same is true for dairy products. A $\frac{1}{2}$-pint of heavy cream always costs much more per ounce than a quart, but if the remaining 3 cups of cream will end up in the sink in a few weeks, go with the smaller size.

- **Buy what you'll eat, not what you should eat.** If your family hates broccoli, the low sale cost doesn't matter; you'll end up throwing it away. We all think about healthful eating when we're in the supermarket, but if you know that the contents of your cart are good thoughts rather than realistic choices, you're wasting money.

- **Buy smart.** Just because you have a coupon doesn't mean you should buy something. We all love bargains, but if you're putting an item into your cart for the first time, you must decide if it's because you really want it, or because you're getting $1.50 off of its cost.

- **Sometimes bigger isn't better.** If you're shopping for snacks for a young child, look for the *small* apples rather than the giant ones. Most kids take a few bites and then toss the rest, so evaluate any purchases you're making by the pound.

- **Ring that bell!** You know the one; it's always in the meat department of the supermarket. It might take you a few extra minutes, but ask the real live human who will appear for *exactly* what you want; many of the recipes in *$3 Chicken Meals* specify less than the weight of packages you find in the meat case. Many supermarkets do not have personnel readily available in departments like the cheese counter, but if there are wedges of cheeses labeled and priced, then someone is in charge. It might be the deli department or the produce department, but find out who it is and ask for a small wedge of cheese if you can't find one the correct size.

- **Check out the bulk bins.** Begin buying from the bulk bins for shelf-stable items, like various types of rice, beans, dried fruits, and nuts. Each of these departments has scales so you can weigh ingredients like dried mushrooms or pasta. If a recipe calls for a quantity rather than a weight you can usually "eyeball" the quantity. If you're unsure of amounts start by bringing a 1-cup measure with you to the market. Empty the contents of the bin into the measuring cup rather than directly into the bag. One problem with bulk food bags is that they are difficult to store in the pantry; shelves were made for sturdier materials. Wash out plastic deli containers or even plastic containers that you bought containing yogurt or salsa. Use those for storage once the bulk bags arrive in the kitchen. Make sure you label your containers of bulk foods both at the supermarket and if you're transferring the foods to other containers at home so you know what they are, especially if you're buying similar foods. Arborio and basmati rice look very similar in a plastic bag, but they are totally different grains and shouldn't be substituted for each other.

- **Shop from the salad bar for tiny quantities.** There's no question that supermarkets charge a premium price for items in those chilled bins in the salad bar, but you get exactly what you need. When to shop there depends on the cost of the item in a larger quantity. At $4 per pound, you're still better off buying a 50-cent can of garbanzo beans, even if it means throwing some of them away. However, if you don't see how you're going to finish the $4 pint of cherry tomatoes, then spend $1 at the salad bar for the handful you need to garnish a salad.

SUPERMARKET ALTERNATIVES

All of the hints thus far in this chapter have been geared to pushing a cart around a supermarket. Here are some other ways to save money:

- **Shop at farmers' markets.** I admit it; I need a 12-step program to help me cure my addiction to local farmers' markets. Shopping *al fresco* on warm summer days turns picking out fruits and vegetables into a truly sensual experience. Also, you buy only what you want. There are no bunches of carrots; there are individual carrots sold by the pound. The U.S. Department of Agriculture began publishing the *National Directory of Farmers' Markets* in 1994, and at that time the number was fewer than 2,000. That figure has now doubled. To find a farmers' market near you, go to www.ams.usda.gov/farmersmarkets. The first cousins of farmers' markets for small quantities of fruits are the sidewalk vendors in many cities. One great advantage to buying from them is that their fruit is always ripe and ready to eat or cook.

- **Shop at ethnic markets.** If you live in a rural area this may not be possible, but even moderately small cities have a range of ethnic markets, and that's where you should buy ingredients to cook those cuisines. All the Asian condiments used in *$3 Meals in Minutes* are far less expensive at Asian markets than in the Asian aisle of your supermarket, and you can frequently find imported authentic brands instead of U.S. versions. Even small cities and many towns have ethnic enclaves, such as a "Little Italy"; each neighborhood has some grocery stores with great prices for those ingredients and the fresh produce used to make the dishes, too.

- **Shop alternative stores.** Groceries aren't only at grocery stores; many "dollar stores" and other discount venues stock shelf-stable items. For example, if you live in New England, Ocean State Job Lot should be on your weekly circuit; this discount store chain is loaded with food bargains.

- **Shop for food in drug stores.** Every national brand of drugstore—including CVS and Walgreens—carries grocery products and usually has great bargains each week. In the same way that food markets now carry much more than foods, drug stores stock thousands of items that have no connection to medicine. Those chains also have circulars in Sunday newspapers, so check them out—even if you're feeling very healthy.

- **Shop online.** In recent years it's become possible to do all your grocery shopping online through such services as Peapod and Fresh Direct. While there is frequently a delivery charge involved, for housebound people this is a true boon. If you really hate the thought of pushing the cart, you should explore it; it's impossible to make impulse buys. There are also a large number of online retailers for ethnic foods, dried herbs and spices, premium baking chocolate, and other shelf-stable items. Letting your cursor do the shopping for these items saves you time, and many of them offer free shipping at certain times of the year.

THAT FRUGAL FRAME OF MIND

In addition to all the tips listed above, you've got to get into a frugal frame of mind. You're out to save money on your food budget, but not feel deprived. You're going to be eating the delicious dishes in this book.

Think about where your food budget goes other than the grocery store. The cost of a few "designer coffee" treats at the local coffee shop is equal to a few dinners at home. Couldn't you brew coffee and take it to work rather than spend $10 a week at the coffee cart? And those cans of soft drinks in the vending machine are four times the cost of bringing a can from home. But do you really need soft drinks at all? For mere pennies you can brew a few quarts of iced tea, which has delicious flavor without chemicals.

Bringing your lunch to work does increase your weekly supermarket tab, but it accomplishes a few good goals. It adds funds to the bottom line of your total budget, and it allows you to control what you're eating—and when. While you may think that your choices for lunch are low-calorie, chances are you're kidding yourself, but you won't be kidding your body. That lean little salad comes with a packet of traditional dressing that may contain upwards of a few hundred calories! That's more than many of the entrees in this book.

If you have a pressured job, chances are there are days that you end up eating from snack food vending machines or eating fast food at your desk. If you bring your lunch you know what it will be—even if you don't know when. Almost every office has a microwave oven, so lunch can frequently be leftovers from a dinner the night or two before, so the extra cost and cooking time are minimal.

So now that you're becoming a grocery guru, you can move on to find myriad ways to save money on your grocery bill while eating wonderfully. That's what *$3 Chicken Meals,* and the other books in the $3 Meals series, is all about.

> A great thing about chicken is that it's really as good cold as it is hot. So make some extra and take it to work for lunch; that's a sure fire way to save money!

Chapter 2:

Chicken 101

Saving dollars by spending a few minutes' work
becomes second nature when you're accustomed to doing it. That
means peeling and cutting up your own carrots rather than buying carrot sticks, and—in the case of this book—it means cutting up your own
chickens; learning that skill leads off this chapter. After you've done it a
few times, you'll see how easy it is to do. All it takes is a pair of poultry
shears (or a strong pair of scissors) and a sharp kitchen knife, and with
a few cuts you're in business and ready to cook whatever part you want
to use that night.

When you cut up your own chickens, *absolutely nothing* goes to
waste. The giblets, wing tips, bones, and skin are used to flavor your
next batch of chicken stock, the cost of which at the supermarket is
more expensive than a quart of milk or orange juice—which are foods
you can't make yourself.

The livers, which don't go into stock, can be saved in a container in
the freezer. When you've got about a dozen, there's enough to make
a yummy treat; look at some of the pâté recipes in Chapter 3, and the
hors d'oeuvre is ready for the next time you've got friends coming for
dinner.

Following the section on poultry production in this chapter are
some easy ways to flavor chicken and turn a simple meal into a real dish
of distinction. All those spice rubs, marinades, and sauces in the aisles
of the supermarket are outrageously expensive, and most of them are
loaded with chemicals and preservatives.

NUTRITIONAL NOTES

Just 4 ounces of chicken provide more than $^2/_3$ of your protein needs for
the day, and that's for only 223 calories. Another health bonus is that
the fat in chicken is less saturated than the fat in beef—discounting the
skin.

One of the other major nutritional contributions of chicken is that
the same size serving contains more than 100 percent of the daily value
for tryptophan. Tryptophan is one of the essential amino acids we have
to eat daily. Amino acids are the building blocks of protein biosynthesis,

and the essential ones are those that have to be part of the diet. Tryptophan raises our level of serotonin, a neurotransmitter that controls our mood and helps regulate appetite. So a diet with a lot of chicken can make you feel emotionally more grounded, as well as financially fitter.

SELECTION AND FOOD SAFETY

Look for packages of chicken that do not have an accumulation of liquid in the bottom. That can be a sign that the chicken has been frozen and defrosted. Chicken should be stored in the coldest part of the refrigerator (40°F or below), sealed as it comes from the market, and used within two or three days.

If it should be necessary to keep it longer, freeze it. While freezing can reduce flavor, moisture, and tenderness, it will preserve freshness. Seal poultry in an airtight container, heavy plastic bag, plastic wrap, foil, or freezer paper. Label the package with the date. Uncooked poultry can be stored frozen up to six months; cooked poultry should be used within three months.

To defrost, place the frozen chicken on a plate in the refrigerator or use the microwave, following manufacturer's instructions. To speed the thawing of uncooked chicken, place package in cold water, changing the water frequently.

Rinse chicken under cold running water when you remove it from the wrapper, and it should have absolutely no aroma. If it has any off smells, take it back to the supermarket if it's before the expiration date, or discard it if it's after that date or you took it out of the freezer.

Illness-causing bacteria such as salmonella can grow in high-protein, low acid foods like poultry, so special handling should always be taken with raw chicken or turkey. To prevent transferring bacteria from one food to another, use warm water and soap to wash your hands, cooking utensils, and work surfaces before and after use. Here are some common foibles when handling chicken:

- **Never put cooked chicken on the same platter that held it raw.** Hospital emergency rooms see many cases of food poisoning in summer because of this. If you transport marinated chicken pieces outside to a grill, bring in the platter and wash it well before placing the cooked chicken on it.

- **Never refrigerate raw chicken with any other foods.** Most of the time it takes to ready food for a stir-fry is cutting it up; the actual cooking is merely minutes. You will note in the stir-fried recipes in this book that you can cut up the foods in advance and keep them refrigerated *with the chicken in a separate bag from the other ingredients.* And cut up the chicken last so there's no chance of exposing your vegetables to bacteria on the cutting board.

- **Never partially cook chicken.** I have been horrified over the years to hear about people partially cooking chicken in the oven and then putting it on the grill a few hours later. Chicken must pass through the "danger zone" of 40°F to 140°F as quickly as possible, which is why I start whole chickens in Chapter 5 at a high temperature.

CUTTING WITH CUNNING

Almost every permutation on how to buy chicken is now available in almost every supermarket—from whole birds of various sizes to delicate breast tenderloins. But it is far more economical to purchase a whole chicken, and cut it up yourself, rather than buying one already cut. If it's a week when whole fryers (chickens between 3 pounds and 4½ pounds) are on sale, take advantage of it. I usually cut up between four and six chickens at a time; that yields enough various pieces for many meals.

Remember that *nothing goes to waste.* The giblets and any bones and skin should go into a bag for making Chicken Stock; the recipe is on page 30. Freeze the livers separately, and when you have about one-half pound amassed, look at the recipes for pâté in Chapter 3. Then freeze the remaining pieces according to what they are. Here's a brief guide to becoming a poultry production line:

- **Cutting up whole chickens.** Start by breaking back the wings until the joints snap, then use the boning knife to cut through the ball joints and detach the wings. When holding the chicken on its side, you will see a natural curve outlining the boundary between the breast and the leg/thigh quarters. Use sharp kitchen shears and cut along this line. Cut the breast in half by scraping away the meat from the breastbone, and using a small paring knife to remove the wishbone. Cut away the breastbone using the shears, and save it for stock. Divide the leg/thigh quarters by turning the pieces over and finding the joint joining them. Cut through the joint and sever the leg from the thigh.

- **Boning chicken breasts.** The price per pound for the edible meat is the lowest when you bone the breasts yourself, especially when they're part of cutting up the whole chicken. Pull off the skin with your fingers, and then make an incision on either side of the breastbone, cutting down until you feel the bone resisting the knife. Working one side at a time, place the blade of your boning knife against the carcass, and scrape away the meat. You will then have two pieces: the large fillet and the small tenderloin. To trim the fillet, cut away any fat, and pound the meat gently between two sheets of plastic wrap to an even thickness. To trim the tenderloin, secure the tip of the tendon that will be visible with your free hand. Using a paring knife, scrape down the tendon, and the meat will push away.

- **Pounding chicken breasts.** Some recipes will tell you to pound the breast to an even thickness so it will cook evenly and quickly. To do so, place the breast between two sheets of plastic wrap, and pound with the smooth side of a meat mallet or the bottom of a small, heavy skillet or saucepan.

- **Butterflying a whole chicken.** Butterflying is a process of partially boning a whole chicken so that it can be pressed down flat on the grill and will cook over direct heat, and therefore in less time than if you kept it whole. Turn the chicken with the breast side down. Using poultry shears, cut away the backbone from the tail to the head end on both sides, and save it for making stock. Open the bird by pulling the halves apart. Use a sharp paring knife to lightly score the top of the breastbone, then run your thumbs along and under the breastbone, and pull them out. Spread the bird flat. It's now time to turn the chicken over. Cut off the wing tips, and you are ready to grill.

COOKING CHICKEN CORRECTLY

The rules have changed for cooking poultry in the last year, and the revision means that you can avoid overcooked dry chicken and turkey. The minimum temperature is now 165°F for both white and dark meat. At that temperature there's no chance for microorganisms to survive.

The best way to test this is to use an instant-read meat thermometer. When the thickest part of the chicken is probed, the reading should be 165°F. If you do not want to take the temperature of every piece of chicken, recognize these visual signals: the chicken should be tender when poked with the tip of a paring knife, there should not be a hint of pink even near the bones, and the juices should run clear. Always test the dark meat before the white meat. Dark meat takes slightly longer to cook, so if the thighs are the proper temperature, you know the breasts will be fine.

SLOW-COOKER ADAPTATION

There are many chicken and even a few turkey recipes in *$3 Slow-Cooked Meals: Delicious, Low-Cost Dishes from Both Your Slow Cooker and Stove*. But if you want to convert some of this book's "wet" recipes with sauce for your slow cooker, here are some pointers:

- Count on 6–8 hours on Low and 3–4 hours on High.

- The chicken should be in pieces and not whole.

- Cut back on the amount of liquid by one quarter because there is little or no evaporation from a slow cooker as there is when cooking conventionally.

- If the chicken dish is made with a cream sauce, it is not a good candidate for the slow cooker because dairy products tend to curdle when subjected to long periods of low heat.

- Add seasonings like pepper at the end of the cooking time.

FLAVORED BUTTER AS A SAUCE

Called "compound butters" in classic French cooking, these are some of the easiest ways to flavor chicken that's been simply baked, broiled, or grilled. You can make a few choices, and then freeze them as individual patties; remove just the amount you need from the freezer when the chicken starts cooking and by the time it's done the butter will have softened. Then merely put the pat on top of the hot chicken when you serve it.

All of these combinations were formulated for $\frac{1}{4}$ pound (1 stick) unsalted butter; add however much salt you would like. Allow the butter to soften, finely chop the ingredients, if necessary, and then beat them into the softened butter by hand or in a food processor, along with salt and freshly ground black pepper to taste. Place the butter on a sheet of wax paper or parchment paper, and form it into a cylinder 2 inches in diameter. Once the butter is chilled, you can cut it into pats to use immediately or freeze the pats. Here are some of the ones I use the most often:

- **Garlic-Herb.** Add 3 garlic cloves, peeled and pressed through a garlic press, 1 tablespoon grated onion, 1 tablespoon chopped fresh parsley, and $\frac{1}{2}$ teaspoon dried thyme.

- **Italian.** Add 1 tablespoon tomato paste, 1 tablespoon chopped fresh parsley, and 1 teaspoon Italian seasoning.

- **Southwestern.** Add 2 tablespoons chili powder, 2 tablespoons chopped fresh cilantro, 1 teaspoon ground cumin, 1 teaspoon dried oregano, and 1 garlic clove, peeled and pressed through a garlic press.

- **Provençal.** Add 2 tablespoons freshly grated Parmesan cheese, 2 teaspoons anchovy paste, 2 teaspoons herbes de Provence, and 1 teaspoon Dijon mustard.

- **Classic French.** Add 3 tablespoons chopped fresh parsley, 2 teaspoons lemon juice, and 2 teaspoons Dijon mustard.

- **Mustard-Dill.** Add 2 tablespoons grainy mustard, 2 tablespoons chopped fresh dill, and 1 tablespoon grated onion.

FLAVORING WITHOUT FUSS

There are basically four ways to flavor chicken before it's baked or grilled—rubs, pastes, marinades, and brines. The amount of time these mixtures need to give the chicken flavor ranges from seconds to days.

Rubs are a relatively new addition to the arsenal of ways to flavor foods; they've only been on the market for about a decade. Rubs are highly concentrated mixtures of herbs and spices that should be applied to the chicken after it has been brushed with oil. And rub is what you should do.

Rather than just giving the chicken pieces a light sprinkle, the mixture should be rubbed into the skin and flesh with your fingertips; a good ratio is 2 tablespoons per pound of chicken pieces with bones and 1 tablespoon per pound if boneless. The rub recipes in this chapter are salt-free because I believe that salting food is a very personal choice. Sprinkle as much salt as you like onto the food at the same time the rub is applied.

Pastes represent the middle ground between rubs and marinades, and the amount of time needed to use them is more than a rub but less than a marinade. Pastes are highly concentrated in the same way as rubs, but they also contain some perishable ingredients for accent flavors so they are moist. Many pastes have oil added to create the proper thick texture.

Pastes should be rubbed into food, and then the food should be allowed to sit for 15–20 minutes to absorb the flavors. Then cook the chicken without removing the paste. Food should be lightly sprinkled with salt just prior to cooking because the pastes are salt-free.

Marinades are a time-honored stalwart of cooking. If given enough time, food will definitely absorb the flavor, and a marinade also tenderizes the chicken because it contains some sort of acid. The heavy resealable plastic bag has revolutionized marinating; far less liquid is now needed because it can surround food in a small space.

If using a mixing bowl, make sure it is made from glass or stainless steel, the so-called "non-reactive" materials. Aluminum will interact with the acid in the marinade and give the food a metallic flavor, while plastic may absorb the flavors from the marinade and give them to inappropriate foods in the future; you really don't want whipped cream to taste like chile peppers!

Once chicken has been marinated, the marinade must be brought to a boil before it can be used to moisten the chicken after cooking. An alternative is to make a larger quantity of the marinade, and reserve some to use on the food later. Chicken pieces with bones and skin should marinate for 4 to 12 hours, while boneless, skinless pieces gain flavor in 30 minutes to 3 hours.

Brining, along with smoking and salting, is the way that food was preserved prior to refrigeration and freezing. It's making a comeback today because the long soaking in flavored salty-sweet water improves the flavor and texture of foods, especially lean foods like chicken and turkey. As is true with marinating, the larger the piece of food, the longer it will take to absorb the flavors; the minimum for chicken pieces is one day, and a large turkey can brine for up to three days.

There is no need to be delicate when amassing ingredients for a brine; due to the length of time, the food will absorb flavor from whole smashed garlic cloves or whole peppercorns.

Be careful not to marinate foods for longer than specified in a recipe. If a marinade contains a strong acid like lemon juice or wine it can actually begin to break down the fibers of the chicken, and will produce mushy flesh once cooked.

South of the Border Rub

Here's a rub with all the flavors you'd expect from Mexican food.

Yield: 1/2 cup | **Active time:** 5 minutes | **Start to finish:** 5 minutes

2 tablespoons chili powder

2 tablespoons paprika

1 tablespoon ground cumin

1 tablespoon ground coriander

1 tablespoon garlic powder

1 tablespoon dried oregano

1 teaspoon freshly ground black pepper

1 teaspoon crushed red pepper

Combine chili powder, paprika, cumin, coriander, garlic powder, oregano, black pepper, and red pepper in a bowl, and mix well.

Note: Store rub in an airtight container in a cool, dry place for up to 1 month.

Aromatic Herb and Spice Rub

There are many herbs and spices that are traditionally used when cooking chicken, and they're all in this rub.

Yield: 1/2 cup | **Active time:** 5 minutes | **Start to finish:** 5 minutes

2 tablespoons ground coriander

2 tablespoons dried thyme

1 tablespoon ground cumin

1 tablespoon freshly ground black pepper

1 tablespoon dried oregano

1 tablespoon dried sage

Combine coriander, thyme, cumin, pepper, oregano, and sage in a bowl, and mix well.

Note: Store in an airtight container in a cool, dry place for up to 1 month.

Asian Five-Spice Rub

Chinese five-spice powder is a blend like chili powder, and it creates a complex flavor when rubbed on the chicken.

Yield: ½ cup | **Active time:** 5 minutes | **Start to finish:** 5 minutes

3 tablespoons Chinese five-spice powder*
2 tablespoons firmly packed light brown sugar
1 teaspoon garlic powder
Cayenne to taste

Combine five-spice powder, brown sugar, garlic powder, and cayenne in a bowl, and mix well.

Note: Store in an airtight container in a cool, dry place for up to 1 month.

*Available in the Asian aisle of most supermarkets and in specialty markets.

Creole Rub

Paprika, oregano, and thyme are three ingredients common to much of Creole cooking, and they're the primary flavors in this rub.

Yield: ½ cup | **Active time:** 5 minutes | **Start to finish:** 5 minutes

3 tablespoons paprika
2 tablespoons garlic powder
1 tablespoon onion powder
1 tablespoon dried oregano
1 tablespoon dried thyme
2 teaspoons freshly ground black pepper
1 teaspoon cayenne

Combine paprika, garlic powder, onion powder, oregano, thyme, pepper, and cayenne in a bowl, and mix well.

Note: Store in an airtight container in a cool, dry place for up to 1 month.

Moroccan Paste

Lemon is a common flavoring in North African cooking, and with parsley and aromatic cilantro it's a dynamite paste for chicken.

Yield: 1 cup | **Active time:** 10 minutes | **Start to finish:** 10 minutes

½ cup chopped fresh parsley
½ cup chopped fresh cilantro
6 garlic cloves, peeled and pushed through a garlic press
1 tablespoon ground cumin
1 tablespoon paprika
1 teaspoon grated lemon zest
Crushed red pepper flakes to taste
⅓ cup olive oil
2 tablespoons lemon juice

Combine parsley, cilantro, garlic, cumin, paprika, lemon zest, and red pepper flakes in a bowl, and mix well. Add oil and lemon juice, and mix into a paste.

Note: Store in an airtight container, refrigerated, for up to 3 days.

Citrus Marinade

The delicacy of chicken takes very well to citrus flavors, especially when they're combined, like in this marinade.

Yield: 1½ cups | **Active time:** 10 minutes | **Start to finish:** 10 minutes

¾ cup orange juice
2 tablespoons lime juice
2 tablespoons soy sauce
2 teaspoons dried rosemary, crumbled
3 garlic cloves, peeled and minced
2 tablespoons chili powder
1 tablespoon grated orange zest
Freshly ground black pepper to taste
½ cup olive oil

Combine orange juice, lime juice, soy sauce, rosemary, garlic, chili powder, orange zest, and pepper in a heavy resealable plastic bag, and mix well. Add oil, and mix well again.

Note: The marinade can be refrigerated for up to 3 days.

Ginger Chile Marinade

Aromatic sesame oil and ginger dominate in this Asian marinade.

Yield: 1 cup | **Active time:** 10 minutes | **Start to finish:** 10 minutes

1/2 cup rice vinegar

2 tablespoons fish sauce (*nam pla*)*

1 tablespoon firmly packed light brown sugar

3 tablespoons grated fresh ginger

2 tablespoons chopped fresh cilantro

2 garlic cloves, peeled and minced

1 jalapeño or serrano chile, seeds and ribs removed, and finely
   chopped

Freshly ground black pepper to taste

1/4 cup vegetable oil

1/4 cup Asian sesame oil*

Combine vinegar, fish sauce, sugar, ginger, cilantro, garlic, chile, and pepper in a heavy resealable plastic bag, and mix well. Add vegetable oil and sesame oil, and mix well again.

Note: The marinade can be refrigerated for up to 3 days.

Spicy Asian Orange Marinade

Chinese chile paste is balanced by orange and sesame.

Yield: 3/4 cup | **Active time:** 5 minutes | **Start to finish:** 5 minutes

1/4 cup mirin or plum wine*

2 tablespoons soy sauce

2 tablespoons orange juice concentrate, thawed

4 garlic cloves, peeled and minced

1 tablespoon Chinese chile paste with garlic*

2 teaspoons grated orange zest

2 tablespoons vegetable oil

2 tablespoons Asian sesame oil*

Combine mirin, soy sauce, orange juice concentrate, garlic, chile paste, and orange zest in a heavy resealable plastic bag, and mix well. Add vegetable oil and sesame oil, and mix well again.

Note: The marinade can be refrigerated for up to 3 days.

*Available in the Asian aisle of most supermarkets and in specialty markets.

Provençal Marinade

You'll enjoy the flavors common to this sunny region in the South of France when your chicken is marinated in this subtle fashion.

Yield: 1 cup | **Active time:** 5 minutes | **Start to finish:** 5 minutes

¼ cup dry white wine
2 tablespoons lemon juice
1 tablespoon dried rosemary, crumbled
2 large garlic cloves, peeled and minced
2 teaspoons grated lemon zest
Salt and freshly ground black pepper to taste
¼ cup olive oil

Combine wine, lemon juice, rosemary, garlic, lemon zest, salt, and pepper in a heavy resealable plastic bag, and mix well. Add oil, and mix well again.

Note: The marinade can be refrigerated for up to 3 days.

Chile Brine

Fresh and dried hot peppers add some spicy flavor to this sweet and sour brine made with honey.

Yield: 2 quarts | **Active time:** 10 minutes | **Start to finish:** 15 minutes

1 cup kosher salt
1½ cups honey
½ cup cider vinegar
2 jalapeño or serrano chiles, halved
1 tablespoon crushed red pepper flakes
6 cups cold water, divided

1. Combine salt, honey, vinegar, chiles, red pepper flakes, and 1 cup water in a large non-reactive saucepan, and stir well. Bring to a boil over medium-high heat, stirring occasionally. Reduce the heat to low and simmer 2 minutes.
2. Add remaining water to the pan, and allow brine to cool. Transfer brine to a large container, and add food to be brined. Cover and refrigerate.

Note: The brine can be prepared up to 2 days in advance and refrigerated, tightly covered.

Citrus and Herb Brine

Once chicken or turkey has soaked in this brine, the subtle flavors of both lemon and orange permeate the meat.

Yield: 2 quarts | **Active time:** 10 minutes | **Start to finish:** 15 minutes

   1 cup kosher salt
   1 cup firmly packed light brown sugar
   2 oranges, sliced
   2 lemons, sliced
   8 garlic cloves, peeled and smashed
   1/4 cup chopped fresh parsley
   2 tablespoons dried thyme
   2 tablespoons black peppercorns
   6 cups cold water, divided

1. Combine salt, brown sugar, oranges, lemons, garlic, parsley, thyme, peppercorns, and 1 cup water in a large nonreactive saucepan, and stir well. Bring to a boil over medium-high heat, stirring occasionally. Reduce the heat to low and simmer 2 minutes.
2. Add remaining water to the pan. Allow brine to cool, transfer brine to a large container, and add food to be brined. Cover; refrigerate.

Note: The brine can be prepared up to 2 days in advance and refrigerated, tightly covered.

Chicken Stock

Now that you're cutting up your own chickens, you'll have a bag for trimmings for stock in your freezer. When it's full, it's time to make stock.

Yield: 4 quarts | **Active time:** 10 minutes | **Start to finish:** 4 hours

6 quarts water
5 pounds chicken bones, skin, and trimmings
4 celery ribs, rinsed and cut into thick slices
2 onions, trimmed and quartered
2 carrots, trimmed, scrubbed, and cut into thick slices
2 tablespoons whole black peppercorns
6 garlic cloves, peeled
4 sprigs parsley
1 teaspoon dried thyme
2 bay leaves

1. Place water and chicken in a large stockpot, and bring to a boil over high heat. Reduce the heat to low, and skim off foam that rises during the first 10–15 minutes of simmering. Simmer stock, uncovered, for 1 hour, then add celery, onions, carrots, peppercorns, garlic, parsley, thyme, and bay leaves. Simmer for 2½ hours.

2. Strain stock through a fine-meshed sieve, pushing with the back of a spoon to extract as much liquid as possible. Discard solids, spoon stock into smaller containers, and refrigerate. Remove and discard fat from surface of stock, then transfer stock to a variety of container sizes.

Note: The stock can be refrigerated and used within 3 days, or it can be frozen for up to 6 months.

Variation:

- For turkey stock, use the same amount of turkey giblets and necks as chicken pieces.

Spicy Maple Barbecue Sauce

This recipe is multicultural, as chipotle chiles—which are smoked jalapeño chiles packed in a spicy sauce—give heat to a thick barbecue sauce sweetened with prized maple syrup native to New England.

Yield: 3 cups | **Active time:** 15 minutes | **Start to finish:** 45 minutes

    3 tablespoons vegetable oil

    2 medium onions, peeled and chopped

    4 garlic cloves, peeled and minced

    4–6 canned chipotle chiles in adobo, drained and finely chopped

    1 cup ketchup

    1 cup pure maple syrup

    3 cups Chicken Stock (recipe on page 30) or purchased chicken or vegetable stock

    $\frac{1}{2}$ teaspoon ground allspice

    3 tablespoons freshly squeezed lemon juice

    Salt and freshly ground black pepper to taste

1. Heat oil in a large sauce pan over medium heat. Add onion and garlic and cook, stirring frequently, for 3 minutes, or until onions are translucent.
2. Stir in chiles, ketchup, maple syrup, stock, and allspice, and bring to a boil over medium-high heat, stirring frequently. Reduce the heat to low, and simmer sauce, uncovered, for 30 minutes or until reduced by $\frac{1}{2}$, stirring occasionally.
3. Stir in lemon juice, and season to taste with salt and pepper.

Note: The sauce can be refrigerated for up to 2 weeks, tightly covered, or it can be frozen for up to 6 months.

My Favorite Barbecue Sauce

When I worked as the food editor for *USA Today,* I spent a lot of time trekking around and meeting "real" cooks as well as restaurant chefs. This sauce was taught to me by a wonderful lady in rural Virginia, and what makes it so special is the combination of ginger and lemon included with more traditional ingredients.

Yield: 4 cups | **Active time:** 10 minutes | **Start to finish:** 40 minutes

> 1 (20-ounce) bottle ketchup
> 1 cup cider vinegar
> 1/2 cup firmly packed dark brown sugar
> 5 tablespoons Worcestershire sauce
> 1/4 cup vegetable oil
> 2 tablespoons dry mustard
> 2 garlic cloves, peeled and minced
> 1 tablespoon grated fresh ginger
> 1 lemon, thinly sliced
> 1/2–1 teaspoon hot red pepper sauce, or to taste

1. Combine ketchup, vinegar, brown sugar, Worcestershire sauce, vegetable oil, mustard, garlic, ginger, lemon, and red pepper sauce in a heavy 2-quart saucepan, and bring to a boil over medium heat, stirring occasionally.

2. Reduce the heat to low and simmer sauce, uncovered, for 30 minutes, or until thick, stirring occasionally. Strain sauce, pressing with the back of a spoon to extract as much liquid as possible. Ladle the sauce into containers and refrigerate, tightly covered.

Note: The sauce can be made up to 1 week in advance and refrigerated, tightly covered. Bring it back to room temperature before serving.

Easy Aioli

Aioli is to Provence what ketchup is to Portland; it's the all-purpose condiment. It's just delicious on grilled chicken, too.

Yield: 2 cups | **Active time:** 10 minutes | **Start to finish:** 10 minutes

1 1/2 cups mayonnaise

6 garlic cloves, peeled and pushed through a garlic press

3 tablespoons freshly squeezed lemon juice

2 tablespoons Dijon mustard

Salt and freshly ground black pepper to taste

Combine mayonnaise, garlic, lemon juice, and mustard in a mixing bowl. Whisk well, and season to taste with salt and pepper. Refrigerate until ready to use.

Note: The sauce can be made up to 3 days in advance and refrigerated, tightly covered. Bring it back to room temperature before serving.

Variations:

- Add 2 tablespoons chili powder to the sauce.
- Add 1/4 cup pureed roasted red bell pepper to the sauce.

Feel free to experiment with this sauce. It's great as the dressing for potato or macaroni salad as well as chicken salad. I also use it thinned with white wine vinegar as a salad dressing.

Instant Asian Barbecue Sauce

This is a wonderful sauce for your grilled or baked chicken, and it has some traditional sweet and sour flavors.

Yield: 2 cups | **Active time:** 10 minutes | **Start to finish:** 10 minutes

- $3/4$ cup unsweetened applesauce
- $1/2$ cup hoisin sauce*
- $1/4$ cup firmly packed dark brown sugar
- 6 tablespoons ketchup
- 2 tablespoons honey
- 2 tablespoons rice vinegar
- 1 tablespoon soy sauce
- 1 tablespoon Chinese chile paste with garlic*, or to taste (or substitute hot red pepper sauce)

Combine applesauce, hoisin sauce, brown sugar, ketchup, honey, rice vinegar, soy sauce, and chile paste in a mixing bowl. Whisk until smooth. Refrigerate until ready to use.

Note: The sauce can be made up to 3 days in advance and refrigerated, tightly covered.

*Available in the Asian aisle of most supermarkets and in specialty markets.

Chapter 3:

$1 Nibbles and Noshes: Snacks, Hors d'Oeuvres, and Appetizers

Chicken is appealing any time of the day, and its versatility extends to snacks and party fare. There are lots of ways to prepare chicken wings in this chapter, and they are wonderful additions to any picnic or tailgate, or in a larger quantity as a kid-friendly meal. Also in this chapter are "little dishes" that could be grouped together as a meal, some classic hors d'oeuvres made with chicken, and some creamy chicken liver pâtés. There are also some meatball recipes made with flavorful ground turkey that delight guests.

All of the recipes in this chapter are far less than $1 per serving—but that's assuming that you're cutting up your own chickens according to the method given in Chapter 2. While chicken livers are sold in containers in the supermarket, they're free in a whole chicken. So save them in a small plastic bag in the freezer, and when you have ½-pound—which is livers from six to eight chickens—then you've got enough to make one of these recipes, which will serve six to eight people as an hors d'oeuvre.

WINGING IT

If you're cutting up your chickens as instructed in Chapter 2, then you only need to supplement the wings in your freezer with a pound or two to make one of these delectable treats.

There are packages of chicken wings on the market, and you'll have to cut off the wing tips to add them to your stock-making trimmings bag. Then there are ones called "drumettes" or "wingettes," which resemble tiny drumsticks and are one-half of the wings from roasting chickens. These are usually larger and meatier—and more expensive.

If you're serving chicken wings as a meal instead of a snack, figure you need 1 pound of wings—which is four or five whole wings—per person. The wing recipes in this chapter are all baked; it's the way I think they come out best and it's the easiest because you put them in the oven and walk away. You'll notice that the wings bake at different temperatures and for different amounts of time. That's because if they were marinated in a marinade containing a lot of sugar, they must bake at a lower temperature for longer. Here are a few other ways to cook wings successfully:

- **Grill the wings.** Cook them, covered, over a medium-hot grill for a total of 12–16 minutes, turning them midway through the cooking time with tongs.

- **Deep-fry the wings.** I really don't approve of deep-frying on a few fronts. First of all, it's adding fat to the food, not allowing it to cook off; and the oil is expensive! If you want to fry them, however, heat 6 cups oil in a saucepan to a temperature of 380°F. Carefully lower in six or seven wings at a time, being careful not to crowd the pan. Cook the wings for 5–8 minutes or until golden and cooked through. Drain well on paper towels.

PÂTÉ POINTERS

A chicken liver pâté is always a hit at a party, and the recipes in this chapter are quick and easy to make, too. Just like the whole birds from which they come, the silky pureed mousses into which they're made take to any number of different seasoning combinations.

When cooking these recipes, the livers should remain slightly pink in the center and feel spongy to the touch. Overcooking the livers will result in a more strongly flavored dish; overcooking is the reason why many people say they don't like chicken livers.

> In common usage, a pâté is a pureed mixture, and a terrine, the other form of classic French charcuterie, is chunky and molded.

Balsamic Chicken Wings

Heady balsamic vinegar, the sweetest of the vinegars, is the basis for a glaze applied after these wings are baked.

Yield: 36 pieces | **Active time:** 15 minutes | **Start to finish:** 50 minutes

> 18 chicken wings, separated into 2 pieces with wing tips reserved
>   for making stock
> 1/4 cup olive oil
> 3 garlic cloves, peeled and minced
> 2 teaspoons Italian seasoning
> Salt and freshly ground black pepper to taste
> 3/4 cup balsamic vinegar
> 1/4 cup sweet vermouth or sweet sherry
> 1 tablespoon granulated sugar
> 2 tablespoons unsalted butter

1. Rinse wings and pat dry with paper towels. Preheat the oven to 425°F, and line 2 baking sheets with heavy-duty aluminum foil.
2. Place wings in a mixing bowl, and add oil, garlic, Italian seasoning, salt, and pepper. Turn wings to coat evenly, and arrange on the baking sheets.
3. Bake wings for 35–40 minutes, turning them with tongs after 15 minutes, or until wings are cooked through and no longer pink.
4. While wings bake, make sauce. Combine vinegar, vermouth, sugar, and butter in a small saucepan, and bring to a boil over high heat, stirring occasionally. Reduce the heat to medium-high and reduce mixture until only 1/2 cup remains. Season to taste with salt and pepper, and set aside.
5. Remove wings from pans, and place them in a mixing bowl. Pour sauce over wings, and toss to coat evenly. Allow to sit for 5 minutes, then toss again. Serve wings hot, at room temperature, or chilled.

Note: The wings can be cooked up to 2 days in advance and refrigerated, tightly covered. Serve them cold, or reheat them, uncovered, in a 350°F oven for 12–15 minutes, or until hot.

Orange Sesame Chicken Wings

The balance of aromatic orange and sesame with garlic and ginger creates a wonderful yin yang of flavor for these wings.

Yield: 36 pieces | **Active time:** 15 minutes | **Start to finish:** 7 hours, including 6 hours for marinating

> 18 chicken wings, separated into 2 pieces with wing tips reserved for making stock
> 1 navel orange
> 3 scallions, trimmed and cut into 2-inch sections
> 6 garlic cloves, peeled
> 4 ($\frac{1}{4}$-inch-thick) slices fresh ginger
> $\frac{1}{4}$ cup soy sauce
> $\frac{1}{4}$ cup Asian sesame oil*
> Freshly ground black pepper to taste

1. Rinse wings and pat dry with paper towels. Remove zest from orange with a sharp paring knife. Squeeze juice from orange, and set aside.
2. Place zest, scallions, garlic, and ginger in a food processor fitted with the steel blade or in a blender. Puree until smooth. Scrape mixture into a heavy resealable plastic bag, add orange juice, soy sauce, sesame oil, and pepper, and mix well. Add chicken wings.
3. Marinate chicken wings, refrigerated, for at least 6 hours, preferably overnight, turning the bag occasionally.
4. Preheat the oven to 425°F, and line 2 baking sheets with heavy-duty aluminum foil.
5. Remove wings from marinade and discard marinade. Arrange wings in a single layer on the baking sheet. Bake wings for 35–40 minutes, turning them with tongs after 20 minutes, or until wings are cooked through and no longer pink. Serve hot, at room temperature, or chilled.

Note: The wings can be cooked up to 2 days in advance and refrigerated, tightly covered. Serve them cold, or reheat them, uncovered, in a 350°F oven for 12–15 minutes, or until hot.

Variation:

- Add 1 tablespoon Chinese chile paste with garlic to the marinade for a spicy dish.

*Available in the Asian aisle of most supermarkets and in specialty markets.

Parmesan Mustard Chicken Wings

Sharp Dijon mustard and flavorful Parmesan cheese enrich the flavor of these crispy wings.

Yield: 36 pieces | **Active time:** 15 minutes | **Start to finish:** 55 minutes

18 chicken wings, separated into 2 pieces with wing tips reserved
    for making stock
1/2 cup Dijon mustard
3 tablespoons olive oil
1 tablespoon cider vinegar
3 garlic cloves, peeled and minced
Salt and freshly ground black pepper to taste
1 1/2 cups Italian bread crumbs
3/4 cup freshly grated Parmesan cheese
Vegetable oil spray

1. Preheat the oven to 400°F, line 2 baking sheets with heavy-duty aluminum foil, and grease the foil with vegetable oil spray. Rinse wings and pat dry with paper towels.

2. Combine mustard, oil, vinegar, garlic, salt, and pepper in a mixing bowl, and whisk well. Combine bread crumbs and Parmesan in a shallow bowl, and stir well to combine.

3. Add wings to mustard mixture, and coat well. Press top of wings (side with the thick skin) into crumb mixture, and arrange wings on the prepared baking sheets, with the crumbed side up.

4. Bake wings for 40–50 minutes, or until cooked through and no longer pink. Serve wings hot or at room temperature.

Note: The wings can be cooked up to 2 days in advance and refrigerated, tightly covered. Reheat them, uncovered, in a 350°F oven for 12–15 minutes, or until hot.

Variation:
- Omit the Parmesan cheese, and substitute panko bread crumbs for the Italian bread crumbs.

Buffalo Chicken Wings

We indeed know the parentage of the Buffalo wing: it's the Anchor Bar where these fiery wings cooled with blue cheese sauce were invented one night on a whim. If you can find Frank's Hot Sauce at your supermarket, it's the authentic one.

Yield: 36 pieces | **Active time:** 15 minutes | **Start to finish:** 50 minutes

> 18 chicken wings, separated into 2 pieces with wing tips reserved for making stock
>
> 1/3 cup olive oil
>
> Salt and freshly ground black pepper to taste
>
> 6 tablespoons (3/4 stick) unsalted butter
>
> 2–3 tablespoons hot red pepper sauce, or to taste
>
> 2 tablespoons balsamic vinegar
>
> 1/2 cup mayonnaise
>
> 1/3 cup sour cream
>
> 3/4 cup crumbled blue cheese
>
> 4–6 celery ribs, rinsed and trimmed

1. Rinse wings and pat dry with paper towels. Preheat the oven to 450°F, and line 2 baking sheets with heavy-duty aluminum foil.

2. Place wings in a mixing bowl, and add oil, salt, and pepper. Turn wings to coat evenly, and arrange on the baking sheets.

3. Bake wings for 30–35 minutes, turning them with tongs after 15 minutes, or until wings are cooked through and no longer pink.

4. While wings bake, make sauce and dressing. Melt butter in a heavy, large skillet over low heat. Stir in hot red pepper sauce and vinegar, and season to taste with salt. Set aside. Combine mayonnaise, sour cream, and blue cheese in a mixing bowl, and whisk well. Season to taste with salt and pepper, and refrigerate until ready to use. Cut each celery rib into thirds lengthwise, and then cut into 3-inch-long pieces. Refrigerate until ready to serve.

5. Remove wings from pans, and place them in the skillet with sauce, tossing to coat. Allow to sit for 5 minutes, then toss again. Serve wings hot or at room temperature, passing celery and blue cheese dressing separately.

Note: The wings can be cooked up to 2 days in advance and refrigerated, tightly covered. Serve them cold, or reheat them, uncovered, in a 350°F oven for 12–15 minutes, or until hot. The blue cheese dressing can also be made in advance and refrigerated, tightly covered.

Variation:

- Substitute ranch dressing for the blue cheese dressing and carrot sticks for the celery sticks.

If you want to cut up celery or carrots a day in advance, wrap the cut sticks in a wet paper towel, and then place them in a plastic bag. This will keep them from drying out.

Santa Fe Quesadillas

The vegetables that flavor the chicken as it cooks then become part of these spicy quesadillas, topped with fiery jalapeño Jack cheese.

Yield: 24 pieces | **Active time:** 15 minutes | **Start to finish:** 45 minutes

> $3/4$ pound boneless, skinless chicken breast halves
> $3/4$ cup refrigerated salsa (found in the produce section of super-markets)
> Salt and freshly ground black pepper to taste
> $1/3$ cup mayonnaise
> 3 tablespoons chopped fresh cilantro
> 1 tablespoon chili powder
> 6 (10-inch) flour or whole-wheat tortillas
> 3 ripe plum tomatoes, rinsed, cored, seeded, and thinly sliced
> 2 cups grated jalapeño Jack cheese
> Vegetable oil spray

1. Preheat the oven to 450°F, and line a 9 x 13-inch baking pan with heavy-duty aluminum foil. Rinse chicken and pat dry with paper towels. Trim chicken of all visible fat. Place chicken between 2 sheets of plastic wrap, and pound to an even thickness of $1/2$ inch. Cut chicken into strips $1/2$ inch wide.

2. Combine chicken and salsa in the pan, and season to taste with salt and pepper. Arrange chicken in one layer. Bake chicken for 10 minutes. Turn chicken with a slotted spatula. Bake for an additional 5 minutes, or until chicken is cooked through and no longer pink. Remove chicken from the pan with a slotted spoon. Drain liquid remaining in the pan, reserving vegetables from salsa. Add vegetables to chicken. Set aside.

3. Combine mayonnaise, cilantro, and chili powder in a small bowl. Stir well. Cover 2 baking sheets with heavy-duty aluminum foil, and grease the foil with vegetable oil spray.

4. Soften tortillas, if necessary, by wrapping them in plastic wrap and heating them in a microwave oven on High (100 percent power) for 10–15 seconds, or until pliable. Place tortillas on a counter. Divide chicken and tomatoes on $1/2$ of each tortilla, and top with cheese. Fold empty side of each tortilla over filling, and press closed with the palm of your hand or a spatula. Arrange tortillas on prepared baking sheets, and spray tops with vegetable oil spray.

5. Bake quesadillas for 5 minutes. Turn them gently with a spatula, and press them down if the top has separated from the filling. Bake for an additional 5–7 minutes, or until crispy. Allow to sit for 2 minutes, then cut each into 4 wedges, and serve immediately.

Note: **The quesadillas can be formed up to 1 day in advance and refrigerated, tightly covered. Add 3 minutes to the baking time if chilled.**

Variation:
• Substitute Monterey Jack cheese for the jalapeño Jack for a milder dish.

> Plum tomatoes are not only less expensive than most on the market, they are also "meatier" so they don't give off very much liquid, which might make a baked sandwich soggy.

Tropical Chicken and Black Bean Quesadillas

Succulent pineapple balances the earthy black beans in these easy to make quesadillas.

Yield: 24 wedges | **Active time:** 15 minutes | **Start to finish:** 30 minutes

2 tablespoons olive oil
1 small onion, peeled and diced
2 garlic cloves, peeled and minced
2 teaspoons ground cumin
1 (15-ounce) can black beans, rinsed and drained
1 (8-ounce) can crushed pineapple packed in juice, drained
Salt and cayenne to taste
$1/4$ cup chopped fresh cilantro
6 (10-inch) flour or whole-wheat tortillas
2 cups shredded cooked chicken
2 cups grated Monterey Jack cheese
Vegetable oil spray

1. Preheat the oven to 450°F, cover 2 baking sheets with heavy-duty aluminum foil, and grease the foil with vegetable oil spray. Set aside.
2. Heat oil in a medium skillet over medium-high heat. Add onion and garlic, and cook, stirring frequently, for 3 minutes, or until onion is translucent. Stir in cumin, and cook for 30 seconds, stirring constantly. Stir in beans and pineapple, and cook for 2 minutes. Season to taste with salt and cayenne, and stir in cilantro.
3. Soften tortillas, if necessary, by wrapping them in plastic wrap and heating them in a microwave oven on High (100 percent power) for 10–15 seconds, or until pliable. Place tortillas on a counter. Divide bean mixture and chicken on $1/2$ of each tortilla, and top with cheese. Fold empty side of each tortilla over filling, and press closed with the palm of your hand or a spatula. Arrange tortillas on prepared baking sheets, and spray tops with vegetable oil spray.
4. Bake quesadillas for 5 minutes. Turn them gently with a spatula, and press them down if the top has separated from the filling. Bake for an additional 5–7 minutes, or until crispy. Allow to sit for 2 minutes, then cut each into 4 wedges, and serve immediately.

Note: The quesadillas can be formed up to 1 day in advance and refrigerated, tightly covered. Add 3 minutes to the baking time if chilled.

Spicy Nachos

Nachos, with sautéed vegetables, beans, chicken, and cheese piled on top of corn chips, are a snack that appeals to all generations.

Yield: 36 pieces | **Active time:** 20 minutes | **Start to finish:** 30 minutes

    2 tablespoons olive oil
    1 small green bell pepper, seeds and ribs removed, and finely
        chopped
    1/2 small red onion, peeled and chopped
    3 garlic cloves, peeled and minced
    1 tablespoon chili powder
    1 teaspoon ground cumin
    1 teaspoon dried oregano
    1 (15-ounce) can red kidney beans, drained and rinsed
    1/2 cup tomato juice
    2 cups shredded cooked chicken
    1/4 cup chopped fresh cilantro
    Salt and freshly ground black pepper to taste
    36 flat corn tortilla chip rounds
    1 1/2 cups grated jalapeño Jack cheese
    2/3 cup sour cream (optional)
    Vegetable oil spray

1. Preheat the oven to 450°F, line 2 baking sheets with heavy-duty aluminum foil, and grease the foil with vegetable oil spray.
2. Heat oil in a large skillet over medium-high heat. Add green bell pepper, onion, and garlic, and cook, stirring frequently, for 5–7 minutes, or until vegetables soften. Stir in chili powder, cumin, and oregano, and cook for 1 minute, stirring constantly. Add beans and tomato juice, and cook for 2 minutes. Stir in chicken and cilantro, and season to taste with salt and pepper.
3. Arrange tortilla chips on the prepared baking sheets. Top each chip with a portion of chicken filling, and then with 1 tablespoon cheese.
4. Bake nachos for 5–7 minutes, or until cheese melts. Serve immediately, garnished with sour cream, if using.

Note: The chicken filling can be made up to 2 days in advance and refrigerated, tightly covered. Reheat it over low heat or in a microwave oven before forming and baking nachos.

Southern Barbecued Meatballs

Meatballs simmered in a barbecue sauce laced with bourbon and mustard have been a hit at parties for decades, and after making this recipe you'll see why.

Yield: 36 meatballs | **Active time:** 20 minutes | **Start to finish:** 45 minutes

2 tablespoons vegetable oil
1 large onion, peeled and chopped
4 garlic cloves, peeled and minced
1 large egg
2 tablespoons whole milk
3 pieces whole-wheat bread
$3/4$ cup chopped canned water chestnuts
2 tablespoons chopped fresh parsley
$1^1/_2$ teaspoons dried sage
$1/2$ teaspoon dried thyme
$1^1/_4$ pounds ground turkey
Salt and freshly ground black pepper to taste
1 cup My Favorite Barbecue Sauce (recipe on page 32) or purchased barbecue sauce
$1/2$ cup Chicken Stock (recipe on page 30) or purchased stock
$1/4$ cup bourbon
$1/4$ cup firmly packed light brown sugar
2 tablespoons grainy mustard
2 teaspoons cornstarch
1 tablespoon cold water
Vegetable oil spray

1. Preheat the oven broiler, line a rimmed baking sheet with heavy-duty aluminum foil, and grease the foil with vegetable oil spray.
2. Heat oil in a large skillet over medium-high heat. Add onion and garlic and cook, stirring frequently, for 3 minutes, or until onion is translucent. While vegetables cook, combine egg and milk in a mixing bowl, and whisk until smooth. Break bread into small pieces and add to the mixing bowl along with water chestnuts, parsley, sage, and thyme, and mix well.
3. Add $1/2$ of onion mixture and turkey, season to taste with salt and pepper, and mix well again. Make mixture into $1^1/_2$-inch meatballs, and

arrange meatballs on the prepared pan. Spray tops of meatballs with vegetable oil spray.

4. Broil meatballs 6 inches from the broiler element, turning them with tongs to brown all sides. While meatballs brown, add barbecue sauce, stock, bourbon, brown sugar, and mustard to the skillet with the vegetables. Bring to a boil over medium-high heat, stirring occasionally. Simmer sauce over low heat, uncovered, for 10 minutes.

5. Remove meatballs from the baking pan with a slotted spoon, and add meatballs to sauce. Bring to a boil, and simmer meatballs, covered, over low heat, turning occasionally with a slotted spoon, for 15 minutes. Mix cornstarch with water in a small bowl, and add to sauce. Cook for 1 minute, or until slightly thickened. Season to taste with salt and pepper, and serve immediately.

Note: The turkey mixture can be prepared up to 1 day in advance and refrigerated, tightly covered. Also, the dish can be cooked up to 2 days in advance and refrigerated, tightly covered. Reheat it in a 350°F oven, covered, for 15–20 minutes, or until hot.

Variation:
- Add 2 chipotle chiles in adobo sauce, finely chopped, to the sauce for a spicier dish.

Our word *barbecue*, which appears in American dictionaries before the Revolutionary War, comes from the Spanish *barbacoa*, which refers to the framework of sticks over which food was cooked. We now use barbecue both as a noun and a verb.

Crunchy Mexican Meatballs

Crushed corn chips are what give these flavorful meatballs additional texture, and a combination of spices adds to their flavor.

Yield: 36 meatballs | **Active time:** 20 minutes | **Start to finish:** 35 minutes

    1 cup corn tortilla chips
    2 tablespoons olive oil
    1/2 small red onion, peeled and finely chopped
    2 garlic cloves, peeled and minced
    1 tablespoon chili powder
    1 teaspoon ground cumin
    1/2 teaspoon dried oregano
    2 slices white bread
    2 tablespoons whole milk
    1 large egg, lightly beaten
    3 tablespoons chopped fresh cilantro
    1 pound ground turkey
    Salt and freshly ground black pepper to taste
    Vegetable oil spray

1. Preheat the oven to 450°F, line a rimmed baking sheet with heavy-duty aluminum foil, and grease the foil with vegetable oil spray. Place tortilla chips in a heavy resealable plastic bag, and pound with the flat side of a meat mallet or the bottom of a small skillet until coarse crumbs form. Set aside.

2. Heat oil in a small skillet over medium-high heat. Add onion and garlic, and cook, stirring frequently, for 3 minutes, or until onion is translucent. Add chili powder, cumin, and oregano, and cook, stirring constantly, for 1 minute.

3. While vegetables cook, tear bread into small pieces, and place bread in a bowl with milk; stir well. Stir in egg, crushed tortilla chips, and cilantro, and mix well.

4. Add onion mixture and turkey to the mixing bowl, season to taste with salt and pepper, and mix well again. Make mixture into 1½-inch meatballs, and arrange meatballs on the prepared pan. Spray tops of meatballs with vegetable oil spray.

5. Bake meatballs for 12–15 minutes, or until cooked through and no longer pink. Remove the pan from the oven, and serve immediately.

Note: The turkey mixture can be prepared up to 1 day in advance and refrigerated, tightly covered. Also, the meatballs can be baked up to 2 days in advance and refrigerated, tightly covered. Reheat them in a 350°F oven, covered, for 10–12 minutes, or until hot.

Variation:
- Add 1–2 finely chopped chipotle chiles in adobo sauce for a spicier dish.

Cilantro, which is a member of the parsley family used extensively in both Hispanic and Asian cooking, is an herb that people either adore or hate. If you fall into the latter category, just substitute fresh parsley for it.

Lemon Rosemary Meatballs

The delicacy of turkey is glorified by the additions of tart lemon and aromatic rosemary, with some garlic and Parmesan cheese thrown in for good measure.

Yield: 4-6 servings | **Active time:** 20 minutes | **Start to finish:** 35 minutes

3 slices white bread
1/4 cup whole milk
1 lemon
2 tablespoons lemon juice
2 tablespoons olive oil
1/2 small onion, peeled and chopped
4 garlic cloves, peeled and minced
1 large egg, lightly beaten
1/4 cup freshly grated Parmesan cheese
2 tablespoons chopped fresh parsley
2 tablespoons dried rosemary, crumbled
1 1/4 pounds ground turkey
Salt and freshly ground black pepper to taste
Vegetable oil spray

1. Preheat the oven to 450°F, line a rimmed baking sheet with heavy-duty aluminum foil, and grease the foil with vegetable oil spray. Tear bread into small pieces, and place bread in a mixing bowl with milk; stir well. Grate zest off lemon, and squeeze juice from lemon. Combine fresh juice with 2 tablespoons juice, and set aside.

2. Heat oil in a small skillet over medium-high heat. Add onion and garlic, and cook, stirring frequently, for 3 minutes, or until onion is translucent. While vegetables cook, whisk egg in a mixing bowl, and add bread mixture, lemon zest, Parmesan, parsley, and rosemary, and mix well.

3. Add onion mixture and turkey to the mixing bowl, season to taste with salt and pepper, and mix well again. Make mixture into 1 1/2-inch meatballs, and arrange meatballs on the prepared pan. Spray tops of meatballs with vegetable oil spray.

4. Bake meatballs for 12-15 minutes, or until cooked through and no longer pink. Remove the pan from the oven, drizzle lemon juice over meatballs, and serve immediately.

Note: The turkey mixture can be prepared up to 1 day in advance and refrigerated, tightly covered. Also, the meatballs can be baked up to 2 days in advance and refrigerated, tightly covered. Reheat them in a 350°F oven, covered, for 10–12 minutes, or until hot.

Variation:
- Substitute 1 tablespoon dried oregano for the rosemary.

> Zest really is zesty; it's the thin, colored outer portion of the citrus skin that contains all the aromatic oils. The white pith just beneath it is bitter, so you should take pains to separate the zest from the fruit without also taking any pith with it. Remove the zest using a special citrus zester, a vegetable peeler, or a paring knife. You can also grate it off using the fine holes of a box grater.

Steamed Cantonese Meatballs

These are an elegant hors d'oeuvre to serve with any Asian meal. Water chestnuts and flaky panko bread crumbs add crunch to the delicately seasoned filling, and the meatballs are then coated with rice.

Yield: 36 meatballs | **Active time:** 20 minutes | **Start to finish:** 5 hours, including 4 hours to soak rice

2 cups glutinous rice*
1/2 cup dried shiitake mushrooms*
1 cup boiling water
1 large egg
2 tablespoons soy sauce
2 tablespoons Chinese black bean sauce*
1 1/2 tablespoons cornstarch
2 teaspoons granulated sugar
1/2 cup finely chopped water chestnuts
1/2 cup panko bread crumbs*
3 tablespoons chopped fresh cilantro
2 garlic cloves, peeled and minced
2 scallions, white parts and 4 inches of green tops, rinsed, trimmed, and chopped
1 tablespoon grated fresh ginger
1 1/4 pounds ground chicken
Vegetable oil spray

1. Soak rice covered with cold water in a mixing bowl for 4 hours, or preferably overnight. Once soaked, drain rice well, and place it on a lint-free cloth.

2. Combine shiitake mushrooms and boiling water, pushing mushrooms down into the water with the back of a spoon. Soak mushrooms for 10 minutes, then drain mushrooms, reserving soaking liquid. Discard stems, and chop mushrooms. Set aside.

3. Combine egg, 2 tablespoons reserved mushroom soaking liquid, soy sauce, black bean sauce, cornstarch, and sugar in a mixing bowl, and whisk until smooth. Add mushrooms, water chestnuts, bread crumbs, cilantro, garlic, scallions, ginger, and chicken, and mix well.

*Available in the Asian aisle of most supermarkets and in specialty markets.

4. Make mixture into 1½-inch balls, and roll balls in rice, pressing it in. Spray bamboo steamer baskets with vegetable oil spray, and arrange meatballs in baskets.

5. Steam meatballs for 30-35 minutes, and serve immediately.

Note: The chicken mixture can be prepared up to 1 day in advance and refrigerated, tightly covered. Also, the meatballs can be steamed up to 2 days in advance and refrigerated, tightly covered. Reheat them in the steamer for 5-10 minutes, or until hot.

Variation:
- Add 1 tablespoon Chinese chile paste with garlic to the meat for a spicy meatball.

I serve these, as well as other Asian hors d'oeuvres, in a bamboo steamer. I line the steamer with plastic wrap and then with leaves of green or red head lettuce. In addition to placing a cup of sauce, if appropriate, in the steamer, I also place a half lime so that people can spear it with used toothpicks.

Southwest Chicken Pinwheels

These are some of the prettiest hors d'oeuvres to serve. The chicken and salsa-flavored cream cheese are rolled around a core of salad greens, and then sliced into pinwheel shapes.

Yield: 24 pieces | **Active time:** 20 minutes | **Start to finish:** 1½ hours, including 1 hour to chill

> 2 ripe plum tomatoes, rinsed, cored, seeded, and finely chopped
> Salt and freshly ground black pepper to taste
> 1 (3-ounce) package cream cheese, softened
> ¼ cup chopped fresh cilantro
> 2 scallions, white parts and 3 inches of green tops, rinsed, trimmed, and chopped
> 1 large garlic clove, peeled and minced
> 1 tablespoon lime juice
> 4 (10-inch) flour or whole-wheat tortillas
> ½ pound thinly sliced cooked chicken
> 2 cups baby greens, rinsed and dried

1. Place tomatoes in a sieve, and sprinkle with salt and pepper. Allow tomatoes to drain for 10 minutes.
2. Combine tomatoes, cream cheese, cilantro, scallions, garlic, and lime juice in a mixing bowl, and stir well. Season to taste with salt and pepper, and stir well again.
3. Wrap tortillas in plastic wrap and microwave on High (100 percent power) for 20–30 seconds, or until soft and pliable. Place tortillas on a counter, and spread each with the cream cheese mixture. Arrange chicken slices on the bottom half of each tortilla. Place ½ cup of salad greens at the bottom edge of each tortilla on top of chicken. Roll tortillas firmly but gently, starting at the filled edge. Place rolls, seam side down, on a platter or ungreased baking sheet, and refrigerate for 1 hour.
4. Trim the end off each roll by cutting on the diagonal to remove the portion of the tortilla that does not meet and form a log. Slice each tortilla into 6 slices and serve chilled.

Note: The tortillas can be filled up to 6 hours in advance and refrigerated, tightly covered. Slice just before serving.

Variations:

- These wraps can also be served as part of a brunch, served like halved egg rolls. Rather than rolling them as described in the recipe, tuck in both sides of the tortillas first, then roll them firmly but gently. Cut them on the diagonal into two halves.
- Add 1-2 jalapeño or serrano chiles, seeds and ribs removed, and finely chopped, to the cream cheese mixture for a spicy dish.
- Substitute smoked turkey or roast turkey for the chicken.

It's important to allow tomatoes to drain when using them in a dish like this. They will give off a lot of liquid, which could make the dish soggy. But save the liquid and use it in soups.

Curried Caribbean Fried Wontons

Wonton skins, found in the produce section of supermarkets, are just thin sheets of pasta dough that can hold any number of fillings that aren't Chinese. In this case, the turkey is scented with curry and contains chopped raisins.

Yield: 36 pieces | **Active time:** 30 minutes | **Start to finish:** 30 minutes

    2 tablespoons olive oil
    6 scallions, white parts and 3 inches of green tops, rinsed,
        trimmed, and chopped
    2 garlic cloves, peeled and minced
    2 teaspoons curry powder (or more to taste)
    ½ teaspoon dried thyme
    ½ pound ground turkey
    ⅓ cup chopped raisins
    Salt and cayenne to taste
    1 large egg, lightly beaten
    3 tablespoons plain bread crumbs
    36 wonton wrappers
    2 cups vegetable oil for frying

1. Preheat the oven to 200°F, and line a baking sheet with paper towels.
2. Heat oil in a heavy, large skillet over medium-high heat. Add scallions and garlic, and cook, stirring frequently, for 3 minutes, or until scallions are translucent. Add curry powder and thyme, and cook for 1 minute, stirring constantly.
3. Add turkey, breaking up lumps with a fork, and cook for 3–5 minutes, or until turkey is no longer pink. Remove mixture from the skillet with a slotted spoon, and place it in a mixing bowl. Stir in raisins, and season to taste with salt and cayenne. Stir in egg and bread crumbs, and mix well.
4. Place 1 tablespoon filling in the center of 1 wrapper. Brush edges with water, and fold dough diagonally to encase filling. Press to seal. Repeat with remaining wrappers and filling.

5. Heat oil in a heavy, large skillet over medium-high heat until oil reaches 375°F on a frying thermometer. Fry 1/3 of dumplings for 1½–2 minutes per side, turning them with a slotted spoon, or until golden brown. Drain well on paper towels, and keep dumplings warm in the oven while frying remaining dumplings. Serve immediately.

Note: The wontons can be fried up to 1 day in advance and refrigerated, tightly covered. Reheat them, uncovered, in a 375°F oven for 5–7 minutes, or until hot and crisp.

Variation:
- Substitute dried cranberries or chopped dried apricots for the raisins.

While a deep fat thermometer, also called a candy thermometer, is a great addition to any kitchen, here's a visual trick to tell if oil is hot enough. Add a few bread cubes, and if the oil bubbles furiously and the cubes brown in about 10 seconds, the oil is at 375°F.

Vietnamese Spring Rolls

Cha gio, crispy Vietnamese spring rolls wrapped in rice paper, are one of my favorite dishes, and baking instead of frying makes them much quicker to prepare and lighter.

Yield: 36 pieces | **Active time:** 25 minutes | **Start to finish:** 1 hour

    5 large dried shiitake mushrooms
    1 ounce bean thread (sometimes called cellophane) noodles*
    1/2 pound ground chicken
    1 cup fresh bean sprouts, rinsed and cut into 1-inch lengths
    1 small carrot, peeled and grated
    5 scallions, white parts and 4 inches of green tops, rinsed, trimmed, and chopped
    6 garlic cloves, peeled and minced
    3 tablespoons fish sauce (*nam pla*)*
    2 large eggs, lightly beaten
    1/2 cup granulated sugar, divided
    Salt and freshly ground black pepper to taste
    18 (8-inch) rice paper pancakes*
    Vegetable oil spray

1. Soak dried mushrooms and bean thread noodles in separate bowls of very hot tap water for 30 minutes. Drain mushrooms, and squeeze well to extract as much water as possible. Discard stems, and finely chop mushrooms. Drain bean thread noodles. Place them on a cutting board in a long log shape, and cut into 1-inch pieces. Measure out 1/2 cup, and discard any additional.

2. Preheat the oven to 400°F, cover a baking sheet with heavy-duty aluminum foil, and grease the foil with vegetable oil spray.

3. Place mushrooms and noodles in a mixing bowl, and add chicken, bean sprouts, carrot, scallions, garlic, fish sauce, eggs, and 1 teaspoon sugar. Season to taste with salt and pepper, and mix well.

4. Fill a wide mixing bowl with very hot tap water, and stir in remaining sugar until it is dissolved. Place a damp tea towel in front of you on the counter. Place rice paper pancakes on a plate, and cover with a barely damp towel.

*Available in the Asian aisle of most supermarkets and in specialty markets.

5. Fill 1 rice paper pancake at a time, keeping remainder covered. Totally immerse pancake in the hot water for 2 seconds. Remove it and place it on the damp tea towel; it will become pliable within a few seconds. Gently fold the front edge of the pancake $1/3$ of the way to the top. Place about 2 tablespoons filling on the folded-up portion, and shape it into a log, leaving a 2-inch margin on each side. Lightly spray the unfilled pancake with vegetable oil spray. Fold the sides over the filling, and roll tightly but gently, beginning with the filled side. Place roll on the prepared baking sheet, and continue until all rice paper pancakes are filled. Spray tops and sides of rolls with vegetable oil spray.

6. Bake for 12 minutes, then turn rolls gently with tongs, and bake an additional 10–12 minutes, or until rolls are browned. Remove the pan from the oven, and blot rolls with paper towels. Slice each in half on the diagonal, and serve immediately.

Note: The filling for the spring rolls can be prepared up to 1 day in advance and refrigerated, tightly covered. The rolls should not be filled and baked until just prior to serving.

Variation:
- Add 1–2 tablespoons Chinese chile paste with garlic to the filling for a spicy dish.

Baked Asian Turkey Rolls

When I wrote a book titled *All Wrapped Up* in 1998 I was experimenting with various wrappers, and discovered that rolled-out slices of basic white bread worked wonderfully! These flavorful Asian morsels are crunchy from water chestnuts as well as from the toast covering.

Yield: 36 pieces | **Active time:** 20 minutes | **Start to finish:** 30 minutes

12 slices white sandwich bread
½ pound ground turkey
2 tablespoons grated fresh ginger
1 tablespoon Asian sesame oil*
1 large egg white
1 tablespoon dry sherry
2 tablespoons cornstarch
1 tablespoon soy sauce
2 scallions, white parts and 3 inches of green tops, rinsed, trimmed, and sliced
⅓ cup finely chopped canned water chestnuts
Salt and freshly ground black pepper to taste
Vegetable oil spray

1. Preheat the oven to 425°F, cover a baking sheet with aluminum foil, and grease the foil with vegetable oil spray.
2. Remove crusts from bread slices using a serrated bread knife. Roll each slice with a rolling pin until bread slice is thin, but still pliable. Set aside.
3. Combine turkey, ginger, sesame oil, egg white, sherry, cornstarch, and soy sauce in a food processor fitted with the steel blade or in a blender. Puree until smooth, stopping a few times to scrape the sides of the work bowl. Scrape mixture into a mixing bowl, and stir in scallions and water chestnuts. Season to taste with salt and pepper.
4. Spread bread slices out on a counter and place 1 heaping tablespoon filling in a line across the long side of each slice. Roll bread around filling so that edges meet and place rolls, seam side down, on the prepared baking sheet. Spray tops with vegetable oil spray.

*Available in the Asian aisle of most supermarkets and in specialty markets.

5. Bake rolls for 5 minutes, turn over gently with tongs, and bake for 4 minutes, or until browned. Cut each into 3 sections with a serrated knife, and serve immediately.

Note: The turkey mixture can be prepared 1 day in advance and refrigerated, tightly covered. Fill the bread and bake the rolls just prior to serving.

> If you don't have a rolling pin, or you're using it to prop open a window, you can use any glass bottle—like wine or vinegar—to roll out the bread slices. Either wash it well, or cover it with foil.

Chicken in Lettuce Cups

Here's another of my favorite Asian hors d'oeuvres. I usually put out the bowl of filling and a plate of lettuce cups, and let guests roll their own; think of them as Chinese tacos.

Yield: 36 pieces | **Active time:** 20 minutes | **Start to finish:** 20 minutes

    2 tablespoons Asian sesame oil*
    2 garlic cloves, peeled and minced
    1 tablespoon grated fresh ginger
    4 scallions, white parts and 3 inches of green tops, rinsed,
        trimmed, and thinly sliced
    1 pound ground chicken
    1 (8-ounce) can water chestnuts, drained, rinsed, and chopped
    1/4 cup soy sauce
    2 tablespoons hoisin sauce*
    1 tablespoon cider vinegar
    2 teaspoons cornstarch
    Salt and freshly ground black pepper to taste
    36 (4-inch) rounds iceberg lettuce, rinsed and dried
    1/2 cup chopped scallions (optional)

1. Heat sesame oil in a large skillet over medium-high heat. Add garlic, ginger, and scallions, and cook for 30 seconds, stirring constantly. Add chicken, and cook for 4–5 minutes, breaking up lumps with a fork, or until chicken has lost all of its pink color and is white and beginning to brown. Stir in water chestnuts, and stir-fry 1 minute.

2. Mix soy sauce, hoisin sauce, vinegar, and cornstarch in a small bowl. Add to the pan, and when mixture boils and thickens, reduce the heat to low, and simmer for 1 minute, stirring frequently. Season to taste with salt and pepper.

3. Spoon mixture into lettuce leaves, and garnish with scallions, if using. Serve immediately.

Note: The filling can be prepared up to 1 day in advance and refrigerated, tightly covered. Reheat it over low heat, covered, stirring occasionally, or in a microwave oven.

*Available in the Asian aisle of most supermarkets and in specialty markets.

Variation:

- Add 1 tablespoon Chinese chile paste with garlic for an interesting, spicy filling.

Hoisin sauce, pronounced *hoy-ZAHN*, is a thick sweet and spicy reddish-brown sauce; it's made from a mixture of soybeans, garlic, chiles, Chinese five-spice powder, and sugar. Like ketchup in our country, it's used both as a condiment and as an ingredient.

Chicken Satay with Spicy Thai Peanut Sauce

Satays are part of many Asian cultures, and these morsels of spicy chicken are inspired by Thai cooking. While these are meant to be served as individual morsels, you can also thread many pieces onto parallel skewers and transform this hors d'oeuvre into an entree.

Yield: 36 pieces | **Active time:** 15 minutes | **Start to finish:** 3½ hours, including 3 hours for marinating

CHICKEN

³⁄₄ pound boneless, skinless chicken breast halves

½ cup soy sauce

½ cup firmly packed dark brown sugar

¼ cup lime juice

2 tablespoons Chinese chile paste with garlic*

4 garlic cloves, peeled and minced

1 tablespoon Asian sesame oil*

SAUCE

1 cup chunky peanut butter

½ cup very hot tap water

½ cup firmly packed dark brown sugar

⅓ cup freshly squeezed lime juice

¼ cup soy sauce

2 tablespoons Asian sesame oil*

2 tablespoons Chinese chile paste with garlic*

6 garlic cloves, peeled and minced

3 scallions, trimmed and chopped

¼ cup chopped fresh cilantro

1. Rinse chicken and pat dry with paper towels. Trim fat from chicken breasts and pull off tenderloins. Remove tendon from the center of each tenderloin by holding down tip with your finger and scraping away meat with the dull side of paring knife. Cut tenderloins in half, and cut the remaining chicken meat into 1-inch cubes.

*Available in the Asian aisle of most supermarkets and in specialty markets.

2. Combine soy sauce, brown sugar, lime juice, chili paste, garlic, and sesame oil in a heavy resealable plastic bag, and blend well. Add chicken pieces and marinate, refrigerated, for 3 hours, turning the bag occasionally.

3. While chicken marinates, make sauce. Combine peanut butter, water, brown sugar, lime juice, soy sauce, sesame oil, and chile paste in a mixing bowl. Whisk until well combined. Stir in garlic, scallions, and cilantro, and chill well before serving.

4. Light a charcoal or gas grill, or preheat the oven broiler. Remove chicken from marinade and discard marinade. Grill or broil chicken pieces for a total of 3–5 minutes, turning pieces with tongs, or until chicken is cooked through and no longer pink. Spear each piece of chicken with a toothpick or bamboo skewer, and serve hot, passing sauce separately.

Note: The chicken can marinate for up to 6 hours, and it can be cooked 1 day in advance and refrigerated, tightly covered. Reheat it in a 350°F oven wrapped in aluminum foil for 5 to 10 minutes, or until hot. The sauce can be made up to 3 days in advance and refrigerated, tightly covered. Bring it back to room temperature before serving.

Variation:
- Substitute boneless, skinless chicken thighs for the chicken breasts, and the cooking time will remain the same.

Creole Chicken Liver Pâté

The butter gives this dish a velvety texture, and it's made in a matter of minutes. It's a variation with American ingredients on a classic French dish.

Yield: 1 pint | **Active time:** 20 minutes | **Start to finish:** 2 hours, including 1½ hours to chill

> ½ pound chicken livers
> 4 tablespoons (½ stick) unsalted butter
> 3 scallions, white parts and 3 inches of green tops, rinsed, trimmed, and sliced
> 2 garlic cloves, peeled and minced
> 1 tablespoon chopped fresh parsley
> ½ teaspoon dried thyme
> ¼ teaspoon dried sage
> Pinch ground allspice
> 1 tablespoon bourbon
> Salt and freshly ground black pepper to taste
> Crackers or toast points for serving

1. Rinse chicken livers in a sieve, and trim them of all fat. Cut livers into ¾-inch pieces, and drain on paper towels.
2. Melt butter in a large skillet over medium-high heat. Add scallions and garlic, and cook, stirring frequently, for 2 minutes. Add parsley, thyme, sage, and allspice, and cook for an additional 1 minute, or until scallions are translucent.
3. Add livers, and cook, stirring frequently, for 4–6 minutes, or until livers are just slightly pink in the center. Sprinkle with bourbon. Puree in a food processor fitted with the steel blade or in a blender. Season to taste with salt and pepper.
4. Line a small mixing bowl with plastic wrap, and scrape mixture into the bowl. Chill pâté for at least 1½ hours, or until cold. To serve, unmold onto a platter and serve with crackers.

Note: The pâté can be made up to 2 days in advance and refrigerated, tightly covered.

Variation:
- Add 1 jalapeño or serrano chile, seeds and ribs removed, and finely chopped, to the skillet along with the scallions and garlic.

Glazed Chicken Liver Pâté with Dried Fruit

The earthiness of chicken livers is enhanced with the additions of succulent dried fruit and jam in this easy pâté.

Yield: 1 pint | **Active time:** 20 minutes | **Start to finish:** 2 hours, including 1½ hours to chill

> ½ pound chicken livers
> 4 tablespoons (½ stick) unsalted butter
> 1 medium onion, peeled and chopped
> ¼ cup port
> ½ cup apricot preserves, divided
> ¼ teaspoon ground cinnamon
> Salt and freshly ground black pepper to taste
> ½ cup finely chopped dried apricots
> Crackers or toast points for serving

1. Rinse chicken livers in a sieve, and trim them of all fat. Cut livers into ³/₄-inch pieces, and drain on paper towels.
2. Melt butter in a large skillet over medium-high heat. Add onion, and cook, stirring frequently, for 3 minutes, or until onion is translucent.
3. Add livers, and cook, stirring frequently, for 4–6 minutes, or until livers are just slightly pink in the center. Transfer liver mixture to a food processor fitted with the steel blade or to a blender.
4. Add port, 2 tablespoons apricot preserves, and cinnamon to the skillet, and cook for 1 minute, stirring constantly. Add liquid to livers, and puree until smooth. Stir in dried apricots, and season to taste with salt and pepper.
5. Line a small mixing bowl with plastic wrap, and scrape mixture into the bowl. Chill pâté for at least 1½ hours, or until cold. To serve, unmold onto a platter, and spread top of pâté with remaining apricot preserves. Serve with crackers.

Note: The pâté can be made up to 2 days in advance and refrigerated, tightly covered.

Variation:
- Substitute chopped dried figs and fig preserves for the apricots and apricot preserves.

Apple Walnut Chicken Liver Pâté

While this pâté is rich, the apples make it lighter than most I have tried, and the slight undertastes from the walnut oil and Calvados are delicious.

Yield: 1 pint | **Active time:** 20 minutes | **Start to finish:** 2 hours, including 1½ hours to chill

> ½ cup chopped walnuts
> ½ pound chicken livers
> 5 tablespoons unsalted butter, divided
> 1 McIntosh apple, peeled, cored, and thinly sliced
> 1 teaspoon granulated sugar
> 1 tablespoon brandy (Calvados recommended)
> Salt and freshly ground black pepper to taste
> Crackers and toast points for serving

1. Preheat the oven to 350°F, and line a baking sheet with foil. Bake walnuts for 5–7 minutes, or until lightly browned. Set aside. Rinse chicken livers in a sieve, and trim them of all fat. Cut livers into ¾-inch pieces, and drain on paper towels.

2. Melt 2 tablespoons butter in a large skillet over medium-high heat. Add livers, and cook, stirring frequently, for 4–6 minutes, or until livers are just slightly pink in the center. Transfer liver mixture to a food processor fitted with the steel blade or to a blender.

3. Add remaining butter to the skillet, add apple slices, and sprinkle apples with sugar. Cook for 4–6 minutes, or until apples are tender. Add brandy, and cook for 1 minute more.

4. Add apples and walnuts to the livers, and puree until smooth. Season to taste with salt and pepper.

5. Line a small mixing bowl with plastic wrap, and scrape mixture into the bowl. Chill pâté for at least 1½ hours, or until cold. To serve, unmold onto a platter, and serve with crackers.

Note: The pâté can be made up to 2 days in advance and refrigerated, tightly covered.

Variation:
- Substitute almonds or pecans for the walnuts.

Chapter 4:
Meals in a Bowl: Entree Soups from the World's Cauldrons

Chicken soups are synonymous with comfort food, and they are delicious, healthful meals even for days when you don't have a cold. They are found in almost all of the world's cuisines, and run the gamut from lean to luscious.

There is evidence to support the idea that chicken stock really does contain medicinal qualities; perhaps your grandma was right all along. In 1993, University of Nebraska Medical Center researcher Dr. Stephen Rennard published a study stating that chicken soup contains a number of substances, including an anti-inflammatory mechanism that eases the symptoms of upper respiratory tract infections. Other studies also showed that the chicken soup was equally medicinal if made without vegetables; the value came from the chicken itself.

There are two ways to create chicken soups, both from "scratch" and to use up leftover cooked chicken cooked another way. If you're doing the latter, then go ahead and use stock from your freezer, and cut up whatever chicken you have around. But if you're specifically cooking stock and chicken to make a soup, then look at the recipes that lead off this chapter; you get a rich stock with chicken meat that is tender but still has texture.

Most stock is made with scraps and trimmings, and after boiling it for many hours there's really nothing left to save. But cooking Chicken Stock for Entree Soups (recipe on page 71) gives you a flavorful broth plus freshly cooked chicken in large pieces to cut up for the soup, and have some leftover, too.

These recipes are written for entree portions of the soups. These are all—as promised in the chapter title—"meals in a bowl." But if you're serving these soups as an appetizer before another entree, they will feed eight to ten people.

GREASY GOODNESS

In other books in the $3 Meals series I've touted the benefits—both for flavor and economy—of using bacon grease for cooking. It's been a part of every Southern woman's kitchen for centuries.

Well, in this chapter the equally saturated fat I'm suggesting you use, especially in soups, is chicken fat—that layer you skim off of stocks. First of all, it's free; you've already bought and cooked the chicken from which it came. And it adds a richness of flavor to soups. Chicken fat can also be used for sautéing potatoes or other vegetables because it has a very high smoke point.

Add vegetables after the stock has simmered for a few minutes. It's easier to remove the scum that rises to the surface if there are no vegetables floating around.

Chicken Stock for Entree Soups

Here is the basis for many of the recipes in this chapter; the whole chicken is cooked for part of the time to create the broth, and then it's removed to preserve the flavor and texture of the meat. The chicken should be refrigerated and/or frozen separately from the stock.

Yield: 3 quarts | **Active time:** 10 minutes | **Start to finish:** 3 hours

1 (3½–4-pound) chicken including giblets, liver reserved for another use
6 quarts water
2 celery ribs, rinsed and cut into thick slices
1 large onion, trimmed and quartered
2 carrots, trimmed, scrubbed, and cut into thick slices
1 tablespoon salt
2 tablespoons whole black peppercorns
4 garlic cloves, peeled
4 parsley sprigs
1 teaspoon dried thyme
2 bay leaves

1. Rinse chicken inside and out. Place chicken and water in a large stockpot, and bring to a boil over high heat. Reduce the heat to low, and skim off foam that rises during the first 10–15 minutes of simmering. Simmer stock, uncovered, for 15 minutes, then add celery, onion, carrots, salt, peppercorns, garlic, parsley, thyme, and bay leaves. Simmer for an additional 1 hour.
2. Remove chicken from the stockpot with a slotted spoon, and set aside. When cool enough to handle, remove meat from bones, and discard bones and skin.
3. Raise the heat to medium, and cook vegetables and remaining stock for an additional 1 hour, or until liquid is reduced by ⅓.
4. Strain stock through a fine-meshed sieve, pushing with the back of a spoon to extract as much liquid as possible. Discard solids, spoon stock into smaller containers, and refrigerate. Remove and discard fat from surface of stock, then transfer stock to a variety of container sizes.

Note: Refrigerate the stock for 3 days, or freeze for up to 6 months.

Variation:
- For turkey stock, substitute ½ turkey breast or 1 leg and thigh quarter for the chicken, and cook the turkey for 30 minutes longer.

Quick Chicken Stock for Entree Soups

While I always try to have homemade chicken stock in the freezer, I'm also enough of a realist to know that occasionally that doesn't happen and I've got to turn to containers of stock. If that's the case, then use this recipe for gently simmering the chicken and adding additional flavor to the commercial stock.

Yield: 3 quarts | **Active time:** 10 minutes | **Start to finish:** 1 hour

> 3 quarts purchased low-sodium chicken stock
> 1 (3½–4-pound) chicken including giblets, liver reserved for another use, cut into serving pieces
> 2 celery ribs, rinsed and cut into thick slices
> 1 onion, trimmed and quartered
> 2 carrots, trimmed, scrubbed, and cut into thick slices
> 2 tablespoons whole black peppercorns
> 4 garlic cloves, peeled
> 4 parsley sprigs
> 1 teaspoon dried thyme
> 2 bay leaves

1. Place stock, chicken, celery, onion, carrots, peppercorns, garlic, parsley, thyme, and bay leaves in a large stockpot, and bring to a boil over high heat. Reduce the heat to low, and skim off foam that rises during the first 10–15 minutes of simmering. Simmer stock, uncovered, for a total of 1 hour.
2. Remove chicken from the stockpot with a slotted spoon, and set aside. When cool enough to handle, remove meat from bones, and discard bones and skin.
3. Strain stock through a fine-meshed sieve, pushing with the back of a spoon to extract as much liquid as possible. Discard solids, spoon stock into smaller containers, and refrigerate. Remove and discard fat from surface of stock, then transfer stock to a variety of container sizes.

Note: The stock can be refrigerated and used within 3 days, or it can be frozen for up to 6 months.

Variation:

- For turkey stock, substitute ½ turkey breast or 1 leg and thigh quarter for the chicken, and cook the turkey for 30 minutes longer.

> You'll notice that there is no salt specified in this recipe—and for good reason. Even the so-called "low-sodium" chicken stocks on the market contain a great quantity of sodium—upwards of 500 mg per serving. That's another good reason to make your own stock: they can be sodium-free if you desire.

Old-Fashioned Chicken Noodle Soup

Tender egg noodles and a variety of vegetables in a richly flavored homemade stock are the hallmarks of this American classic.

Yield: 4-6 servings | **Active time:** 15 minutes | **Start to finish:** 35 minutes

2 cups medium egg noodles
2 tablespoons unsalted butter or chicken fat
1 medium onion, peeled and diced
2 celery ribs, rinsed, trimmed, and sliced
2 carrots, peeled and sliced
8 cups Chicken Stock for Entree Soups (recipe on page 71) or purchased stock
3 tablespoons chopped fresh parsley
1 teaspoon dried thyme
1 bay leaf
2-3 cups diced cooked chicken
$2/3$ cup frozen cut green beans, thawed
$1/2$ cup frozen peas, thawed
Salt and freshly ground black pepper to taste

1. Bring a large pot of salted water to a boil over high heat. Add egg noodles and cook according to package directions until al dente. Drain, and set aside.
2. While water heats, melt butter in a 4-quart saucepan over medium-high heat. Add onion, celery, and carrots, and cook, stirring frequently, for 3 minutes, or until onion is translucent. Add stock, parsley, thyme, and bay leaf, and bring to a boil over high heat.
3. Reduce the heat to low and simmer soup, uncovered, for 15 minutes, or until vegetables are tender. Add chicken, green beans, and peas, and simmer for 5 minutes. Remove and discard bay leaf, stir in noodles, and season to taste with salt and pepper. Serve immediately.

Note: The soup can be prepared up to 3 days in advance and refrigerated, tightly covered. To serve, reheat it, covered, over low heat, stirring frequently.

Variations:
- Add 1 (14.5-ounce) can diced tomatoes, undrained, to the soup.
- Add 1 (15-ounce) can garbanzo beans, kidney beans, or cannellini beans, drained and rinsed.
- Substitute cooked pasta or rice for the egg noodles.
- Substitute 2 large redskin potatoes, scrubbed and cut into 3/4-inch dice, for the noodles. Add the potatoes to the soup along with the stock.

You can save money on your energy bills if every time you bring a pot of salted water to a boil to cook pasta or noodles, you cover the pot until it begins to boil. Five minutes here and there add up on your gas or electric bill.

Chicken Vegetable Soup with Matzo Balls

While this recipe might be the epitome of "Jewish penicillin," you don't have to be sick to enjoy it. Matzo balls, when made properly, are fluffy and light dumplings that can be personalized in many ways.

Yield: 4-6 servings | **Active time:** 15 minutes | **Start to finish:** 1½ hours, including 30 minutes for dough to chill

MATZO BALLS

4 large eggs
¼ cup chicken stock
¼ cup vegetable oil or melted chicken fat
1 cup matzo meal
Salt and freshly ground black pepper to taste

SOUP

6 cups Chicken Stock for Entree Soups (recipe on page 71) or purchased stock
2 carrots, peeled and sliced
1 small onion, peeled and diced
1 celery rib, rinsed, trimmed, and sliced
1½ cups diced cooked chicken
½ cup frozen peas, thawed
½ cup frozen cut green beans, thawed
Salt and freshly ground black pepper to taste

1. For matzo balls, place eggs in a mixing bowl, and whisk well with stock and oil. Stir in matzo meal, and season to taste with salt and pepper. Refrigerate mixture for at least 30 minutes.
2. Bring a large pot of salted water to a boil over high heat. Using wet hands, form matzo dough into 1½-inch balls, and drop them into water. Cover the pot, reduce the heat to low, and simmer matzo balls for 35 minutes *without removing the cover from the pan.*
3. While matzo balls simmer, heat stock in a large saucepan to a boil over medium-high heat. Add carrots, onion, and celery, reduce the heat to low, and cook vegetables, uncovered, for 10–12 minutes, or until carrots are tender. Add chicken, peas, and green beans, and cook for an additional 5 minutes.

4. Remove matzo balls from the pan with a slotted spoon, and transfer them to soup. Season to taste with salt and pepper, and serve immediately.

Note: **The soup can be made up to 3 days in advance and refrigerated, tightly covered. Reheat it over low heat, covered.**

Variations for matzo balls:
- Add ¾ cup frozen chopped spinach, thawed and squeezed dry.
- Add ¼ cup chopped fresh dill.
- Add 2 tablespoons chopped fresh parsley, 2 teaspoons fresh thyme, and 2 teaspoons chopped fresh sage.
- Add ¼ pound sautéed chopped fresh mushrooms.
- Add 2 tablespoons of tomato paste.

Perhaps it's not authentic matzo, also spelled matzah, but if you've eaten a water cracker you know what it is. This traditional unleavened bread is eaten yearly by Jews worldwide for the week they celebrate Passover. The holiday commemorates the Jews' flight from Egypt, during which they had no time for their bread to rise.

Cream of Chicken Soup with Pasta

Lots of healthful mushrooms and other vegetables dot this easy to make soup. While it contains half-and-half, it remains light.

Yield: 4–6 servings | **Active time:** 15 minutes | **Start to finish:** 35 minutes

1 cup macaroni
3 tablespoons unsalted butter or chicken fat
1 medium onion, peeled and diced
$1/4$ pound mushrooms, wiped with a damp paper towel, trimmed, and sliced
1 celery rib, rinsed, trimmed, and thinly sliced
1 carrot, peeled and thinly sliced
3 tablespoons all-purpose flour
4 cups Chicken Stock for Entree Soups (recipe on page 71) or purchased stock
2 cups half-and-half
2 tablespoons chopped fresh parsley
$1/2$ teaspoon dried thyme
2–3 cups cooked chicken, cut into $3/4$-inch cubes
$2/3$ cup frozen peas, thawed
Salt and freshly ground black pepper to taste

1. Bring a large pot of salted water to a boil over high heat. Add pasta, and cook according to package directions until al dente. Drain, and set aside.
2. While water heats, melt butter in 3-quart saucepan over medium-high heat. Add onion, mushrooms, celery, and carrot, and cook, stirring frequently, for 5 minutes, or until mushrooms soften.
3. Stir in flour and cook for 1 minute, stirring constantly. Add stock, half-and-half, parsley, and thyme. Bring to a boil over medium-high heat, stirring frequently. Reduce the heat to low, and simmer soup, uncovered, for 10 minutes. Add pasta, chicken, and peas, and simmer for an additional 5 minutes. Season to taste with salt and pepper, and serve immediately.

Note: The soup can be prepared up to 3 days in advance and refrigerated, tightly covered. To eat, reheat it, covered, over low heat, stirring frequently.

Variation:

- Substitute rice or egg noodles for the macaroni.

It's always important to cook the flour as specified in a recipe. This creates what's called a *roux* (pronounced *roo* as in kangaroo) to thicken the soup or sauce, and cooking the flour keeps it from tasting pasty.

Corn and Chicken Chowder

Thick and hearty chowders are quintessentially American soups, and this version contains corn in three forms to enhance its flavor and texture.

Yield: 4–6 servings | **Active time:** 15 minutes | **Start to finish:** 40 minutes

- 2 tablespoons unsalted butter or chicken fat
- 1 medium onion, peeled and diced
- 6 cups Chicken Stock for Entree Soups (recipe on page 71) or purchased stock
- $1/2$ pound redskin potatoes, scrubbed and cut into $3/4$-inch dice
- $1/4$ small acorn squash, peeled and cut into $3/4$-inch dice
- 2 tablespoons chopped fresh parsley
- $1/2$ teaspoon dried thyme
- $1/2$ cup heavy cream
- 1 (8-ounce) can creamed corn
- 3 tablespoons yellow cornmeal
- 1 (10-ounce) package frozen corn kernels
- 2–3 cups diced cooked chicken
- Salt and freshly ground black pepper to taste
- $1/4$ cup chopped chives (optional)

1. Heat butter in a 3-quart saucepan over medium-high heat. Add onion, and cook, stirring frequently, for 3 minutes, or until onion is translucent. Add stock, potatoes, squash, parsley, and thyme. Bring to a boil over high heat, stirring occasionally. Reduce the heat to low, and simmer soup, uncovered, for 10–12 minutes, or until vegetables are tender.

2. Add cream, creamed corn, and cornmeal, and stir well. Bring to a boil, and simmer 2 minutes. Add corn kernels and chicken, and cook for 5 minutes. Season to taste with salt and pepper, and serve immediately, sprinkling servings with chives, if using.

Note: The soup can be made up to 3 days in advance and refrigerated, tightly covered. Reheat it, covered, over low heat, stirring frequently.

Variations:

- Cook 6 bacon slices, cut into 1-inch sections, in the saucepan for 5-7 minutes, or until crisp. Remove bacon from the pan, and set aside. Discard all but 2 tablespoons bacon grease from the pan, and substitute the bacon grease for the butter to sauté the onion.
- Add 1 green bell pepper, seeds and ribs removed, and chopped, to the saucepan along with the onion.
- Substitute cilantro for the parsley, and add 1 (4-ounce) can chopped mild green chiles, drained, to the soup along with the stock.

Cornmeal can be used as a thickener instead of all-purpose flour in many soups and stews. Unlike flour, it needs no precooking. But it does add a distinctive taste to dishes.

Italian Wedding Soup

Wedding soup is actually Italian-American, rather than tied to any region of Italy. It is a mistranslation of *minestra maritata,* which has nothing to do with nuptials, but is a reference to the fact that green vegetables and meats go well together. Serve it with a loaf of garlic bread and your meal is complete.

Yield: 4–6 servings | **Active time:** 15 minutes | **Start to finish:** 40 minutes

SOUP

6 cups Chicken Stock (recipe on page 71) or purchased stock
1 pound curly endive, rinsed, cored, and coarsely chopped
2 large eggs
½ cup freshly grated Parmesan cheese, divided
Salt and freshly ground black pepper to taste

MEATBALLS

1 large egg
½ cup Italian bread crumbs
¼ cup whole milk
1 small onion, peeled and grated
2 garlic cloves, peeled and minced
¼ cup freshly grated Parmesan cheese
¼ cup chopped fresh parsley
2 teaspoons Italian seasoning
1 pound ground turkey
Salt and freshly ground black pepper to taste

1. Combine chicken stock and endive in a 3-quart saucepan, and bring to a boil over medium-high heat. Reduce the heat to low, and simmer soup, uncovered, for 10 minutes.
2. While soup simmers, make meatballs. Combine egg, bread crumbs, milk, onion, garlic, ¼ cup Parmesan, parsley, and Italian seasoning, and mix well. Add turkey, season to taste with salt and pepper, and mix well to form a paste.

3. Using wet hands, form meatball mixture into 1-inch balls, and drop them into simmering soup. Cook, uncovered, for 7–10 minutes, or until meatballs are cooked through and no longer pink.

4. Whisk remaining 2 eggs with 2 tablespoons of remaining Parmesan. Stir soup and gradually add egg mixture to form thin strands. Season to taste with salt and pepper, and serve immediately, passing remaining cheese separately.

Note: The soup can be made up to 3 days in advance and refrigerated, tightly covered. Reheat it over low heat, covered.

Variations:

- If you can't find curly endive, or want a more prominent flavor, try this soup with escarole.
- Add 1 cup cooked orzo or other small pasta to the soup.

Whisk is both a noun (the item itself) and a verb (what it does). The whisk is a cone made up of interlocking wires that converge in a handle. To whisk is to use the gadget. Rotate it in a circular motion through the food in the mixing bowl.

Minestrone

Minestrone is a catch-all phrase for most Italian vegetable soups. Most, like this one, contain a number of vegetables, beans, and pasta, and—of course—chicken.

Yield: 6–8 servings | **Active time:** 20 minutes | **Start to finish:** 1 hour

1/4 cup olive oil

1 large onion, peeled and diced

1 large carrot, peeled and sliced

1 celery rib, rinsed, trimmed, and sliced

3 garlic cloves, peeled and minced

4 cups shredded green cabbage

5 cups Chicken Stock for Entree Soups (recipe on page 71) or purchased stock

1 (28-ounce) can diced tomatoes, undrained

1/4 cup chopped fresh parsley

1 tablespoon Italian seasoning

1 small zucchini, rinsed, trimmed, and diced

1 (15-ounce) can garbanzo beans, drained and rinsed

1 (15-ounce) can kidney beans, drained and rinsed

2 cups diced cooked chicken

1 cup frozen cut green beans, thawed

1/4 pound small shells or other small pasta

Salt and freshly ground black pepper to taste

1/2 cup freshly grated Parmesan cheese

1. Heat olive oil in a 5-quart saucepan over medium-high heat. Add onion, carrot, celery, and garlic. Cook, stirring frequently, for 3 minutes, or until onion is translucent. Add cabbage, and cook for 1 minute.

2. Add stock, tomatoes, parsley, and Italian seasoning, and bring to a boil over medium-high heat, stirring occasionally. Reduce the heat to low, and simmer soup, partially covered, for 40 minutes. Add zucchini, garbanzo beans, and kidney beans, and simmer an additional 10 minutes. Add chicken and green beans and simmer an additional 5 minutes.

3. While soup simmers, bring a large pot of salted water to a boil over high heat. Cook pasta according to package directions until al dente. Drain, and set aside.

4. Add pasta to soup, and season to taste with salt and pepper. Serve hot, passing Parmesan cheese separately.

Note: The soup can be made up to 3 days in advance and refrigerated, tightly covered. Reheat it, covered, over low heat, stirring frequently.

Variations:
- Substitute kale for the green cabbage.
- Substitute kidney beans or cannellini beans for the garbanzo beans.
- Add ¼ pound diced Genoa salami for additional flavor.

While it might seem like a silly waste of time to wash an additional pot to cook the pasta rather than cooking it in the soup, this is not a shortcut to take. The pasta gives off a lot of starch into the water as it boils, and this starch would add a nasty taste to the soup.

Golden Lentil Soup with Turkey Meatballs

The lentil, a small lens-shaped legume, is an important part of the diet of people from the Middle East all the way to India. This pureed soup is flavored with aromatic cumin and coriander, and the meatballs contain some chopped raisins for sweetness.

Yield: 4-6 servings | **Active time:** 20 minutes | **Start to finish:** 50 minutes

SOUP

3 tablespoons olive oil
1 small onion, peeled and finely chopped
1 carrot, scrubbed, trimmed, and finely chopped
1 celery rib, rinsed, trimmed, and finely chopped
3 garlic cloves, peeled and minced
2 teaspoons ground cumin
1 teaspoon ground coriander
6 cups Chicken Stock (recipe on page 71) or purchased stock
1 pound golden lentils, rinsed
3 tablespoons chopped fresh cilantro
Salt and freshly ground black pepper to taste

MEATBALLS

2 tablespoons olive oil
1 medium onion, peeled and finely chopped
2 garlic cloves, peeled and minced
1 large egg
1/2 cup plain bread crumbs
1/4 cup milk
1 1/4 pounds ground turkey
1/3 cup chopped raisins
3 tablespoons chopped fresh cilantro
Salt and freshly ground black pepper to taste

1. For soup, heat olive oil in a 3-quart saucepan over medium-high heat. Add onion, carrot, celery, and garlic, and cook, stirring frequently, for 3 minutes, or until onion is translucent. Add cumin and coriander, and cook for 1 minute, stirring constantly.

2. Stir in chicken stock, lentils, and cilantro, and bring to a boil over medium-high heat, stirring occasionally. Reduce the heat to low, and simmer soup, uncovered, for 20–25 minutes, or until lentils are tender. Remove soup from the heat, and puree mixture with an immersion blender, in a food processor fitted with the steel blade, or in a blender. Set aside.

3. While soup simmers, make meatballs. Heat oil in a small skillet over medium-high heat. Add onion and garlic, and cook, stirring frequently, for 3 minutes, or until onion is translucent. While vegetables cook, whisk egg in a mixing bowl, and add bread crumbs and milk. Add turkey, raisins, and cilantro, and mix well. Add onion mixture to the mixing bowl, season to taste with salt and pepper, and mix well.

4. Bring pureed soup back to a simmer. Using wet hands, form meatball mixture into 1-inch balls, and drop them into simmering soup. Cook for 7–10 minutes, or until meatballs are cooked through and no longer pink. Season to taste with salt and pepper, and serve immediately.

Note: The soup can be made up to 3 days in advance and refrigerated, tightly covered. Reheat it over low heat, covered.

Variation:

- Substitute finely chopped dried apricots or dried currants for the raisins.

Greek Lemon Egg Soup

This soup, called *avgolemono,* is part of classic Greek cooking, and the addition of cooked chicken transforms it from a starter to your dinner. Serve a Greek salad with it to harmonize with the theme.

Yield: 4–6 servings | **Active time:** 20 minutes | **Start to finish:** 30 minutes

> 7 cups Chicken Stock for Entree Soups (recipe on page 71) or purchased stock
> ¾ cup orzo
> 2–3 cups diced cooked chicken
> 4 large eggs
> ⅓ cup lemon juice
> Salt and freshly ground black pepper to taste

1. Bring stock to a boil over medium-high heat. Add orzo and cook, covered, for 9–12 minutes, or until orzo is tender; the length of time depends on the brand of pasta. Stir in chicken, and simmer for 1 minute.
2. While stock simmers, whisk eggs well with lemon juice. Remove the pan from the heat, and stir for 45 seconds to cool soup. The liquid should not be bubbling or simmering at all. Stir in egg-lemon mixture, cover the pan, and let soup sit for 5 minutes to thicken.
3. Season soup to taste with salt and pepper, and serve immediately.

Note: The soup can be prepared 1 day in advance and refrigerated, tightly covered. Reheat it over very low heat, stirring frequently, and do not allow it to boil or the eggs will scramble.

Variations:
- Substitute rice for the orzo. Cook rice for 12–15 minutes, or until rice is tender.
- Add 1 (10-ounce) box frozen mixed vegetables along with the orzo.

African Peanut Soup

Peanuts were one of the crops brought over from Africa by the slaves in the seventeenth century, and on their native continent they are frequently used to flavor creamy soups.

Yield: 4–6 servings | **Active time:** 15 minutes | **Start to finish:** 35 minutes

3 tablespoons unsalted butter or chicken fat
1 large onion, peeled and diced
2 celery ribs, rinsed, trimmed, and sliced
1 large carrot, peeled and thinly sliced
3 tablespoons all-purpose flour
5 cups Chicken Stock for Entree Soups (recipe on page 71) or purchased stock
$\frac{1}{2}$ cup heavy cream
$\frac{1}{2}$ cup peanut butter (creamy or chunky)
1 (14.5-ounce) can diced tomatoes, drained
2–3 cups diced cooked chicken
1 (15-ounce) can black-eyed peas, drained and rinsed
Salt and hot red pepper sauce to taste

1. Melt butter in a 3-quart saucepan over medium-high heat. Add onion, celery, and carrot, and cook, stirring frequently, for 3 minutes, or until onion is translucent. Add flour, and cook for 1 minute, stirring constantly.

2. Add stock, cream, peanut butter, and tomatoes, and whisk well to dissolve peanut butter. Bring to a boil over medium heat, stirring occasionally. Reduce the heat to low, and simmer soup, partially covered, for 12–15 minutes, or until vegetables are tender.

3. Add chicken and black-eyed peas, and simmer for 5 minutes. Season to taste with salt and hot red pepper sauce, and serve immediately.

Note: The soup can be prepared up to 3 days in advance and refrigerated, tightly covered. To serve, reheat it, covered, over low heat, stirring frequently.

Variation:

- Substitute 2 medium zucchini, rinsed, trimmed, and cut into $\frac{3}{4}$-inch dice, for the celery and carrot.

Chinese Vegetable, Egg Drop, and Noodle Soup

The stock in which the vegetables are cooked is infused with ginger and garlic to make this a two-step cooking process. While most egg drop soup in Chinese restaurants is merely thickened stock with eggs, this one is a whole meal.

Yield: 4–6 servings | **Active time:** 15 minutes | **Start to finish:** 45 minutes

1 cup fine egg noodles
6 cups Chicken Stock for Entree Soups (recipe on page 71) or purchased stock
¼ cup soy sauce
2 tablespoons dry sherry
1 (2-inch) piece fresh ginger, thinly sliced
3 garlic cloves, peeled and sliced
1 tablespoon Asian sesame oil*
1 carrot, peeled and cut into fine julienne
1 celery rib, rinsed, trimmed, and thinly sliced
½ pound bok choy, rinsed, trimmed, and thinly sliced
¼ pound green beans, rinsed, trimmed, and cut into ¾-inch pieces
2 tablespoons cornstarch
2 tablespoons cold water
3 large eggs, well beaten
2–3 cups diced cooked chicken
3 scallions, white parts and 4 inches of green tops, rinsed, trimmed, and thinly sliced
Salt and freshly ground black pepper to taste

1. Bring a medium pot of salted water to a boil over high heat. Cook egg noodles according to package direction until al dente. Drain, and set aside.

2. While water heats, combine stock, soy sauce, sherry, ginger, garlic, and sesame oil in a 3-quart saucepan. Bring to a boil over high heat, reduce the heat to low, and simmer soup, uncovered, for 15 minutes. Strain soup, and discard ginger and garlic. Return soup to the saucepan.

*Available in the Asian aisle of most supermarkets and in specialty markets.

3. Bring stock back to a boil over high heat. Add carrot and celery, reduce the heat to low, and simmer for 5 minutes. Add bok choy and green beans, and simmer for an additional 5–7 minutes, or until vegetables are crisp-tender.

4. Combine cornstarch and cold water in a small cup. Add to soup, and cook for 2 minutes, or until slightly thickened. Slowly add egg while stirring. Simmer 1 minute, and stir in chicken, noodles, and scallions. Season to taste with salt and pepper, and serve immediately.

Note: The soup can be made up to 3 days in advance and refrigerated, tightly covered. Reheat it, covered, over low heat, stirring frequently.

Variation:

- Soak 6 large dried shiitake mushrooms in boiling water for 10 minutes, pushing them into the liquid with the back of a spoon. Drain mushrooms, reserving soaking liquid. Discard mushroom stems, slice thinly, and add to soup. Strain soaking liquid through a sieve lined with a paper coffee filter or a paper towel. Substitute soaking liquid for 1 cup of chicken stock.

I believe in saving time whenever possible. For a dish like this in which the ginger is strained out, there's no need to peel it.

Szechwan Hot and Sour Soup

Unlike many dishes found on Chinese restaurant menus in the United States, hot and sour soup is authentically Chinese; it comes from the Szechwan province. Healthful tofu and other vegetables join the chicken in this satisfying dish.

Yield: 4–6 servings | **Active time:** 20 minutes | **Start to finish:** 40 minutes

6 large dried shiitake mushrooms*
1 cup boiling water
1 tablespoon vegetable oil
1 tablespoon Asian sesame oil*
6 scallions, white parts and 4 inches of green tops, rinsed, trimmed, and sliced
3 garlic cloves, peeled and minced
5 cups Chicken Stock for Entree Soups (recipe on page 71) or purchased stock
$1/3$ cup rice vinegar
$1/4$ cup soy sauce
2 tablespoons dry sherry
$1/2$–1 teaspoon freshly ground black pepper
2–3 cups cooked diced chicken
$1/2$ pound firm tofu, drained, rinsed, and cut into $3/4$-inch cubes
2 tablespoons cornstarch
2 tablespoons cold water
3 large eggs, lightly beaten
Salt and freshly ground black pepper to taste

1. Combine shiitake mushrooms and boiling water, pushing them down into the water with the back of a spoon. Soak mushrooms for 10 minutes, then drain mushrooms, reserving soaking liquid. Discard stems, and chop mushrooms. Strain liquid through a sieve lined with a paper coffee filter or a paper towel. Set aside.

*Available in the Asian aisle of most supermarkets and in specialty markets.

2. Heat vegetable oil and sesame oil in a heavy 3-quart saucepan over medium-high heat. Add scallions and garlic and cook, stirring frequently, for 1 minute. Stir in stock, rice vinegar, soy sauce, sherry, reserved mushroom soaking liquid, and pepper. Bring to a boil, and simmer soup, uncovered, for 5 minutes. Add chicken and tofu, and simmer for an additional 10 minutes.

3. Combine cornstarch and cold water in a small bowl. Add to soup, and simmer for 2 minutes, or until slightly thickened. Slowly add egg while stirring. Simmer 1 minute, season to taste with salt and pepper, and serve immediately.

Note: The soup can be made up to 3 days in advance and refrigerated, tightly covered. Reheat it over low heat, covered.

Variations:
- Add 1 cup fresh bean sprouts, rinsed, along with the cornstarch mixture.
- Add 1 cup shredded Napa cabbage along with the chicken and tofu.

Tofu, sometimes called bean curd, is a white custard-like food made in a manner similar to cheese. Soy milk, which is a great source of iron and other nutrients, is curdled and then the curds are pressed to extract the whey. The texture depends on how much whey is removed, and can range from very soft to hard.

Chinese Chicken Vegetable Soup

This soup is similar to wonton soup, but it's much faster and easier to make because the additions are chicken meatballs flavored like wonton filling, which require far less time than handcrafting wontons in wrappers.

Yield: 6-8 servings | **Active time:** 20 minutes | **Start to finish:** 1 hour

MEATBALLS

2 tablespoons soy sauce

2 tablespoons cornstarch

3 large egg whites

1 tablespoon Asian sesame oil*

3 scallions, white parts and 3 inches of green tops, rinsed, trimmed, and chopped

3 tablespoons chopped fresh cilantro

1 tablespoon grated fresh ginger

2 garlic cloves, peeled and minced

1 pound ground chicken

½ cup finely chopped water chestnuts

Salt and freshly ground black pepper to taste

SOUP

7 cups Chicken Stock (recipe on page 71) or purchased stock

6 scallions, white parts and 3 inches of green tops, rinsed, trimmed, and chopped

2 garlic cloves, peeled and minced

1 tablespoon grated fresh ginger

2 tablespoons soy sauce

1 large carrot, peeled and cut into a fine julienne

2 cups chopped iceberg lettuce or Napa cabbage

1 cup thinly sliced green beans

Salt and freshly ground black pepper to taste

1. For meatballs, mix soy sauce with cornstarch. Combine egg whites, soy sauce mixture, sesame oil, scallions, cilantro, ginger, and garlic

*Available in the Asian aisle of most supermarkets and in specialty markets.

in a mixing bowl, and whisk well. Add chicken and water chestnuts, season to taste with salt and pepper, and mix well into a paste. Chill mixture for 30 minutes.

2. For soup, combine stock, scallions, garlic, ginger, soy sauce, and carrot in a 3-quart saucepan, and bring to a boil over medium-high heat. Reduce the heat to low, and simmer soup, uncovered, for 10 minutes.

3. Using wet hands, form meatball mixture into 1-inch balls, and drop them into simmering soup. Cook for 7–10 minutes, or until meatballs are cooked through and no longer pink. Add lettuce and green beans, and simmer for 2 minutes. Season to taste with salt and pepper, and serve hot.

Note: The soup can be prepared up to 3 days in advance and refrigerated, tightly covered. Reheat it, covered, over low heat, stirring frequently.

Variations:
- Use some rehydrated shiitake mushrooms in addition to the water chestnuts in the meatballs.
- Add some fresh spinach leaves to the broth to up the nutrient content without changing the flavor.

Classic French cooking is full of fancy terms used when cutting beyond the basic slice and dice. Julienne (pronounced *julie-en)* is a long, rectangular cut used for vegetables. For hard vegetables like carrots or potatoes, trim them so that the sides are straight, which will make it easier to make even cuts. Slice the vegetable lengthwise, using parallel cuts of the proper thickness. Stack the slices, aligning the edges, and make parallel cuts of the same thickness through the stack.

Chapter 5:

Slowly Does It: Dishes Made with Whole and Cut-Up Chickens

Eating the whole chicken is a great way to save money, and you'll find whole-chicken recipes in this chapter. Your family only likes the white meat? Don't worry. You can disguise the dark meat by "hiding" it in one of the delicious dishes for precooked chicken in Chapter 9 or as part of a salad using the recipes in Chapter 10.

It does take a few hours to properly roast a large chicken; that's why that meal becomes one for a lazy Sunday dinner. But there are other recipes in this chapter that bake chicken as its component pieces (which you've cut from the whole bird) that are ready in as little as 35 or 40 minutes. Those are the ones for that midweek meal.

RITUALS OF ROASTING

Roasting a chicken is a no-brainer; you rinse it out and season it. But there are some small steps that make it easier down the road. All roasted chickens are far easier to carve if the wishbone has been removed. Also cut off the wing tips, and save them for stock. They will burn before the chicken is roasted, and the chicken has a better line if they are removed.

Then there's the age-old debate of to truss or not to truss. I do not believe in trussing any poultry before roasting since it compresses the dark meat, which means it takes longer to cook, and there is more of a chance that the breast meat will be dry. The reason supermarket rotisserie chickens are trussed is to keep them from falling off the spit.

If you insist on tying up the chicken, however, this is the two-tie approach: Tie the wings to the body by pushing a needle through the bird at the knees, where the legs join the body. The second tie is made by pushing the needle through the ends of the drumsticks and the tip of the breastbone in the middle. When you wrap the string around the back of the chicken and pull it taut, the cavity naturally closes.

STUFFING SAVVY

Much of what Grandma taught you about cooking is true, especially if part of that knowledge was the warning that you should never stuff poultry in advance. Warm, moist stuffing provides a great breeding ground for bacteria, especially such nasty ones as salmonella and *E. coli*. That's why I would never buy one of the pre-stuffed chickens or chicken breasts in the supermarket.

If you want to bake the chicken stuffed, make the stuffing right before you plan to roast the chicken. That way it's starting out warm and will pass through the "danger zone" of 40°F to 140°F as quickly as possible. If you've made it in advance, reheat it in a microwave oven and then stuff the chicken.

Another answer is to bake the stuffing outside of the chicken in a casserole. I've given you the procedure for doing that with the stuffing recipes in this chapter. A key to remember is that stuffing in a casserole doesn't absorb moisture from the chicken as it roasts, so it needs additional stock to keep it from drying out.

VERSATILE VEGGIES

If you've got your carbohydrate (aka stuffing) inside of the bird, why not have your vegetables bake outside of the bird? That way the whole dinner is in the same roasting pan. And there's nothing like the flavor of crunchy potatoes and sweet root vegetables that have benefited from the juices in the roasting pan to complete a meal.

The plan is to use a larger roasting pan than you would for just the chicken itself so there's room for the vegetables to brown, and try to use a roasting pan with fairly low sides for that reason as well. Add the vegetables to the roasting pan after the chicken has baked for 30 minutes. If there's not enough chicken fat in the pan to coat them, use a few tablespoons of olive oil. Then sprinkle them with salt and pepper, and you're ready to roast. Here are some options:

- **Shallots.** All you have to do is peel them.
- **Onions.** Use small ones, and cut them in half lengthwise, trimming the root but leaving it attached.
- **Potatoes.** If you use redskin potatoes they don't need peeling, and they should but cut into 1½-inch cubes.
- **Carrots.** Peeled and cut into 2-inch sections.
- **Parsnips.** Peeled and cut into 2-inch sections.
- **Turnips.** Peeled and cut into 1-inch cubes.

Basic Roast Chicken

There are few foods as wonderful as a perfectly roasted chicken, filling the house with aromas and exiting the oven with crisp skin like a Caribbean suntan. While a roasting chicken can feed a crowd, make a few at a time so that you'll have cooked chicken with which to feed the family later in the week.

Yield: 6–8 servings | **Active time:** 15 minutes | **Start to finish:** 2 hours

> 1 roasting chicken (5–7 pounds)
> 4 sprigs fresh parsley, divided
> 4 sprigs fresh rosemary, divided
> 6 garlic cloves, peeled, divided
> 2 sprigs fresh thyme
> Salt and freshly ground black pepper to taste
> 4 tablespoons (½ stick) unsalted butter, softened
> 1 large onion, peeled and roughly chopped
> 1 carrot, peeled and thickly sliced
> 1 celery rib, rinsed, trimmed, and sliced
> 1 cup Chicken Stock (recipe on page 30) or purchased stock

1. Preheat the oven to 425°F. Rinse chicken, and pat dry with paper towels. Place 2 sprigs parsley, 2 sprigs rosemary, 4 garlic cloves, and thyme in cavity of chicken. Sprinkle salt and pepper inside cavity, and close it with skewers and string.
2. Chop remaining parsley, rosemary, and garlic. Mix with butter, and season to taste with salt and pepper. Gently stuff mixture under the skin of breast meat. Rub skin with salt and pepper. Place chicken on a rack in a roasting pan, breast side up.
3. Bake for 30 minutes, reduce the oven temperature to 350°F, and add onion, carrot, and celery to the roasting pan. Cook an additional 1–1½ hours, or until chicken is cooked through and no longer pink, and an instant-read thermometer registers 165°F when inserted into the thigh. Remove the chicken from the oven, and allow it to rest on a heated platter for 10 minutes.
4. Spoon grease out of the pan, discard grease, and add chicken stock to the pan. Stir over medium-high heat until the liquid is reduced to a syrupy consistency. Strain sauce into a sauce boat, and add to it any liquid that accumulates on the platter when the chicken is carved. Serve immediately.

Note: The chicken can be roasted up to 3 hours in advance and kept at room temperature, covered with aluminum foil.

Variations: While the method remains the same, here are some other seasoning blends to flavor the chicken:

- Use 3 tablespoons smoked Spanish paprika, 1 tablespoon ground cumin, 1 tablespoon dried thyme, and 3 minced garlic cloves.
- Use 3 tablespoons Italian seasoning, 3 tablespoons chopped fresh parsley, and 3 garlic cloves.
- Use 3 tablespoons dried oregano and 5 garlic cloves, and add 1 sliced lemon to the cavity.
- Rather than chicken stock, deglaze the pan with white wine.

Here's how to carve a roast chicken or turkey: To add a flourish to carving that also assures crisp skin for all, first "unwrap" the breast. Use a well-sharpened knife and fork. Carve and serve one side at a time. From neck, cut just through skin down middle of breast and around side. Hook fork on skin at tail and roll skin back to neck. Holding bird with fork, remove leg by severing hip joint. Separate drumstick from thigh and serve. Cut thin slices of breast at slight angle and add a small piece of rolled skin to each serving. Repeat all steps for other side. Remove wings last.

Basic Roast Turkey

There are two schools of thought to roasting a turkey—either relatively low heat or high heat—and I prefer the latter. Using this roasting method, the turkey basically steams; the meat remains moist since it is being cooked by a moist rather than dry heat method.

Yield: 8–10 servings, plus enough for lots of leftovers | **Active time:** 15 minutes | **Start to finish:** at least 2 hours, but varies by the weight of the turkey

    1 (12–16-pound) turkey
    6 tablespoons (¾ stick) unsalted butter, softened and divided
    3 garlic cloves, peeled and minced
    3 tablespoons smoked Spanish paprika
    1 tablespoon dried thyme
    Salt and freshly ground black pepper to taste
    1 large onion, peeled and diced
    1½ cups Chicken Stock (recipe on page 30) or purchased stock
    1 tablespoon cornstarch
    2 tablespoons cold water

1. Preheat the oven to 450°F. Rinse turkey inside and out under cold running water, and place it in a large roasting pan.

2. Combine 3 tablespoons butter, garlic, paprika, thyme, salt, and pepper in a small bowl, and mix well. Rub mixture over skin of turkey and inside cavity. Place onion and stock in the roasting pan, and place turkey on top of it. Create a tent with two sheets of heavy-duty aluminum foil, crimping foil around the edges of the roasting pan, and joining the two sheets in the center by crimping.

3. Place turkey in the oven, and roast for 12–15 minutes per pound. After 2 hours, remove the foil, and remove liquid from the roasting pan with a bulb baster. Return turkey to the oven, covered as before.

4. Reduce the oven temperature to 350°F, and uncover turkey for the last 1 hour of roasting so skin browns. Rub skin with remaining butter after removing the foil. Turkey is done when it is cooked through and no longer pink, and dark meat registers 165°F on an instant-read thermometer. Remove turkey from the oven, and allow it to rest on a heated platter for 10–15 minutes, lightly covered with foil.

5. While turkey rests, prepare gravy. Pour all juices and flavoring ingredients from the roasting pan into a saucepan. If there are any brown bits clinging to the bottom of the pan, add 1 cup of turkey or chicken stock. Stir over medium heat, scraping brown bits from bottom of pan. In a small bowl, mix cornstarch and water, and set aside. Remove as much fat as possible from the surface of juices with a soup ladle, and then reduce liquid by at least $\frac{1}{4}$ to concentrate flavor. Stir cornstarch mixture into the pan, and cook for 3–5 minutes, or until liquid boils and slightly thickens. Season gravy to taste with salt and pepper.

6. To serve, carve turkey, and pass gravy separately.

Note: The turkey can be left at room temperature for up to 1 hour after removing it from the oven; keep it lightly tented with aluminum foil.

Variations: While the method remains the same, here are some other seasoning blends to flavor the turkey:

- Use 2 tablespoons herbes de Provence or Italian seasoning along with 3 garlic cloves.
- Use $\frac{1}{4}$ cup chopped fresh rosemary, 1 tablespoon grated lemon zest, and 3 garlic cloves.

All-Purpose Herbed Stuffing

If you're going to make a whole roasting chicken, it only seems right to stuff it and have your meal complete. Here is my basic stuffing, with lots of variations at the end to dress it up.

Yield: 4-6 servings | **Active time:** 25 minutes | **Start to finish:** 1 hour, if baking stuffing outside of the chicken

> 6 tablespoons (³/₄ stick) unsalted butter
> 1 large onion, peeled and diced
> 3 celery ribs, rinsed, trimmed, and diced
> 1 ¹/₂ cups Chicken Stock (recipe on page 30) or purchased stock, divided
> 3 tablespoons chopped fresh parsley
> 1 tablespoon dried sage
> 1 teaspoon dried thyme
> 3 cups herb stuffing cubes
> Salt and freshly ground black pepper to taste

1. Heat butter in a large, covered skillet over medium-high heat. Add onion and celery, and cook, stirring frequently, for 3 minutes, or until onion is translucent. Add 1 cup stock, parsley, sage, and thyme, and bring to a boil, stirring occasionally. Reduce the heat to low, cover the skillet, and simmer mixture for 15 minutes, or until vegetables are tender.

2. Stir in stuffing cubes, and season to taste with salt and pepper. Stuff cavity of chicken or turkey lightly with stuffing, and skewer cavity closed. Place any remaining stuffing mixture in an ovenproof casserole, and sprinkle with some of remaining stock to moisten well.

3. Bake chicken or turkey according to the recipe; stuffing should register 165°F on an instant-read thermometer. Remove stuffing from cavity as soon as chicken or turkey has rested, and refrigerate any leftovers separately. Place remaining stuffing in the oven for the last 20 minutes of baking.

If cooking all of the stuffing outside the bird: Preheat the oven to 350°F, and grease a 9 x 13-inch baking pan. Moisten stuffing with remaining stock, and transfer it to the prepared pan. Cover pan with aluminum foil, and bake for 30 minutes. Remove the foil, and bake for an additional 10 minutes, or until slightly crisp.

Note: The stuffing can be prepared for baking up to 2 days in advance and refrigerated, tightly covered. Reheat it in a microwave oven until it is warm before stuffing mixture into the cavity.

Variations:

- Sauté ½ pound bulk pork sausage over medium-high heat, breaking up lumps with a fork, for 5–7 minutes, or until browned. Reduce butter to 4 tablespoons (½ stick), increase sage to 2 tablespoons, and omit thyme.
- Add ½ pound cooked chopped chestnuts.
- Add ½ pound mushrooms, wiped with a damp paper towel, trimmed, and chopped, to the skillet along with the onion and celery.
- Preheat the oven to 350°F, and line a baking sheet with foil. Bake ½ cup chopped walnuts for 5–7 minutes, or until lightly browned. Soak ½ cup raisins in very hot tap water for 15 minutes, and add ½ teaspoon ground cinnamon to the skillet along with the other ingredients.
- Substitute 1 small fennel bulb for the celery.
- Dice olive bread into ½-inch cubes, and bake the cubes in a 375°F oven for 10–15 minutes, or until toasted. Substitute 3 cups olive bread cubes for the herbed stuffing cubes.

For dishes such as stuffings, it's fine to use the celery leaves as well as the ribs. The celery basically melts away into the stuffing, so its texture doesn't matter.

Fruited Cornbread Stuffing

Poultry melds well with subtle fruit flavors, and the fresh apples and dried apricots and cranberries dotting the cornbread make this a real treat. It's not sweet, but it's luscious.

Yield: 4–6 servings | **Active time:** 25 minutes | **Start to finish:** 1 hour, if cooking stuffing outside of the chicken

> 6 tablespoons (¾ stick) unsalted butter
> 1 large onion, peeled and diced
> 2 celery ribs, rinsed, trimmed, and diced
> 1 ¼ cups Chicken Stock (recipe on page 30) or purchased stock, divided
> 2 Golden Delicious apples, peeled, cored, and diced
> ½ cup chopped dried apricots
> ¼ cup dried cranberries
> 2 tablespoons chopped fresh parsley
> 1 teaspoon dried thyme
> 3 cups cornbread stuffing cubes
> Salt and freshly ground black pepper to taste

1. Heat butter in a large, covered skillet over medium-high heat. Add onion and celery, and cook, stirring frequently, for 3 minutes, or until onion is translucent. Add ¾ cup stock, apples, dried apricots, dried cranberries, parsley, and thyme, and bring to a boil, stirring occasionally. Reduce the heat to low, cover the skillet, and simmer mixture for 15 minutes, or until vegetables are tender.

2. Stir in stuffing cubes, and season to taste with salt and pepper. Stuff cavity of chicken or turkey lightly with stuffing, and skewer cavity closed. Place any remaining stuffing mixture in an ovenproof casserole, and sprinkle with some of remaining stock to moisten well.

3. Bake chicken or turkey according to the recipe; stuffing should register 165°F on an instant-read thermometer. Remove stuffing from cavity as soon as chicken or turkey has rested, and refrigerate any leftovers separately. Place remaining stuffing in the oven for the last 20 minutes of baking.

If cooking all of the stuffing outside the bird: Preheat the oven to 350°F, and grease a 9 x 13-inch baking dish. Moisten stuffing with remaining stock, and transfer it to the prepared pan. Cover pan with aluminum foil, and bake for 30 minutes. Remove the foil, and bake for an additional 10 minutes, or until slightly crisp.

Note: The stuffing can be prepared for baking up to 2 days in advance and refrigerated, tightly covered. Reheat it in a microwave oven until it is warm before stuffing mixture into the cavity.

Variations:
- Substitute chopped dried apple for the dried apricots and dried cranberries, and add ½ teaspoon ground cinnamon to the skillet with the other ingredients.
- Substitute 3 fresh peaches, peeled and diced, for the Golden Delicious apples.
- Add ½ pound cooked and diced sweet potatoes along with the stuffing cubes.

Southwestern Cornbread Stuffing

Cornbread is part of the tradition in the Southwest as well as the South, and this savory stuffing contains many of the hearty flavors of traditional Southwestern cooking.

Yield: 4–6 servings | **Active time:** 25 minutes | **Start to finish:** 1 hour, if cooking stuffing outside of the chicken

6 tablespoons (³/₄ stick) unsalted butter
1 large red onion, peeled and diced
¹/₂ green bell pepper, seeds and ribs removed, and chopped
1 celery rib, rinsed, trimmed, and diced
2 garlic cloves, peeled and minced
1 tablespoon ground cumin
1 teaspoon dried oregano
1¹/₄ cups Chicken Stock (recipe on page 30) or purchased stock, divided
¹/₄ cup chopped fresh cilantro
2 tablespoons canned chopped mild green chiles, drained
3 cups cornbread stuffing cubes
Salt and freshly ground black pepper to taste

1. Heat butter in a large, covered skillet over medium-high heat. Add onion, green bell pepper, celery, and garlic, and cook, stirring frequently, for 3 minutes, or until onion is translucent. Add cumin and oregano, and cook for 1 minute, stirring constantly.

2. Add 1 cup stock, cilantro, and chiles, and bring to a boil, stirring occasionally. Reduce the heat to low, cover the skillet, and simmer mixture for 15 minutes, or until vegetables are tender.

3. Stir in stuffing cubes, and season to taste with salt and pepper. Stuff cavity of chicken or turkey lightly with stuffing, and skewer cavity closed. Place any remaining stuffing mixture in an ovenproof casserole, and sprinkle with some of remaining stock to moisten well.

4. Bake chicken or turkey according to the recipe; stuffing should register 165°F on an instant-read thermometer. Remove stuffing from cavity as soon as chicken or turkey has rested, and refrigerate any leftovers separately. Place remaining stuffing in the oven for the last 20 minutes of baking.

If cooking all of the stuffing outside the bird: Preheat the oven to 350°F, and grease a 9 x 13-inch baking dish. Moisten stuffing with remaining stock, and transfer it to the prepared pan. Cover pan with aluminum foil, and bake for 30 minutes. Remove the foil, and bake for an additional 10 minutes, or until slightly crisp.

Note: The stuffing can be prepared for baking up to 2 days in advance and refrigerated, tightly covered. Reheat it in a microwave oven until it is warm before stuffing mixture into the cavity.

Variations:
- Add 2 chipotle chiles in adobo sauce, finely chopped, to the skillet along with the other ingredients for a spicy stuffing.
- Add 1 small zucchini, rinsed, trimmed, and diced, to the skillet when sautéing the onion and celery.
- Add ¾ cup cooked corn kernels to the skillet along with the stuffing cubes.
- Sauté ½ pound bulk pork sausage over medium-high heat, breaking up lumps with a fork, for 5–7 minutes, or until browned. Reduce butter to 4 tablespoons (½ stick) before cooking vegetables.

Basic Oven-Fried Chicken

Using this easy method chicken emerges from the oven with skin as crisp as if it was deep-fried on top of the stove, but there's no mess! And you can read a book while it bakes, or prepare the rest of dinner.

Yield: 4-6 servings | **Active time:** 10 minutes | **Start to finish:** 35 minutes

> 1 (3½–4-pound) frying chicken, cut into serving pieces, with each breast half cut crosswise in half
> 1 cup buttermilk
> 2 large eggs, lightly beaten
> 1½ cups finely crushed corn flakes
> ½ cup bread crumbs
> 1 cup vegetable oil, divided
> 3 tablespoons Cajun seasoning
> Salt and freshly ground black pepper to taste

1. Preheat the oven to 400°F, and place a 10 x 14-inch baking pan in the oven as it heats. Rinse chicken and pat dry with paper towels.

2. Combine buttermilk and eggs in a shallow bowl, and whisk well. Combine crushed corn flakes, bread crumbs, 2 tablespoons oil, Cajun seasoning, salt, and pepper in a second large bowl, and mix well.

3. Dip chicken pieces into buttermilk mixture, letting any excess drip back into the bowl. Dip pieces into corn flake mixture, coating all sides. Set aside.

4. Add remaining oil to hot baking dish, and heat for 3 minutes. Add chicken pieces and turn gently with tongs to coat all sides with oil. Bake for a total of 25 minutes, turning pieces gently with tongs after 15 minutes, or until chicken is cooked through and no longer pink, and an instant-read thermometer registers 165°F when inserted into the thigh. Remove chicken from the pan, and pat with paper towels. Serve immediately.

Note: The chicken can be prepared for baking up to 6 hours in advance and refrigerated, tightly covered.

Variations: This is really a method as much as a recipe. Here are other coatings:

- Use seasoned Italian bread crumbs, and add $1/4$ cup freshly grated Parmesan cheese to the mixture.
- Use rice cereal in place of the corn flakes.
- Use fluffy panko bread crumbs, and season them with herbes de Provence.
- Substitute smoked Spanish paprika for the Cajun seasoning, and season egg mixture to taste with salt and pepper.

Breasts are clearly the largest single piece of chicken, and they are the favorite of most folks. That's why I believe in cutting them in half. You make more people happy!

Chicken Cooked in Red Wine (*Coq au Vin*)

Everyone needs a good chicken in red wine recipe in their collection, if for no other reason than to serve a hearty red wine with a white meat on a cold winter night. I like this rendition since the smoky taste of the bacon emerges.

Yield: 4–6 servings | **Active time:** 20 minutes | **Start to finish:** 1¼ hours

> 1 (3½–4-pound) frying chicken, cut into serving pieces, with each breast half cut crosswise in half
> ¼ pound bacon, cut into 1-inch pieces
> Salt and freshly ground black pepper to taste
> ½ cup all-purpose flour
> 6 scallions, white parts and 3 inches of green tops, rinsed, trimmed, and sliced
> 1 pound small mushrooms, wiped with a damp paper towel, and trimmed
> 2 garlic cloves, peeled and minced
> 12–18 small redskin potatoes, scrubbed and halved (quartered if larger than a walnut)
> 2 cups dry red wine
> 1 cup Chicken Stock (recipe on page 30) or purchased stock
> 2 tablespoons chopped fresh parsley
> 2 teaspoons dried thyme
> 2 bay leaves
> 1 (1-pound) package frozen pearl onions, thawed and drained

1. Preheat the oven to 350°F. Rinse chicken and pat dry with paper towels.
2. Place a large Dutch oven or roasting pan over medium-high heat, and cook bacon for 5–7 minutes, or until crisp. Remove bacon from the pan with a slotted spoon, and set aside; discard all but 3 tablespoons bacon fat. Sprinkle chicken with salt and pepper, and dust chicken pieces with flour, shaking off any excess.
3. Brown chicken on all sides over medium-high heat. Remove chicken from the pan, and add scallions, mushrooms, and garlic. Cook, stirring frequently, for 3 minutes, or until scallions are translucent.

4. Return chicken to the pan, along with reserved bacon, potatoes, wine, chicken stock, parsley, thyme, salt, pepper, and bay leaves. Bring to a boil on top of the stove, and then cover the pan and bake in the center of the oven for 45 minutes. Add onions, and bake an additional 15 minutes, or until the potatoes are tender. Remove and discard bay leaves, season to taste with salt and pepper, and serve immediately.

Note: The dish can be made up to 2 days in advance and refrigerated, tightly covered. Reheat it over low heat or in a 350°F oven for 30 minutes, or until hot.

Variation:
- Substitute white wine for the red wine, and substitute dried tarragon for the thyme.

While it would be nice, I no longer subscribe to the philosophy of not using a wine in cooking that I wouldn't drink. I've discovered that the best way to buy "cooking wines"—both red and white—is in boxes. A box is equivalent to four bottles, and because the wine is dispensed through a spigot, the wine never touches air and stays fresh for months.

Mexican Chicken and Rice (*Arroz con Pollo*)

This is one of those wonderful all-in-one dishes; the rice cooks in the same savory Mexican sauce as the pieces of chicken. It's incredibly flavorful, without being overly spicy.

Yield: 4–6 servings | **Active time:** 20 minutes | **Start to finish:** 50 minutes

> 1 (3½–4-pound) frying chicken, cut into serving pieces, with each breast half cut crosswise in half
> Salt and freshly ground black pepper to taste
> 3 tablespoons olive oil
> 1 large onion, peeled and diced
> 3 garlic cloves, peeled and minced
> 1 cup long-grain white rice
> 1 (14.5-ounce) can diced tomatoes, drained
> 1 (4-ounce) can diced mild green chiles, drained
> 1¾ cups Chicken Stock (recipe on page 30) or purchased stock
> 1 tablespoon ground cumin
> 2 teaspoons dried oregano
> 1 bay leaf
> ½ cup sliced pimiento-stuffed green olives
> 1 (10-ounce) package frozen peas, thawed

1. Rinse chicken, pat dry with paper towels, and sprinkle chicken with salt and pepper. Heat oil in a large skillet over medium-high heat. Add chicken pieces to the pan, and brown well on all sides, turning gently with tongs, and being careful not to crowd the pan. Remove chicken from the pan, and set aside.

2. Add onion and garlic to the pan, and cook, stirring frequently, for 3 minutes, or until onion is translucent. Add rice to the pan, and cook for 1 minute, stirring constantly. Add tomatoes, green chiles, stock, cumin, oregano, and bay leaf to the pan, and bring to a boil over high heat, stirring frequently.

3. Return chicken to the pan, cover the pan, reduce the heat to medium-low, and cook for 25–35 minutes, or until chicken is tender and no longer pink, an instant-read thermometer registers 165°F when inserted into the thigh, and almost all liquid has been absorbed.

4. Stir olives and peas into the pan, recover the pan, and cook for 2–3 minutes, or until hot and remaining liquid is absorbed. Remove and discard bay leaf, season to taste with salt and pepper, and serve immediately.

Note: The dish can be cooked up to 2 days in advance and refrigerated, tightly covered. Reheat in a 350°F oven, covered, for 20–25 minutes, or until hot.

Variation:

- Substitute 1–2 chipotle chiles in adobo sauce, finely chopped, for the mild green chiles for a spicier dish.

There are two types of chiles in small cans in the Hispanic food section of supermarkets. What is specified here are the mild green chiles, but the small cans of fiery jalapeño peppers look very similar. Look at the cans carefully; not only would jalapeño peppers waste your money, they would ruin this dish.

Italian Chicken with White Beans and Tomatoes

This is a hearty dish for a cold winter's night. The chicken is cooked in an herbed tomato sauce with lots of healthful (and inexpensive) beans. Serve it with a tossed salad.

Yield: 4-6 servings | **Active time:** 20 minutes | **Start to finish:** 50 minutes

> 1 (3½-4-pound) frying chicken, cut into serving pieces, with each breast half cut crosswise in half
> Salt and freshly ground black pepper to taste
> ½ cup all-purpose flour
> ¼ cup olive oil
> 1 large onion, peeled and diced
> 4 garlic cloves, peeled and minced
> 1 (28-ounce) can stewed tomatoes
> 2 cups Chicken Stock (recipe on page 30) or purchased stock
> ½ cup dry white wine
> 3 tablespoons chopped fresh parsley
> 1 tablespoon Italian seasoning
> 2 (15-ounce) cans cannellini beans, drained and rinsed

1. Rinse chicken and pat dry with paper towels. Sprinkle chicken with salt and pepper. Place flour on a sheet of plastic wrap.
2. Heat oil in a large, covered skillet over medium-high heat. Dredge chicken in flour, shaking off any excess. Brown chicken for 2-3 minutes per side, or until browned, turning chicken with tongs. Remove chicken from the skillet, and set aside.
3. Add onion and garlic to the skillet, and cook, stirring frequently, for 3 minutes, or until onion is translucent. Return chicken to the pan, and add tomatoes, stock, wine, parsley, and Italian seasoning.
4. Bring to a boil over medium-high heat, then reduce the heat to low, and simmer chicken, covered, for 15 minutes. Add beans to the skillet, and cook for an additional 10-15 minutes, or until chicken is cooked through and no longer pink, and an instant-read thermometer registers 165°F when inserted into the thigh. Season to taste with salt and pepper, and serve immediately.

Note: The dish can be cooked up to 2 days in advance and refrigerated, tightly covered. Reheat in a 350°F oven, covered, for 20–25 minutes, or until hot.

Variation:
- Substitute 2 tablespoons chili powder, 2 teaspoons ground cumin, and 1 teaspoon dried oregano for the Italian seasoning, and substitute kidney beans for the cannellini beans.

Canned beans are fully cooked, that's why you can combine varieties that take different amounts of time to cook in the same recipe. It also means that beans should be added at the end of the cooking time. You want them to absorb flavor, but not become mushy.

Chicken with Root Vegetables

In the middle of winter, you know you'll still find root vegetables at a reasonable cost in the supermarket, and these homey and healthful accompaniments create a whole meal when cooked with chicken.

Yield: 4-6 servings | **Active time:** 25 minutes | **Start to finish:** 55 minutes

1 (3½-4-pound) frying chicken, cut into serving pieces, with each breast half cut crosswise in half

Salt and freshly ground black pepper to taste

½ cup all-purpose flour, divided

3 tablespoons olive oil

2 large onions, peeled and diced

4 garlic cloves, peeled and minced

¾ cup dry white wine

2 large redskin potatoes, scrubbed and cut into 1-inch dice

2 carrots, peeled and cut into ¾-inch slices

2 large parsnips, peeled and cut into ¾-inch slices

2 small turnips, peeled and cut into 1-inch dice

4 cups Chicken Stock (recipe on page 30) or purchased stock

3 tablespoons chopped fresh parsley

1½ teaspoons dried thyme

1 bay leaf

½ cup heavy cream

1. Rinse chicken and pat dry with paper towels. Sprinkle chicken with salt and pepper. Reserve 2 tablespoons flour, and place remaining flour on a sheet of plastic wrap.

2. Heat oil in a large skillet over medium-high heat. Dredge chicken in flour, shaking off any excess. Brown chicken for 2-3 minutes per side, or until browned, turning chicken with tongs. Remove chicken from the skillet, and transfer it to a large, deep saucepan.

3. Add onions to the skillet, and cook for 5-7 minutes, stirring frequently, or until onions are lightly browned. Add garlic to the skillet, and cook for 1 minute.

4. Reduce the heat to low, stir in reserved flour, and cook for 1 minute, stirring constantly. Whisk in wine, and cook for 2 minutes.

5. Arrange potatoes, carrots, parsnips, and turnips in the pot with the chicken, and scrape in onion mixture. Add stock, parsley, thyme, and bay leaf. Bring to a boil over medium-high heat, then reduce the heat to low, and simmer chicken, covered, for 25–35 minutes, or until chicken is cooked through and no longer pink, an instant-read thermometer registers 165°F when inserted into the thigh, and vegetables are tender.

6. Remove chicken and vegetables from the pot, and keep warm. Raise the heat to high, and cook sauce until reduced by $\frac{1}{3}$. Remove and discard bay leaf, and add cream. Return chicken and vegetables to the pan, season to taste with salt and pepper, and serve immediately.

Note: The dish can be cooked up to 2 days in advance and refrigerated, tightly covered. Reheat in a 350°F oven, covered, for 20–25 minutes, or until hot.

Variation:

- Substitute rutabagas or celery root for any of the vegetables listed.

Chicken with Herb Pan Gravy

A simple pan gravy made with the same herbs used in the butter that moistens this chicken is a way to turn a quick, midweek meal into something special. Serve it with mashed potatoes and a steamed green vegetable.

Yield: 4–6 servings | **Active time:** 15 minutes | **Start to finish:** 40 minutes

1 (3½–4-pound) frying chicken, cut into serving pieces, with each breast half cut crosswise in half
Salt and freshly ground black pepper to taste
3 tablespoons unsalted butter, softened
2 garlic cloves, peeled and minced
¼ cup chopped fresh parsley, divided
2 teaspoons dried thyme, divided
2 teaspoons dried rosemary, crushed, divided
3 tablespoons all-purpose flour
1 cup Chicken Stock (recipe on page 30) or purchased stock
Vegetable oil spray

1. Preheat the oven to 425°F, and grease a metal 10 x 14-inch baking pan with vegetable oil spray. Rinse chicken and pat dry with paper towels. Sprinkle chicken with salt and pepper.
2. Combine butter, garlic, 2 tablespoons parsley, 1 teaspoon thyme, and 1 teaspoon rosemary in a small bowl. Season to taste with salt and pepper, and mix well. Stuff butter under skin of chicken pieces, and arrange pieces in the prepared pan skin side up.
3. Bake chicken for 25 minutes, or until chicken is cooked through and no longer pink, and an instant-read thermometer registers 165°F when inserted into the thigh. Remove chicken from the pan, and keep warm.
4. Place the pan over a burner on low heat. Stir in flour, and cook for 2 minutes, stirring constantly. Whisk in stock, and add remaining parsley, thyme, and rosemary. Simmer for 2 minutes, then serve immediately, spooning sauce over chicken.

Note: The dish can be cooked up to 2 days in advance and refrigerated, tightly covered. Reheat in a 350°F oven, covered, for 20–25 minutes, or until hot.

Variation:

- Substitute 4 teaspoons Italian seasoning or herbes de Provence for the combination of thyme and rosemary.

A pan gravy is made by a process called "deglazing." All the juices that escaped while the chicken cooked are incorporated into the sauce to give it flavor.

Old-Fashioned Chicken and Dumplings

Dumplings are biscuits that are steamed on the top of a simmering liquid, and they are a part of traditional colonial American cooking. Their addition on top of stewed chicken and vegetables makes this a one-dish meal.

Yield: 4-6 servings | **Active time:** 20 minutes | **Start to finish:** 1¼ hours

CHICKEN

> 1 (3½-4-pound) frying chicken, cut into serving pieces, with each breast half cut crosswise in half
> Salt and freshly ground black pepper to taste
> 3 tablespoons vegetable oil
> 3 tablespoons unsalted butter
> 1 large onion, peeled and diced
> 2 carrots, peeled and sliced
> 2 celery ribs, rinsed, trimmed, and sliced
> 3 tablespoons all-purpose flour
> 3 cups Chicken Stock (recipe on page 30) or purchased stock
> 3 tablespoons chopped fresh parsley
> 2 teaspoons herbes de Provence
> 1 bay leaf
> 1 (10-ounce) package frozen peas, thawed

DUMPLINGS

> 1 cup all-purpose flour
> 1½ teaspoons baking powder
> Pinch of salt
> Pinch of freshly ground black pepper
> 1 tablespoon dried sage
> 3 tablespoons unsalted butter
> ⅓ cup milk

1. Rinse chicken, pat dry with paper towels, and sprinkle chicken with salt and pepper. Heat oil in a large skillet over medium-high heat. Add chicken pieces to the pan, and brown well on all sides, turning gently with tongs, and being careful not to crowd the pan. Remove chicken from the pan, and set aside. Discard fat from the pan.

2. Return the pan to the stove, and melt butter over medium heat. Add onion, carrots, and celery, and cook, stirring frequently, for 3 minutes, or until onion is translucent. Add flour, and cook for 2 minutes, stirring constantly. Add stock, parsley, herbes de Provence, and bay leaf to the pan, and bring to a boil.

3. Return chicken to the pan, cover the pan, and cook chicken over medium-low heat for 20–30 minutes, or until chicken is tender and no longer pink, and an instant-read thermometer registers 165°F when inserted into the thigh.

4. While chicken simmers, prepare dumpling dough. Combine flour, baking powder, salt, pepper, and sage in a mixing bowl. Cut in butter using a pastry blender, two knives, or your fingertips until mixture resembles coarse crumbs. Add milk, and stir to blend. Knead dough lightly on lightly floured counter, then cut into 12 parts and make each part into a patty.

5. Add peas to chicken, remove and discard bay leaf, and place dough rounds on top of chicken. Cover the pan and cook for 15 minutes, or until dumplings are puffed and cooked through. Do not uncover the pan while dumplings steam. Serve immediately.

Note: The chicken can be cooked up to 1 day in advance and refrigerated, tightly covered. Reheat it over medium heat to a simmer, stirring occasionally, before completing recipe. Do not make dumpling dough until just prior to serving.

Variation:

- Substitute frozen mixed vegetables for the peas.

Baking powder does not live forever, and if you don't do very much baking it's a good idea to test the potency before using it. Stir a few teaspoons into a glass of cold water. It should fizz furiously. If not, buy a new box.

Plum Chicken à la Fox

Fox Wetle is a dear friend and great cook, in addition to being most proficient in her "real" life as an academic dean. She improvised this recipe one night, and shared it with me. The combination of fresh plums with herbs is fantastic. Serve it over rice, with a steamed green vegetable.

Yield: 4–6 servings | **Active time:** 20 minutes | **Start to finish:** 50 minutes

> 1 (3½–4-pound) frying chicken, cut into serving pieces, with each breast half cut crosswise in half
> Salt and freshly ground black pepper to taste
> ½ cup all-purpose flour, divided
> 3 tablespoons unsalted butter
> 2 tablespoons olive oil
> 1 cup Chicken Stock (recipe on page 30) or purchased stock
> ½ cup dry white wine
> 1 tablespoon dried tarragon
> 1 tablespoon firmly packed dark brown sugar
> 3–4 ripe plums, rinsed, stoned, and sliced

1. Rinse chicken and pat dry with paper towels. Sprinkle chicken with salt and pepper. Reserve 2 tablespoons flour, and place remaining flour on a sheet of plastic wrap.
2. Heat butter and oil in a large, covered skillet over medium-high heat. Dredge chicken in flour, shaking off any excess. Brown chicken for 2–3 minutes per side, or until browned, turning chicken with tongs. Remove chicken from the skillet, and set aside.
3. Reduce the heat to low, stir in reserved flour, and cook for 1 minute, stirring constantly. Whisk in stock, wine, tarragon, and brown sugar, and bring to a boil over medium-high heat. Return chicken to the skillet, reduce the heat to low, and cook chicken, covered, for 15 minutes.
4. Add plums to the skillet, and cook for an additional 10–15 minutes, or until chicken is cooked through and no longer pink, and an instant-read thermometer registers 165°F when inserted into the thigh. Season to taste with salt and pepper, and serve immediately.

Note: The dish can be cooked up to 2 days in advance and refrigerated, tightly covered. Reheat in a 350°F oven, covered, for 20–25 minutes, or until hot.

Variation:
- Substitute 2–3 ripe peaches for the plums.

Tongs are one of the most important utensils you can have in a kitchen. They make it possible to turn food without puncturing it, which allows juices to escape. You should use tongs for any recipe dealing with whole chicken pieces and also when turning all food on the grill.

Chapter 6:

The Daily Grind: Dishes Based on Ground Turkey and Chicken

Ground turkey is the chopped beef of the twenty-first century. And with good reason. It's always reasonably priced, it's easy to work with, and it cooks fast. That's why there's a whole chapter of recipes in *$3 Chicken Meals* that uses this cousin in the poultry family.

While ground chicken is becoming more available, it's usually more expensive than ground turkey, and it doesn't deliver the same depth of flavor. There are a few recipes written for ground chicken because I wanted its delicacy to emerge. Feel free to substitute the two meats interchangeably, however.

There's no need to brown ground poultry as there is with ground beef. The turkey never really browns, and it wastes time to try. For foods such as meatballs, which are baked in the oven, the exterior of the food browns from the heat and from a dusting with vegetable oil spray.

You'll find a great range of recipes in this chapter. Some are for "dry" meatballs and meatloaves, while others have a sauce. Some are casseroles, and others are burgers. But they're all delicious, and they all fit within your budget.

MEAT LOAF IN THE FAST LANE

Just as small pieces of food for a stir-fry cook in less time than a large roast, so a meat loaf mixture baked in muffin cups is ready in far less time. While the meat loaf recipes in this chapter are written to be baked as one unit, you can change that to speed them up. Another advantage of baking meat loaves as "muffins" is that you can take them to the office for lunch; the muffins don't fall apart the way slices tend to do.

Here's how to do it: Preheat the oven to 400°F, and spray 8–12 muffin cups with vegetable oil spray. Divide the meat loaf mixture into the prepared muffin cups, and bake for 20–25 minutes, or until an instant-read thermometer inserted into the center registers 165°F.

An alternative, if you don't have a muffin pan, is to form the meat mixture into individual "logs" that are about 3 inches high. Bake them at 375°F for 25–30 minutes.

Turkey Burgers Provençal

Fresh basil is the dominant herb used to flavor these delicate turkey burgers, and the same mayonnaise-based sauce tops them as well as flavoring the patties.

Yield: 4-6 servings | **Active time:** 15 minutes | **Start to finish:** 45 minutes

1 cup mayonnaise
1 cup tightly packed chopped fresh basil
¼ cup chopped fresh parsley
2 garlic cloves, peeled and minced
1 large shallot, peeled and chopped
2 teaspoons herbes de Provence
Salt and freshly ground black pepper to taste
1¼ pounds ground turkey
4-6 rolls of your choice, sliced in half
For serving: Lettuce, tomato, and thinly sliced red onion

1. Prepare a dual-temperature hot and medium grill according to the instructions given on page 177, or preheat the oven broiler.
2. Combine mayonnaise, basil, parsley, garlic, shallot, herbes de Provence, salt, and pepper in a mixing bowl, and stir well.
3. Combine ½ cup mayonnaise mixture and turkey in a mixing bowl, and mix gently. Form mixture into 4-6 (¾-inch-thick) burgers.
4. Grill rolls on the hot side of the grill cut side down until toasted. Sear burgers over high heat for 2 minutes per side, uncovered if using a charcoal grill, and then transfer burgers to the cooler side of the grill. Continue to cook, covered, for 3-5 minutes per side or until burgers register 165°F on an instant-read thermometer and are cooked through and no longer pink.
5. Serve immediately with remaining mayonnaise mixture, lettuce, tomato, and onion.

Note: The turkey mixture can be prepared up to 1 day in advance and refrigerated, tightly covered.

Variation:
- Omit the salt and add 1 tablespoon anchovy paste to the sauce.

Shepherd's Pie with Swiss Cheese Potato Topping

This classic English dish is quintessential comfort food, and it's very easy to make. The potato topping and vegetables in the flavorful filling mean that your dinner is done with this one dish.

Yield: 4–6 servings | **Active time:** 20 minutes | **Start to finish:** 1¼ hours

FILLING

2 tablespoons unsalted butter

1 large onion, peeled and diced

2 garlic cloves, peeled and minced

1 pound ground turkey

1¼ cups Chicken Stock (recipe on page 30) or purchased stock

2 tablespoons chopped fresh parsley

1 tablespoon herbes de Provence

1 (10-ounce) package frozen mixed vegetables, thawed

1 tablespoon cornstarch

1 tablespoon cold water

Salt and freshly ground black pepper to taste

TOPPING

1½ pounds redskin potatoes, scrubbed and cut into ¾-inch dice

⅓ cup heavy cream

3 tablespoons unsalted butter

1 cup grated Swiss cheese

Salt and freshly ground black pepper to taste

1. Preheat the oven to 400°F, and grease a 9 x 13-inch baking pan.
2. Heat butter in a heavy, large skillet over medium-high heat. Add onion and garlic, and cook, stirring frequently, for 3 minutes, or until onion is translucent. Add turkey, breaking up lumps with a fork.
3. Add stock, parsley, and herbes de Provence to the skillet, and bring to a boil, stirring occasionally. Reduce the heat to low, and simmer mixture, uncovered, for 15 minutes, stirring occasionally. Add mixed vegetables for the last 5 minutes of cooking.

4. Combine cornstarch and water in a small cup. Add mixture to turkey and simmer for 2 minutes or until slightly thickened. Season filling to taste with salt and pepper.

5. While filling simmers, prepare topping. Place potatoes in a saucepan of salted water, and bring to a boil over high heat. Reduce the heat to medium and boil potatoes, uncovered, for 10–15 minutes, or until soft. Drain potatoes in a colander. Heat cream, butter, and cheese in the saucepan over medium heat until cheese melts, stirring occasionally. Return potatoes to saucepan, and mash well with a potato masher. Season to taste with salt and pepper, and set aside.

6. Scrape turkey mixture into the prepared pan. Spoon potatoes on top of turkey, smoothing them into an even layer. Bake for 15 minutes, or until filling is bubbly and the potatoes are lightly browned. Serve immediately.

Note: The turkey mixture can be prepared up to 2 days in advance and refrigerated, tightly covered; reheat it over low heat before baking. Or the dish can be prepared for baking up to 6 hours in advance and kept at room temperature. Add 5–10 minutes to the baking time if turkey is not hot.

Variation:
- Substitute sharp cheddar cheese for the Swiss cheese.

Mushroom Meat Loaf

This is a family-pleasing favorite, and is really a variation on the beef meat loaf recipe I've used for decades—including glazing the top with ketchup. Serve it with some coleslaw.

Yield: 4–6 servings | **Active time:** 20 minutes | **Start to finish:** 1½ hours

2 tablespoons unsalted butter
2 tablespoons olive oil
1 medium onion, peeled and chopped
2 garlic cloves, peeled and minced
¼ pound mushrooms, wiped with a damp paper towel, trimmed,
   and chopped
1 small carrot, peeled and finely chopped
1 large egg
¼ cup whole milk
1 tablespoon Worcestershire sauce
⅔ cup Italian bread crumbs
2 tablespoons chopped fresh parsley
1 teaspoon dried thyme
½ cup ketchup, divided
1 pound ground turkey
Salt and freshly ground black pepper to taste

1. Preheat the oven to 350°F, and line a 9 x 13-inch baking pan with heavy-duty aluminum foil.
2. Heat butter and oil in a large skillet over medium-high heat. Add onion and garlic, and cook, stirring frequently, for 3 minutes, or until onion is translucent. Add mushrooms and carrot, and cook, stirring frequently, for 4–6 minutes, or until vegetables soften.
3. While vegetables cook, combine egg, milk, Worcestershire sauce, bread crumbs, parsley, thyme, and 2 tablespoons ketchup in a mixing bowl, and stir well. Add vegetable mixture and turkey to the mixing bowl, and mix well again. Season to taste with salt and pepper, and form mixture into a loaf 9 inches long and 5 inches wide in the prepared pan. Spread top of meat loaf with remaining ketchup.
4. Bake meat loaf for 1–1¼ hours, or until an instant-read thermometer inserted into the center registers 165°F. Allow meat loaf to rest for 5 minutes, then serve.

Note: The turkey mixture can be prepared up to 1 day in advance and refrigerated, tightly covered. Also, the meat loaf can be baked up to 2 days in advance and refrigerated, tightly covered. Reheat it in a 350°F oven, covered, for 20–25 minutes, or until hot.

Variation:
- Substitute ½ green bell pepper, seeds and ribs removed, and chopped, for the carrot.

Mushrooms give off a lot of liquid as they begin to cook, so it's important to cook them long enough that the liquid evaporates. Otherwise the meat loaf could be too moist.

Creole Meat Loaf

Certain ingredient combinations are hallmarks of various regions of American cuisine. In this case, the combination of onion, green bell pepper, and celery, flavored with thyme and oregano, defines Creole cooking. I like a tossed salad with vinaigrette dressing with this meat loaf.

Yield: 4–6 servings | **Active time:** 20 minutes | **Start to finish:** 1½ hours

3 tablespoons olive oil

1 medium onion, peeled and chopped

1 small green bell pepper, seeds and ribs removed, and chopped

2 celery ribs, rinsed, trimmed, and chopped

3 garlic cloves, peeled and minced

1 large egg

¼ cup whole milk

2 tablespoons tomato paste

½ cup plain bread crumbs

¼ cup chopped fresh parsley

1 teaspoon dried thyme

½ teaspoon dried oregano

1 pound ground turkey

½ cup grated Monterey Jack cheese

Cajun seasoning to taste

½ cup bottled chili sauce

1. Preheat the oven to 350°F, and line a 9 x 13-inch baking pan with heavy-duty aluminum foil.
2. Heat oil in a medium skillet over medium-high heat. Add onion, green bell pepper, celery, and garlic, and cook, stirring frequently, for 5–7 minutes, or until vegetables soften.
3. Combine egg, milk, and tomato paste in a mixing bowl, and whisk well to dissolve tomato paste. Add bread crumbs, parsley, thyme, and oregano, and mix well. Add vegetable mixture, turkey, and cheese to the mixing bowl, and mix well again. Season to taste with Cajun seasoning. Form mixture into a loaf 9 inches long and 5 inches wide in the prepared pan. Spread top of meat loaf with chili sauce.
4. Bake meat loaf for 1–1¼ hours, or until an instant-read thermometer inserted into the center registers 165°F. Allow meat loaf to rest for 5 minutes, then serve.

Note: The turkey mixture can be prepared up to 1 day in advance and refrigerated, tightly covered. Also, the meat loaf can be baked up to 2 days in advance and refrigerated, tightly covered. Reheat it in a 350°F oven, covered, for 20–25 minutes, or until hot.

Variation:

- Substitute sharp cheddar cheese for the Monterey Jack.

Contrary to its name, chili sauce is closer to a chunky ketchup than a fiery sauce. It's a tomato-based condiment that contains onions, green peppers, vinegar, sugar, and spices. It serves as the basis for traditional cocktail sauce, too, so it's worth it to keep a bottle in the house.

Meatballs in Fruit Sauce

Ground turkey in particular, and poultry in general, take very well to being cooked with fruit and flavored with spices like aromatic cinnamon. The cider and apples in this dish are an example of that pairing. I serve these over buttered egg noodles with a steamed green vegetable.

Yield: 4–6 servings | **Active time:** 20 minutes | **Start to finish:** 50 minutes

> 2 tablespoons unsalted butter
> 1 medium onion, peeled and chopped
> 1 carrot, peeled and chopped
> 3 garlic cloves, peeled and minced
> 1 Granny Smith apple, peeled, cored, and chopped
> 1 cup apple cider, divided
> ³/₄ cup medium-dry sherry
> ½ cup raisins
> 2 tablespoons chopped fresh parsley
> ½ teaspoon dried thyme
> ½ teaspoon ground cinnamon
> 1 large egg
> ½ cup plain bread crumbs
> 1 pound ground turkey
> Salt and freshly ground black pepper to taste
> 1 tablespoon cornstarch
> 1 tablespoon cold water
> Vegetable oil spray

1. Heat butter in a large skillet over medium-high heat. Add onion, carrot, and garlic, and cook, stirring frequently, for 3 minutes, or until onion is translucent. Remove ½ of vegetable mixture, and set aside. Add apple, ³/₄ cup cider, sherry, raisins, parsley, thyme, and cinnamon to the skillet, and bring to a boil over medium-high heat, stirring occasionally. Simmer sauce over low heat, uncovered, for 15 minutes.

2. While sauce simmers, preheat the oven broiler, line a rimmed baking sheet with heavy-duty aluminum foil, and grease the foil with vegetable oil spray.

3. Combine egg, remaining ¼ cup cider, and bread crumbs in a mixing bowl, and whisk until smooth. Add reserved vegetable mixture, and turkey. Season to taste with salt and pepper, and mix well. Make mixture into 1½-inch meatballs, and arrange meatballs on the prepared pan. Spray tops of meatballs with vegetable oil spray.

4. Broil meatballs 6 inches from the broiler element, turning them with tongs to brown all sides. Remove meatballs from baking pan with a slotted spoon, and add meatballs to sauce. Bring to a boil, and simmer meatballs over low heat, covered, turning occasionally with a slotted spoon, for 15 minutes. Mix cornstarch with water in a small bowl, and add to sauce. Cook for 1 minute, or until slightly thickened. Season sauce to taste with salt and pepper, and serve immediately.

Note: The meatball mixture can be prepared up to 1 day in advance and refrigerated, tightly covered. Also, the dish can be made up to 2 days in advance and refrigerated, tightly covered. Reheat it in a 350°F oven, covered, for 15 to 20 minutes, or until hot.

Variation:
- Instead of the raisins use a combination of chopped dried apricots and dried cranberries.

Some time-honored methods of cutting fruits and vegetables made sense when chefs had hundreds of hands to work for them, but they don't make sense in our busy lives. If it matters how the apples in the dish look, then peeling, coring, and then slicing each half or quarter is still the best method. But if the apples are going to be hidden, as in this dish, there's a faster way: Peel the apple and keep turning it in your hand as you cut off slices. Soon all you'll be left with is the core, which you can discard. It's much faster.

Turkey Chili

It's just like the chili con carne your family loves, but in this case the carne in question is turkey. The addition of a bit of cocoa powder adds a depth of flavor to the dish. Serve it with a tossed salad, and place it over rice.

Yield: 6–8 servings | **Active time:** 15 minutes | **Start to finish:** 45 minutes

> 2 tablespoons olive oil
> 1 large onion, peeled and diced
> 3 garlic cloves, peeled and minced
> 1 large green bell pepper, seeds and ribs removed, and chopped
> 1½ pounds ground turkey
> 2 tablespoons all-purpose flour
> 3 tablespoons chili powder
> 2 tablespoons ground cumin
> 2 teaspoons dried oregano
> 2 teaspoons unsweetened cocoa powder
> 1 (28-ounce) can diced tomatoes, undrained
> 2 (15-ounce) cans kidney beans, drained and rinsed
> Salt and cayenne to taste

1. Heat oil in a large saucepan over medium-high heat. Add onion, garlic, and green bell pepper. Cook, stirring frequently, for 3 minutes, or until onion is translucent. Add turkey and cook, stirring constantly, for 5 minutes, breaking up lumps with a fork.
2. Stir in flour, chili powder, cumin, oregano, and cocoa. Cook over low heat, stirring frequently, for 2 minutes. Add tomatoes and bring to a boil over medium heat. Simmer chili, partially covered and stirring occasionally, for 25 minutes, or until thick. Add beans, and cook for an additional 5 minutes.

Note: The dish can be prepared up to 2 days in advance and refrigerated, tightly covered. Reheat it, covered, in a saucepan over low heat.

Variation:

- There's a related dish in Mexican cooking called *picadillo*. Omit the oregano, and add ½ teaspoon ground cinnamon, ½ cup raisins, and 1 tablespoon cider vinegar to the chili.

Any chili can become a finger food by turning it into nachos. Pile the chili on large nacho corn chips, top with some grated Monterey Jack cheese, and pop them under the broiler until the cheese is melted.

Southwestern Meat Loaf with Smoked Cheddar

Two ingredients—chipotle peppers and smoked cheese—give this easy-to-make meat loaf its distinctive flavor. Serve it with some Mexican rice and a salad.

Yield: 4–6 servings | **Active time:** 20 minutes | **Start to finish:** 1½ hours

3 tablespoons olive oil

1 medium onion, peeled and chopped

3 garlic cloves, peeled and minced

2 jalapeño or serrano chiles, seeds and ribs removed, and finely chopped

2 teaspoons dried oregano

2 teaspoons ground cumin

2 large eggs, lightly beaten

¼ cup whole milk

⅓ cup plain bread crumbs

¼ cup chopped fresh cilantro

1 chipotle chile in adobo sauce, finely chopped

¾ cup crushed corn tortilla chips

¾ cup grated smoked cheddar cheese

1 pound ground turkey

Salt and freshly ground black pepper to taste

1. Preheat the oven to 350°F, and line a 9 x 13-inch baking pan with heavy-duty aluminum foil.
2. Heat oil in a medium skillet over medium-high heat. Add onion, garlic, and chiles, and cook, stirring frequently, for 5 minutes, or until vegetables soften. Add oregano and cumin, and cook for 1 minute, stirring constantly.
3. While vegetables cook, combine eggs, milk, bread crumbs, cilantro, chipotle chile, and tortilla chips, and mix well. Add vegetable mixture, cheese, and turkey to the mixing bowl, and mix well again. Season to taste with salt and pepper. Form mixture into a loaf 9 inches long and 5 inches wide in the prepared pan.
4. Bake meat loaf for 1–1¼ hours, or until an instant-read thermometer inserted into the center registers 165°F. Allow meat loaf to rest for 5 minutes, then serve.

Note: The turkey mixture can be prepared up to 1 day in advance and refrigerated, tightly covered. Also, the meat loaf can be baked up to 2 days in advance and refrigerated, tightly covered. Reheat it in a 350°F oven, covered, for 20-25 minutes, or until hot.

Variation:

- Omit the chipotle chile for a milder dish.

It's a shame to waste much of a bunch of an herb like parsley, cilantro, and dill, when you need but a few tablespoons for a recipe. Trim off the stems, and then wrap small bundles in plastic wrap, and freeze them. When you need some, you can "chop" it with the blunt side of a knife. It will chop easily when frozen, and this method produces far better flavor than dried herbs.

Spicy Mexican Meatballs

This is not a dish for delicate palates; it's both aromatic and spicy and contains many of the essential ingredients of Mexican cooking. Serve it with some Mexican rice or saffron rice, and cold beer.

Yield: 4-6 servings | **Active time:** 25 minutes | **Start to finish:** 40 minutes

> 1/4 cup olive oil
> 1 large onion, peeled and chopped
> 4 garlic cloves, peeled and minced
> 1 large egg
> 2 tablespoons whole milk
> 1/2 cup plain bread crumbs
> 2/3 cup chopped fresh cilantro, divided
> 1 tablespoon chili powder
> 1 tablespoon dried oregano
> 1 1/4 pounds ground turkey
> Salt and freshly ground black pepper to taste
> 1 (15-ounce) can tomato sauce
> 2 teaspoons ground cumin
> 2 chipotle chiles in adobo sauce, drained and finely chopped

1. Preheat the oven broiler, line a rimmed baking sheet with heavy-duty aluminum foil, and grease the foil with vegetable oil spray.
2. Heat oil in a skillet over medium-high heat. Add onion and garlic, and cook, stirring frequently, for 3 minutes, or until onion is translucent. While vegetables cook, combine egg and milk in a mixing bowl, and whisk until smooth. Add bread crumbs, 1/3 cup cilantro, chili powder, and oregano, and mix well.
3. Add 1/2 of onion mixture and turkey, season to taste with salt and pepper, and mix well again. Make mixture into 1 1/2-inch meatballs, and arrange meatballs on the prepared pan. Spray tops of meatballs with vegetable oil spray.
4. Broil meatballs 6 inches from the broiler element, turning them with tongs to brown all sides. While meatballs brown, add tomato sauce, cumin, and chipotle chiles to the skillet containing remaining onions and garlic. Bring to a boil over medium-high heat, stirring occasionally.

5. Remove meatballs from the baking pan with a slotted spoon, and add meatballs to sauce. Bring to a boil, and simmer meatballs over low heat, covered, turning occasionally with a slotted spoon, for 15 minutes. Serve immediately.

Note: The meatball mixture can be prepared up to 1 day in advance and refrigerated, tightly covered. Also, the dish can be cooked up to 2 days in advance and refrigerated, tightly covered. Reheat it in a 350°F oven, covered, for 15–20 minutes, or until hot.

Variation:
- Add ½ cup crushed tortilla chips to the turkey mixture for crunchy meatballs.

Chipotle chiles in adobo sauce are a canned Mexican product, and both the peppers, which are smoked jalapeños, and the rich, dark red sauce are used to flavor dishes. The sauce also contains herbs and vinegar, so it's similar to a hot red pepper sauce but with a more complex, richer flavor.

Tex-Mex Tamale Pie

This is one of my favorite dishes for a buffet because the cornbread topping is stunning when the casserole is put on the table. The filling is similar to a chili con carne, and a tossed salad is all you need to complete the meal.

Yield: 4–6 servings | **Active time:** 15 minutes | **Start to finish:** 1 hour

FILLING

2 tablespoons olive oil

1 large onion, peeled and chopped

2 celery ribs, rinsed, trimmed, and diced

$\frac{1}{2}$ green bell pepper, seeds and ribs removed, and chopped

1 jalapeño or serrano chile, seeds and ribs removed, and finely chopped

3 garlic cloves, peeled and minced

3 tablespoons chili powder

1 pound ground turkey

1 (14.5-ounce) can diced tomatoes, undrained

1 (8-ounce) can tomato sauce

1 cup frozen corn, thawed

Salt and cayenne to taste

TOPPING

2 large eggs, lightly beaten

1 cup well-stirred buttermilk

4 tablespoons unsalted butter, melted

$1\frac{1}{2}$ cups yellow cornmeal

$\frac{1}{2}$ cup all-purpose flour

$2\frac{1}{2}$ teaspoons baking powder

$\frac{1}{2}$ teaspoon salt

1. Preheat the oven to 400°F, and grease a 9 x 13-inch baking pan.
2. For filling, heat oil in a large skillet over medium-high heat. Add onion, celery, green bell pepper, chile, and garlic. Cook, stirring frequently, for 3 minutes, or until onion is translucent. Stir in chili powder, and stir 1 minute. Add turkey, breaking up lumps with a fork.

3. Add tomatoes and tomato sauce, and bring to a boil over medium-high heat, stirring occasionally. Reduce the heat to low, and simmer, uncovered, for 15 minutes. Add corn, and simmer 5 minutes. Season to taste with salt and cayenne, and spread mixture into the prepared pan.
4. While filling simmers, prepare topping. Combine eggs, buttermilk, melted butter, cornmeal, flour, baking powder, and salt in a mixing bowl, and whisk well. Spoon batter over filling, leaving a 1/2-inch margin around the edges.
5. Bake for 15–20 minutes, or until golden and a toothpick inserted into the topping comes out clean. Serve immediately.

Note: The filling can be prepared up to 2 days in advance and refrigerated, tightly covered. Reheat it over low heat until hot before baking.

Variations:
- Instead of corn, use 1 (15-ounce) can kidney beans, drained and rinsed.
- Sprinkle 1/2 cup grated cheddar cheese or Monterey Jack cheese on top of the cornbread for the last 3 minutes of baking.

Chili powder is actually a spice blend, and can be made as follows: Combine 2 tablespoons ground red chile, 2 tablespoons paprika, 1 tablespoon ground coriander, 1 tablespoon garlic powder, 1 tablespoon onion powder, 2 teaspoons ground cumin, 2 teaspoons ground red pepper or cayenne, 1 teaspoon ground black pepper, and 1 teaspoon dried oregano.

Italian Stuffed Peppers

Green peppers stuffed with a mixture of turkey and cheeses, then baked in a tomato sauce, are a hearty and filling entree that is visually attractive when it comes to the table. I usually serve some pasta to enjoy all the sauce, and a tossed salad.

Yield: 4–6 servings | **Active time:** 15 minutes | **Start to finish:** 1 hour

4–6 small green bell peppers
2 tablespoons olive oil
1 large onion, peeled and chopped
2 garlic cloves, peeled and minced
3 tablespoons chopped fresh parsley
2 teaspoons Italian seasoning
Salt and freshly ground black pepper to taste
½ cup bread crumbs
2 tablespoons whole milk
½ cup grated whole-milk mozzarella cheese
1½ cups marinara sauce, divided
1 large egg, lightly beaten
1 pound ground turkey
½ cup freshly grated Parmesan cheese

1. Preheat the oven to 375°F, and grease a 9 x 13-inch baking pan. Bring a large pot of water to a boil over high heat.
2. Cut off top ½ inch of peppers, and reserve. Scoop out seeds and ribs with your hands. Discard stems, and chop flesh from pepper tops. Add pepper shells to boiling water, and cook for 5 minutes. Remove peppers from water with tongs and invert over paper towels to drain.
3. While peppers blanch, heat oil in a large skillet over medium-high heat. Add onion, garlic, and chopped pepper pieces. Cook, stirring frequently, for 5 minutes, or until onion softens. Transfer mixture to a large mixing bowl, and add parsley, Italian seasoning, salt, pepper, bread crumbs, milk, mozzarella, ¼ cup marinara sauce, and egg. Mix well, add turkey, and mix well again.

4. Fill pepper cavities with turkey mixture. Stand peppers up in the prepared pan, and pour remaining sauce over them. Cover the pan with aluminum foil, and bake for 25 minutes. Remove the foil, baste peppers with sauce, and sprinkle with Parmesan cheese. Return pan to the oven, and bake an additional 20 minutes. Serve immediately, spooning sauce over tops of peppers.

Note: The dish can be cooked up to 2 days in advance and refrigerated, tightly covered. Reheat, covered with foil, in a 350°F oven for 25–30 minutes, or until hot.

Variations:
- Substitute turkey Italian sausage, casings discarded, for the ground turkey.
- Substitute chopped cooked pasta for the bread crumbs in the recipe.

When selecting green peppers for this dish, try to pick ones that stand firmly when you place them on a flat surface rather than ones that are free-form or long and skinny.

Meatballs Normandy

The French province of Normandy is known for its creamy sauces made with apple, and that's what you've got in this dish. Serve it over buttered egg noodles with a steamed green vegetable.

Yield: 4–6 servings | **Active time:** 20 minutes | **Start to finish:** 55 minutes

    2 tablespoons unsalted butter
    1 medium onion, peeled and chopped
    2 garlic cloves, peeled and minced
    1 large egg
    2 tablespoons whole milk
    $1/2$ cup plain bread crumbs
    $1/4$ pounds ground turkey
    Salt and freshly ground black pepper to taste
    2 Granny Smith apples, peeled, cored, and chopped
    1 cup apple cider, divided
    1 cup Chicken Stock (recipe on page 30) or purchased stock
    2 tablespoons smooth Dijon mustard
    $1/2$ cup heavy cream
    1 tablespoon cornstarch
    Vegetable oil spray

1. Preheat the oven broiler, line a rimmed baking sheet with heavy-duty aluminum foil, and grease the foil with vegetable oil spray.
2. Heat butter in a large skillet over medium-high heat. Add onion and garlic and cook, stirring frequently, for 3 minutes, or until onion is translucent. While vegetables cook, combine egg and milk in a mixing bowl, and whisk until smooth. Add bread crumbs to the mixing bowl, and mix well.
3. Add $1/2$ of onion mixture and turkey, season to taste with salt and pepper, and mix well again. Make mixture into $1/2$-inch meatballs, and arrange meatballs on the prepared pan. Spray tops of meatballs with vegetable oil spray.
4. Broil meatballs 6 inches from the broiler element, turning them with tongs to brown all sides. Remove the pan from the oven, and set aside.

5. Add apples, $3/4$ cup cider, stock, and mustard to the skillet, and bring to a boil over medium-high heat, stirring occasionally. Simmer sauce, uncovered, for 10 minutes, or until volume is reduced by $1/3$. Add meatballs and cream to sauce, bring to a boil, and simmer meatballs, covered, over low heat, turning occasionally with a slotted spoon, for 15 minutes.

5. Combine cornstarch and remaining $1/4$ cup cider in a small bowl, and stir well. Add mixture to sauce, and cook for an additional 2 minutes, or until lightly thickened. Season sauce to taste with salt and pepper, and serve immediately.

Note: The meatball mixture can be prepared up to 1 day in advance and refrigerated, tightly covered. Also, the dish can be cooked up to 2 days in advance and refrigerated, tightly covered. Reheat it in a 350°F oven, covered, for 15 to 20 minutes, or until hot.

Variation:
- Rather than using fresh apples, add $2/3$ cup chopped dried apples for a more assertive apple flavor.

Keep in mind that ground pork can be substituted for ground turkey in all recipes, so if you like one of these dishes, you can adapt it for those times you want "the other white meat."

Dilled Swedish Meatballs

Swedish meatballs, called *köttbullar* in Sweden, have been a favorite in this country since Scandinavian settlers brought them in the nineteenth century. Serve these over buttered egg noodles to enjoy every drop of the aromatic sauce.

Yield: 4–6 servings | **Active time:** 20 minutes | **Start to finish:** 45 minutes

> 4 tablespoons (½ stick) unsalted butter, divided
> 1 small onion, peeled and chopped
> ¼ cup whole milk
> 1 large egg
> 1 large egg yolk
> 3 slices fresh white bread
> ¼ teaspoon ground allspice
> ¼ teaspoon freshly grated nutmeg
> 1¼ pounds ground turkey
> Salt and freshly ground black pepper to taste
> ¼ cup all-purpose flour
> 2 cups Chicken Stock (recipe on page 30) or purchased stock
> ½ cup heavy cream
> ¼ cup chopped fresh dill
> Vegetable oil spray

1. Preheat the oven broiler, line a rimmed baking sheet with heavy-duty aluminum foil, and grease the foil with vegetable oil spray.
2. Heat 2 tablespoons butter in a large skillet over medium-high heat. Add onion, and cook, stirring frequently, for 3 minutes, or until onion is translucent. Combine milk, egg, and egg yolk in a mixing bowl, and whisk until smooth. Break bread into small pieces, add it to the mixing bowl along with allspice and nutmeg, and mix well.
3. Add onion and turkey, season to taste with salt and pepper, and mix well again. Make mixture into 1½-inch meatballs, and arrange meatballs on the prepared pan. Spray tops of meatballs with vegetable oil spray.

4. Broil meatballs 6 inches from the broiler element, turning them with tongs to brown all sides. While meatballs brown, add remaining butter to the skillet and heat over low heat. Stir flour into the skillet, and cook over low heat for 2 minutes, stirring constantly. Raise the heat to medium-high, whisk in stock, cream, and dill, and bring to a boil over medium-high heat, whisking constantly.

5. Remove meatballs from the baking pan with a slotted spoon, and add meatballs to sauce. Bring to a boil, and simmer meatballs over low heat, covered and turning occasionally with a slotted spoon, for 15 minutes. Season to taste with salt and pepper, and serve immediately.

Note: The meatball mixture can be prepared up to 1 day in advance and refrigerated, tightly covered. Also, the dish can be cooked up to 2 days in advance and refrigerated, tightly covered. Reheat in a 350°F oven, covered, for 15–20 minutes, or until hot.

Variation:

- Substitute 2 teaspoons Italian seasoning or herbes de Provence for the dill, and add ½ cup freshly grated Parmesan cheese to the sauce at the end of the time the meatballs are simmering.

Nutmeg is one spice that loses its flavor and aroma almost immediately after being grated, so it's worth it to buy the whole nutmeg and grate it yourself. While there are special nutmeg graters on the market, you can use the small side of a box grater.

Sweet and Sour Stuffed Cabbage

Stuffed cabbage, which comes from traditional German and Eastern European cooking, was brought to this country in the nineteenth century. This is my favorite version because it includes sweet and succulent fruits.

Yield: 4–6 servings | **Active time:** 25 minutes | **Start to finish:** 2 hours

> 1 (2-pound) head green cabbage
> 1 pound ground turkey
> 1¼ cups cooked rice
> 1 small onion, peeled and grated
> Salt and freshly ground black pepper to taste
> 2 Golden Delicious apples, peeled, cored, and cut into ¾-inch dice
> ½ cup raisins
> 1 (15-ounce) can tomato sauce
> ¾ cup cider vinegar
> ¾ cup firmly packed dark brown sugar

1. Preheat the oven to 375°F, and grease a 10 x 14-inch baking pan. Bring a large pot of water to a boil. Remove and discard broken outer leaves of cabbage. Core cabbage by cutting around all 4 sides of the core with a heavy, sharp knife. Discard core, and spear cabbage with meat fork in the hole made by discarding core.

2. Hold cabbage in boiling water, and pull off leaves with tongs as they become pliable. Continue until you have 8–12 leaves separated. Remove cabbage from water, and shred 2 additional cups cabbage. Scatter shredded cabbage into the bottom of the baking pan. Set leaves aside.

3. Combine turkey, rice, onion, salt, and pepper in mixing bowl, and mix well. Place 1 cabbage leaf in front of you, and scoop ⅓ cup meat mixture into large end. Fold sides over meat, and roll leaf. Place in baking pan, stem side down, and repeat with remaining leaves and meat. Scatter apple and raisins over meat rolls. Combine tomato sauce, vinegar, and brown sugar in mixing bowl, and stir well. Pour mixture over cabbage rolls.

4. Cover the pan with aluminum foil, and bake for 1¼ hours. Remove foil, and bake an additional 15 minutes, or until lightly browned. Serve immediately.

Note: The dish can be cooked up to 2 days in advance and refrigerated, tightly covered. Reheat, covered with foil, in a 350°F oven for 25–30 minutes, or until hot.

Variation:
- Substitute chopped dried apricots or dried cranberries for the raisins.

After the cabbage has been submerged in the boiling water, some of the inner leaves will be hot and blanched, and the central core will still be cold and crisp. Shred the cabbage from the exterior in, and save the portion that is still crisp to make a batch of coleslaw.

Turkey Moussaka

The traditional version of this Greek dish, popular in *tavernas*, is made with lamb. But you'll find that the lighter turkey filling, still melded with hearty eggplant, scented with cinnamon, and topped with a custard sauce, is equally delicious, and not as filling. I usually serve it with just a salad because the dish is really a whole meal.

Yield: 6–8 servings | **Active time:** 20 minutes | **Start to finish:** 1½ hours

FILLING

1 large eggplant (1½ pounds), cap discarded, and cut into ¾-inch dice
Salt and freshly ground black pepper to taste
¼ cup olive oil
1 large onion, peeled and diced
3 garlic cloves, peeled and minced
1½ pounds ground turkey
1 (15-ounce) can tomato sauce
¾ cup dry white wine
2 tablespoons chopped fresh parsley
1 teaspoon dried oregano
½ teaspoon ground cinnamon

TOPPING

4 tablespoons (½ stick) unsalted butter
¼ cup all-purpose flour
2 cups whole milk
3 large eggs, lightly beaten
¾ cup freshly grated Parmesan cheese, divided
3 tablespoons chopped fresh dill (optional)

1. Place eggplant in a mixing bowl, and cover with heavily salted water; use 1 tablespoon table salt per 1 quart water. Soak eggplant for 30 minutes, then drain and squeeze hard to remove water. Wring out remaining water with a cloth tea towel, and set aside.
2. Preheat the oven to 375°F, and grease a 9 x 13-inch baking pan.

3. Heat oil in a large skillet over medium-high heat. Add onion and garlic, and cook, stirring frequently, for 3 minutes, or until onion is translucent. Add eggplant, and cook for 3 minutes. Add turkey, breaking up lumps with a fork, and cook for 2 minutes. Add wine, parsley, oregano, and cinnamon. Simmer for 20 minutes, stirring occasionally. Season to taste with salt and pepper.

4. While turkey simmers, prepare sauce. Heat butter in saucepan over low heat. Stir in flour and cook, stirring constantly, for 2 minutes. Whisk in milk, and simmer 2 minutes, or until thick. Whisk ½ cup milk mixture into eggs, then whisk egg mixture back into the saucepan. Remove custard from the stove, and stir in ½ cup Parmesan cheese and dill, if using. Season to taste with salt and pepper.

5. Spread turkey mixture into the prepared pan. Pour hot custard cheese sauce over filling, and sprinkle with remaining ¼ cup Parmesan. Bake dish for 45 minutes, or until custard is set and top is browned. Cool 5 minutes, then serve immediately.

Note: The turkey mixture can be prepared up to 2 days in advance and refrigerated, tightly covered; reheat it over low heat before baking. Or the dish can be prepared for baking up to 6 hours in advance and kept at room temperature. Add 5–10 minutes to baking time if filling is not hot.

While it may seem like a small step, whisking some of the hot liquid into the eggs is crucial to the success of this dish, or any dish done with an egg-enriched custard. It's called "tempering" the eggs, and it makes the sauce smooth rather than like scrambled eggs.

Chinese Turkey Burgers

Traditional Chinese cooking has a dish called lion's head, which is basically large meatballs flavored with myriad ingredients and crisp with water chestnuts. These burgers are a grilled version, and the sweet mustard topping glorifies them even more.

Yield: 4-6 servings | **Active time:** 20 minutes | **Start to finish:** 45 minutes

1¼ pounds ground turkey

8 scallions, white parts and 4 inches of green tops, rinsed, trimmed, and thinly sliced, divided

2 tablespoons grated fresh ginger

¼ cup chopped fresh cilantro

3 garlic cloves, peeled and minced

3 tablespoons soy sauce

2 tablespoons dry sherry

½ cup finely chopped water chestnuts

Freshly ground black pepper to taste

½ cup Dijon mustard

¼ cup hoisin sauce*

4-6 sesame rolls, sliced in half

For serving: Lettuce and tomato slices

1. Prepare a dual-temperature medium and hot grill according to the instructions given on page 177, or preheat the oven broiler.
2. Combine turkey, ½ of scallions, ginger, cilantro, garlic, soy sauce, sherry, water chestnuts, and pepper in a mixing bowl. Mix well and form into 4-6 (¾-inch thick) burgers. Combine mustard and hoisin sauce in a bowl, whisk well, and divide into 2 bowls.
3. Grill rolls on the hot side of the grill cut side down until toasted. Sear burgers over high heat for 2 minutes per side, uncovered if using a charcoal grill, and then transfer burgers to the cooler side of the grill. Continue to cook, covered, for 3-5 minutes per side, or until burgers register 165°F on an instant-read thermometer and are cooked through and no longer pink. Baste burgers with sauce for last 4 minutes of grilling.

*Available in the Asian aisle of most supermarkets and in specialty markets.

4. Add remaining scallions to second bowl of sauce. Serve burgers immediately on rolls with lettuce and tomato. Pass sauce separately.

Note: The turkey mixture can be prepared up to 1 day in advance and refrigerated, tightly covered.

Variation:
- Add 1 tablespoon Chinese chile paste with garlic to the sauce for a spicy dish.

You can transform any burger recipe into a meatball dish. Make the mixture as directed, and then bake the meatballs on a greased baking sheet in a 425ºF oven for 10–12 minutes, or until cooked through and no longer pink.

Beijing Meat Loaf

This flavorful dish is really a whole meal. It contains lots of vegetables, as well as cooked rice. Some cucumbers marinated in rice vinegar are a good addition to the meal.

Yield: 4–6 servings | **Active time:** 20 minutes | **Start to finish:** 1½ hours

>   2 tablespoons Asian sesame oil*
>   1 tablespoon vegetable oil
>   3 scallions, white parts and 4 inches of green tops, rinsed, trimmed, and chopped
>   3 garlic cloves, peeled and minced
>   1 tablespoon grated fresh ginger
>   1 carrot, peeled and finely chopped
>   1 celery rib, rinsed, trimmed, and finely chopped
>   1 large egg
>   ½ cup hoisin sauce*, divided
>   1 tablespoon soy sauce
>   1 tablespoon Chinese chile paste with garlic*
>   1 tablespoon fermented black beans, chopped*
>   ¾ cup cooked white rice
>   1 pound ground chicken

1. Preheat the oven to 350°F, and line a 9 x 13-inch baking pan with heavy-duty aluminum foil.
2. Heat sesame oil and vegetable oil in a small skillet over medium-high heat. Add scallions, garlic, and ginger, and cook, stirring frequently, for 30 seconds, or until fragrant. Add carrot and celery, and cook, stirring frequently, for 3 minutes. While vegetables cook, whisk egg, 3 tablespoons hoisin sauce, soy sauce, chile paste, and fermented black beans in a mixing bowl. Add rice, and mix well.
3. Add vegetable mixture and chicken to the mixing bowl, and mix well again. Form mixture into a loaf 9 inches long and 5 inches wide in the prepared pan. Spread top of meat loaf with remaining hoisin sauce.
4. Bake meat loaf for 1–1¼ hours, or until an instant-read thermometer inserted into the center registers 165°F. Allow meat loaf to rest for 5 minutes, then serve.

*Available in the Asian aisle of most supermarkets and in specialty markets.

Note: The chicken mixture can be prepared up to 1 day in advance and refrigerated, tightly covered. Also, the meat loaf can be baked up to 2 days in advance and refrigerated, tightly covered. Reheat it in a 350°F oven, covered, for 20–25 minutes, or until hot.

Variation:
- Add ½–¾ cup chopped water chestnuts to the meat loaf mixture to make it crunchy.

Fermented black beans are tiny black soybeans that are preserved in salt, so they have a very pungent flavor. They should be chopped to release their flavor prior to cooking. Because they are salted as a preservative, they last for up to 2 years if refrigerated once opened.

Chapter 7:
Redefining Fast Food: Dishes Made with Boneless, Skinless Chicken Breasts

Breasts are the chickens' filet mignon, and luckily they're often on sale—which is when you should buy them.

Boneless, skinless breasts are the form of chicken that cooks the fastest—especially when it's cut up into small nuggets, as is the case with most of these recipes. The Asian concept of stir-fry has been applied to many Western cuisines in the past few decades, and those are the recipes you'll find in this chapter.

SUCCESS WITH STIR-FRIES

For stir-frying, advance planning, speed, and control are the keys to success. The ancient Chinese invented stir-frying as one of their more than fifty methods of food preparation. However, many recipes—including some in this chapter—now utilize the technique for non-Asian dishes.

Because the final cooking is a quick process, the food must be sitting in bowls or dishes placed within arm's reach, ready to be cooked. Cut all pieces of the same ingredient the same size, have your seasonings at hand, and make sure that any required partial cooking of vegetables—such as blanching green beans—has already been done.

The game plan is that when the dish comes to the table all the ingredients are properly cooked, so there are two options: Either cut food that takes longer to cook into smaller pieces and cook everything at the same time, or start with the longer-cooking food and keep adding ingredients in their decreasing need of cooking time. Both strategies produce good results. Never place too much food in the wok or skillet at one time. The food must be able to be seared on all sides, without steaming from being buried under a layer of food.

While it's possible to adapt many recipes to stir-frying, oil rather than butter should be used. The dairy solids in butter burn at a very low temperature, 250°F, so it can only be added as a flavoring agent once food is cooked. Oil, on the other hand, does not begin to smoke until it is heated to more than 400°F, so it is the better choice. There is no consensus as to what oil to use; that's why I lump them together as vegetable oil in the ingredient lists. Peanut, corn, soy, or canola all work well. Olive oil will give the dish a pronounced flavor, and it smokes at too low a temperature to be effective in sealing the food.

Place the wok or skillet over a high flame, and heat it very hot. Listen for the sound of sizzles; if a few drops of water evaporate immediately the pan is ready. Add the required amount of oil to the pan, and swirl it around gently to coat all sides.

Add the food, and keep it moving in the pan. If stir-frying in a wok, use a wire mesh spoon designed for the job. If stir-frying in a skillet, use a spoon that will reach to all places on the bottom, and with which you can keep food moving. In some recipes, liquid is added and the pan is covered for a brief time. In other recipes, it's fry and eat.

Not fond of white meat? No problem. Substitute boneless, skinless chicken thighs for the breasts in any of these recipes. Because the nuggets are so small, the thighs will cook in the same short amount of time.

Potato-Crusted Chicken

This is my favorite way to eat a boneless chicken breast, since it's marinated with herbs and garlic and then sandwiched between two potato pancakes; it could be called a "chicken *latke.*" Serve it with a tossed salad.

Yield: 4-6 servings | **Active time:** 25 minutes | **Start to finish:** 40 minutes

    1 pound boneless, skinless chicken breast halves
    Salt and freshly ground black pepper to taste
    1 teaspoon dried thyme
    2 tablespoons olive oil
    2 garlic cloves, peeled and minced
    1 large onion, peeled and diced
    2 large eggs
    1 cup all-purpose flour, divided
    1½ pounds russet potatoes, peeled
    2-3 cups vegetable oil for frying

1. Rinse chicken and pat dry with paper towels. Pound chicken between 2 sheets of plastic wrap to an even thickness of ½ inch. Cut chicken into 4-6 serving pieces. Mix salt, pepper, thyme, olive oil, and garlic together in a small bowl. Spread this mixture on the chicken.

2. Puree onion, eggs, ½ cup flour, salt, and pepper in a food processor fitted with the steel blade or in a blender. Scrape mixture into a mixing bowl. Shred the potatoes in a food processor fitted with a coarse shredding disk or through the large holes of a box grater. Squeeze out excess moisture, and mix potatoes into onion mixture. Push a sheet of plastic wrap directly into the surface of the mixture to prevent discoloration.

3. To cook, heat 1 inch of oil in a large skillet over high heat to a temperature of 375°F. Dust chicken with remaining flour, shaking off any excess over the sink or a garbage can, and coat on both sides with ⅓ inch of the potato mixture. Fry for 5-6 minutes per side, turning pieces gently with a slotted spatula, or until golden. Drain on paper towels, and serve immediately.

Note: The potato mixture and chicken can be prepared up to 6 hours in advance and refrigerated, tightly covered. Do not fry it until just prior to serving.

Variation:

- Substitute sweet potatoes for the russet potatoes.

Potatoes have a lot of liquid, although we think of them as a dry vegetable. That's why it's important to press the moisture out of them when making any sort of potato pancake or French fry.

Tarragon Chicken

This is a delicately flavored "skillet supper" that's scented with tarragon, an herb with a slightly licorice flavor that is used often in dishes containing cream. Serve this over some buttered egg noodles; your vegetables are right in the sauce.

Yield: 4–6 servings | **Active time:** 20 minutes | **Start to finish:** 35 minutes

> 1 pound boneless, skinless chicken breast halves
> Salt and freshly ground black pepper to taste
> 2 large leeks, white parts only
> 3 tablespoons unsalted butter
> 2 garlic cloves, peeled and minced
> 1 cup Chicken Stock (recipe on page 30) or purchased stock
> 1/2 cup dry white wine
> 1/2 cup heavy cream
> 1 tablespoon dried tarragon
> 2 carrots, peeled and thinly sliced
> 2 small zucchini, rinsed, trimmed, and sliced
> 1 cup frozen peas, thawed

1. Rinse chicken and pat dry with paper towels. Trim chicken of all visible fat. Cut chicken into 1-inch cubes. Sprinkle chicken with salt and pepper to taste. Trim leeks, slice in half lengthwise, slice thinly, and rinse slices well in a colander. Set aside.
2. Heat butter in a heavy, large skillet over medium heat. Add chicken cubes, and cook for 3 minutes, or until chicken is opaque. Add leek and garlic, and cook, stirring occasionally, for 3 minutes, or until leek is translucent.
3. Stir stock, wine, cream, tarragon, and carrot into the skillet. Bring to a boil, reduce the heat to medium-low, and simmer for 5 minutes. Add zucchini and peas, and simmer for an additional 5 minutes, or until chicken is cooked through and no longer pink. Season to taste with salt and pepper. Serve immediately.

Note: The dish can be prepared up to 2 days in advance and refrigerated, tightly covered. Reheat it over low heat, covered, stirring occasionally, until hot.

Variation:

- Substitute ¼ cup chopped fresh dill for the tarragon.

While the green tops of leeks are not used very often in cooking, if you're making a stock save them and use them in place of onion. They give stocks a rich color as well as an improved flavor.

Chicken with Herb Butter Sauce

Classic French cooking includes a whole category of sauces called compound butters; all they are is unsalted butter flavored in different ways. This is a fast and refreshing dish, with some tangy lemon juice added to balance the richness of the other flavors.

Yield: 4-6 servings | **Active time:** 20 minutes | **Start to finish:** 20 minutes

> 1¼ pounds boneless, skinless chicken breast halves
> 3 tablespoons all-purpose flour
> Salt and freshly ground black pepper to taste
> ¼ cup olive oil
> 4 garlic cloves, peeled and minced
> ¼ cup chopped fresh parsley
> 1 tablespoon dried rosemary, crushed
> 1 teaspoon dried thyme
> 4 tablespoons (½ stick) unsalted butter
> 2 tablespoons lemon juice

1. Rinse chicken and pat dry with paper towels. Trim chicken of all visible fat. Cut chicken into ¾-inch cubes. Toss chicken with flour, salt, and pepper in a bowl. Heat oil in a 12-inch skillet over high heat, add chicken cubes, and cook, stirring frequently, for 4–5 minutes, or until chicken is cooked through and no longer pink.

2. Add garlic, parsley, rosemary, thyme, and butter to the skillet and cook for 1 minute, shaking the skillet occasionally to coat chicken. Add lemon juice, and season to taste with salt and pepper. Serve immediately.

Note: The dish can be prepared for cooking up to 6 hours in advance, and refrigerated, tightly covered.

Variation:
- Substitute cilantro for the parsley, substitute lime juice for the lemon juice, omit the rosemary and thyme, and add 2 tablespoons chili powder and 1 teaspoon ground cumin to the skillet along with the butter.

Garlicky Spanish Chicken

It doesn't get much easier than this recipe; there are just a few ingredients and it's on the table in a matter of minutes. I usually serve it with a loaf of crusty bread, along with a tossed salad, to enjoy every drop of the garlicky sauce.

Yield: 4–6 servings | **Active time:** 10 minutes | **Start to finish:** 20 minutes

1¼ pounds boneless, skinless chicken breast halves
½ cup olive oil
8 garlic cloves, peeled and minced
2 tablespoons smoked Spanish paprika
3 tablespoons chopped fresh parsley
Salt and crushed red pepper flakes to taste

1. Rinse chicken and pat dry with paper towels. Trim chicken of all visible fat, and cut into ¾-inch cubes.
2. Heat oil in a large skillet over medium-high heat. Add garlic and paprika, and cook for 1 minute, stirring constantly. Add chicken and parsley, and cook, stirring constantly, for 3–4 minutes, or until chicken is cooked through and no longer pink. Season to taste with salt and red pepper flakes, and serve immediately.

Note: The chicken can be prepared up to 3 hours in advance and served at room temperature.

Chicken Parmesan

There's no reason that many favorite restaurant dishes can't be served on your table, and Chicken Parmesan is one of them. It's really easy to make, and what makes it special is the homemade sauce. Serve it over pasta with more of the sauce.

Yield: 4–6 servings | **Active time:** 25 minutes | **Start to finish:** 1 hour

SAUCE

3 tablespoons olive oil
1 medium onion, peeled and diced
3 garlic cloves, peeled and minced
1 teaspoon dried oregano
1 teaspoon dried basil
1 (28-ounce) can crushed tomatoes in tomato puree
$1/4$ cup dry red wine
Salt and crushed red pepper flakes to taste

DISH

$1/2$ pound fettucine
4–6 (4-ounce) boneless, skinless chicken breast halves
Salt and freshly ground black pepper to taste
1 cup milk
$1/2$ cup all-purpose flour
3 large eggs, lightly beaten
3 cups Italian bread crumbs
1 cup olive oil
$1^1/2$ cups grated mozzarella cheese
$1/3$ cup freshly grated Parmesan cheese
2 scallions, green tops only, rinsed and thinly sliced (optional)

1. For sauce, heat olive oil in a saucepan over medium-high heat. Add onion, garlic, oregano, and basil. Cook, stirring frequently, for 3 minutes, or until onion is translucent. Add tomatoes and wine, and season to taste with salt and crushed red pepper flakes. Bring to a boil, stirring occasionally. Reduce heat to low, and simmer sauce for 30 minutes, uncovered, stirring occasionally.

2. Bring a large pot of salted water to a boil over high heat. Add pasta and cook according to package directions until al dente. Drain, and return pasta to the pan to keep warm.

3. While sauce simmers, prepare chicken. Rinse chicken and pat dry with paper towels. Pound chicken between 2 sheets of plastic wrap to an even thickness of $1/2$ inch. Sprinkle chicken with salt and pepper. Place milk, flour, eggs, and bread crumbs in individual shallow bowls. Dip chicken breasts in milk, then in flour, shaking off any excess. Dip then in egg, and finally in bread crumbs, pressing into bread crumbs to make them adhere.

4. Preheat the oven broiler, placing the oven rack 8–10 inches from the broiler element, and grease a 10 x 14-inch baking pan.

5. Heat olive oil in large skillet over medium-high heat. Add chicken breasts, being careful not to crowd the pan. This will have to be done in two batches. Cook until golden brown, 3–4 minutes per side, turning chicken gently with a slotted spatula. Remove chicken to paper towels, and drain well.

6. To serve, arrange warm pasta in bottom of the prepared pan, and spread with 1 cup tomato sauce. Arrange chicken breasts on top of pasta, overlapping if necessary. Coat with remaining sauce, and sprinkle top with mozzarella and Parmesan cheeses. Broil for about 5 minutes, or until cheese melts and browns. Serve immediately, sprinkling each serving with scallions, if using.

Note: The sauce can be made up to 2 days in advance and refrigerated, tightly covered; it can also be frozen for up to 3 months. The chicken can be breaded up to 1 day in advance and refrigerated, tightly covered. Do not cook the dish until just prior to serving.

If time permits, it's always a good idea to coat food destined for frying at least 15 minutes in advance of cooking it. The layers of coating then have a chance to merge with each other and the chance of the breading falling off is reduced.

Baked Chicken and Broccoli Risotto

Risotto is a traditional Italian rice dish that dates back to the Renaissance. The key ingredient is Arborio rice, which is a short, fat-grained Italian rice with a high starch content. Traditional risotto recipes require many minutes of laborious stirring, but this recipe achieves the same results with far less work.

Yield: 4–6 servings | **Active time:** 15 minutes | **Start to finish:** 50 minutes

> 4 cups Chicken Stock (recipe on page 30) or purchased stock
> 1 (1-pound) package frozen chopped broccoli, thawed and drained, divided
> 3 (6-ounce) boneless, skinless chicken breast halves, cut into 1-inch cubes
> Salt and freshly ground black pepper to taste
> 3 tablespoons unsalted butter
> 1 large onion, peeled and chopped
> 3 garlic cloves, peeled and chopped
> 2 cups Arborio rice
> 1/2 cup dry white wine
> 3/4 cup freshly grated Parmesan cheese

1. Preheat the oven to 400°F, and grease a 10 x 14-inch baking pan.
2. Combine stock and 1/3 of broccoli in a food processor fitted with the steel blade or in a blender. Puree until smooth, and set aside.
3. Rinse chicken, pat dry with paper towels, and sprinkle chicken with salt and pepper. Heat butter in a large skillet over medium-high heat. Add chicken and cook, stirring frequently, for 2 minutes, or until chicken is opaque. Remove chicken from the pan with a slotted spoon, and set aside. Add onion and garlic to the pan, and cook for 3 minutes, stirring frequently, or until onion is translucent. Add rice to the pan, and cook for 2 minutes, stirring constantly.
4. Add wine to the pan, raise the heat to high, and cook for 3 minutes, stirring constantly, or until wine is almost evaporated. Add stock and chicken to pan, and bring to a boil. Scrape mixture into the prepared baking pan, cover the pan with aluminum foil, and bake for 10 minutes. Remove foil, stir in remaining broccoli, and return the pan to

oven for 15–20 minutes, or until rice is soft and has absorbed liquid. Stir in Parmesan cheese, season to taste with salt and pepper, and serve immediately.

Note: The dish can be cooked up to 2 days in advance and refrigerated, tightly covered. Reheat in a 350°F oven, covered, for 20–25 minutes, or until hot.

Variation:

- In the spring when fresh asparagus is in season and inexpensive, substitute it for the broccoli.

Dishes such as these can also become a way to use up precooked chicken. If using precooked chicken, add an additional ½ cup of chicken stock to a recipe to compensate for the fact that the chicken won't be giving off moisture, and add it later in the cooking process. In this case, the chicken should be added along with the broccoli.

Sweet and Sour Chicken

Most Americans were introduced to Chinese-American food with some sort of sweet and sour dish, and these flavors appeal to all generations. This recipe has lots of vegetables in it, so some rice is all you need to complete the meal.

Yield: 4–6 servings | **Active time:** 25 minutes | **Start to finish:** 25 minutes

> 1 pound boneless, skinless chicken breast halves
> 3/4 cup pineapple juice
> 1/2 cup ketchup
> 1/3 cup firmly packed light brown sugar
> 1/4 cup cider vinegar
> 1/4 cup water
> 2 tablespoons soy sauce
> 1 tablespoon cornstarch
> 2 tablespoons Asian sesame oil*
> 1 tablespoon vegetable oil
> 3 scallions, white parts and 4 inches of green tops, rinsed, trimmed, and chopped
> 2 garlic cloves, peeled and minced
> 2 tablespoons grated fresh ginger
> 1/2 teaspoon crushed red pepper flakes, or to taste
> 1 sweet onion, such as Vidalia or Bermuda, peeled, and sliced lengthwise
> 1 green bell pepper, seeds and ribs removed, and sliced
> 2 cups diced fresh pineapple

1. Rinse chicken and pat dry with paper towels. Trim chicken of all visible fat, and cut it into 3/4-inch cubes. Set aside. Combine pineapple juice, ketchup, brown sugar, vinegar, water, soy sauce, and cornstarch in a bowl, and stir well to dissolve sugar. Set aside.

2. Heat sesame oil and vegetable oil in a wok or large skillet over high heat, swirling to coat. Add chicken, scallions, garlic, ginger, and red pepper flakes, and stir-fry for 2 minutes. Add onion and bell peppers and stir-fry for 3 minutes, or until chicken is cooked through and no

*Available in the Asian aisle of most supermarkets and in specialty markets.

longer pink. Add sauce and pineapple, and cook, stirring frequently, for 2 minutes, or until slightly thickened. Serve immediately.

Note: The dish can be cooked up to 1 day in advance and refrigerated, tightly covered. Reheat it in a 350°F oven, covered, for 15–20 minutes, or until hot.

Variation:
- Substitute mango or papaya for the pineapple.

To make sweet and sour dishes, most restaurants fry the cubes of chicken rather than stir-frying them. This adds many unnecessary calories and fat grams to the dish. Try to avoid deep frying whenever possible.

Mock Mu Shu Chicken

Easy to find and inexpensive flour tortillas are substitutes for Mandarin pancakes in this healthful stir-fried dish. Serve it with some fried rice.

Yield: 4–6 servings | **Active time:** 25 minutes | **Start to finish:** 25 minutes

>   6 large dried shiitake mushrooms*
>   1 ounce dried wood ear mushrooms*
>   1 cup boiling water
>   ³/₄ pound boneless, skinless chicken breast halves
>   ¹/₄ cup soy sauce
>   1 tablespoon dry sherry
>   2 tablespoons cornstarch
>   2 tablespoons vegetable oil
>   4 scallions, white parts and 4 inches of green tops, rinsed, trimmed, and sliced
>   3 garlic cloves, peeled and minced
>   1¹/₂ cups shredded green cabbage
>   3 large eggs, lightly beaten
>   Salt and freshly ground black pepper to taste
>   ¹/₂ cup plum sauce*
>   12 (6-inch) flour or whole-wheat tortillas

1. Place dried shiitake mushrooms and wood ear mushrooms into a small mixing bowl. Pour boiling water over mushrooms, pressing them into water with the back of a spoon. Soak mushrooms for 10 minutes, then drain, squeezing out as much liquid as possible. Discard stems, and slice mushrooms thinly. Set aside.

2. Rinse chicken and pat dry with paper towels. Trim chicken of all visible fat. Cut chicken into thin slivers by cutting into thin slices and then cutting slices lengthwise. Combine soy sauce, sherry, and cornstarch in a mixing bowl. Stir well, and add chicken to mixing bowl. Toss to coat chicken evenly.

3. Heat oil in a wok or large skillet over medium-high heat. Add scallions and garlic and stir-fry for 30 seconds, or until fragrant. Add cabbage and chicken and stir-fry for 2 minutes, or until chicken is

*Available in the Asian aisle of most supermarkets and in specialty markets.

cooked through and no longer pink. Add mushrooms and eggs to the skillet, and stir. Cook for 1 minute, then scrape the bottom of the pan to dislodge cooked egg. Cook for an additional 1–2 minutes, or until eggs are just set. Season to taste with salt and pepper.

4. To serve, spread plum sauce on the surface of each tortilla. Place a portion of filling in the center. Tuck one edge over filling, and roll tortillas firmly to enclose filling. Serve immediately.

Note: The dish can be prepared up to cooking 6 hours in advance. Refrigerate chicken separately from vegetables.

Wood ear mushrooms, also called cloud ear, are a form of Asian dried mushroom with a slightly crunchy texture and very delicate flavor. They are almost brownish black and expand to five times their size when rehydrated.

Szechwan Chicken with Green Beans

This fast stir-fry is definitely spicy, with the heat tempered a bit by honey. No need to go to the Asian grocery for this dish; all the ingredients are found in your supermarket.

Yield: 4-6 servings | **Active time:** 25 minutes | **Start to finish:** 25 minutes

> 1 pound boneless, skinless chicken breast halves
> 1/3 cup soy sauce, divided
> 2 tablespoons honey, divided
> 4 garlic cloves, peeled and minced, divided
> 1/2 teaspoon crushed red pepper flakes, or to taste, divided
> 3/4 cup Chicken Stock (recipe on page 30) or purchased stock
> 1 tablespoon cornstarch
> 1 tablespoon cold water
> 3 tablespoons vegetable oil
> 3 scallions, white parts and 4 inches of green tops, rinsed, trimmed, and thinly sliced
> 2 tablespoons grated fresh ginger
> 1/2 pound fresh green beans, rinsed, trimmed, and cut into 1-inch pieces on the diagonal
> Salt and freshly ground black pepper to taste

1. Rinse chicken and pat dry with paper towels. Trim chicken of all visible fat. Cut chicken into 3/4-inch cubes. Combine 2 tablespoons soy sauce, 1 tablespoon honey, 2 garlic cloves, and 1/4 teaspoon red pepper flakes in a mixing bowl. Stir well, add chicken, and mix well. Set aside.

2. Combine remaining soy sauce, honey, red pepper flakes, and chicken stock in a small bowl, and set aside. Combine cornstarch with water in a small bowl, stir well, and set aside.

3. Heat vegetable oil in a heavy wok or skillet over high heat, swirling to coat the pan. Add scallions, remaining garlic, and ginger, and stir-fry for 30 seconds, or until fragrant. Add chicken and cook for 2 minutes, stirring constantly. Add green beans, and stir-fry for 2 minutes more, stirring constantly.

4. Add sauce mixture and cook, stirring constantly, for 2 minutes, or until chicken is cooked through and no longer pink. Add cornstarch mixture and simmer for 1 minute, or until slightly thickened. Season to taste with salt and pepper, and serve immediately.

Note: The dish can be prepared up to cooking 6 hours in advance. Refrigerate chicken separately from vegetables.

Variation:

- Substitute broccoli, cut into florets, or asparagus, woody stems discarded and cut into 1-inch pieces on the diagonal, for the green beans.

Here's a way to minimize the number of bowls you'll have to wash after cooking a stir-fried dish: Layer the vegetables starting with the one added last at the bottom of the bowl, and separate the layers with plastic wrap. When it's time to add the next ingredients just reach in, grab the sheet of plastic wrap, and toss it in.

Chapter 8:

Everything Tastes Better Outdoors: Grilled Chicken and Chicken Parts

Firing up the "barbie" is part and parcel of warm-weather living around the world. And grilled chicken is part of that summertime life, if not all year. Chicken, be it whole or in pieces, absorbs all the wonderful smoky nuances created by the grill.

I have to admit my partiality to charcoal grills, and using soaked wood chips to add an intense depth of flavor to grilled chicken. If cooking a recipe that includes a long bath in a vibrant marinade, using a gas grill is just as good.

As is true in other chapters of *$3 Chicken Meals*, most of the recipes use cost-effective whole chickens and chicken parts. For the recipes for parts, you'll notice that I don't suggest the wings but just the breasts and dark meat. That's because I really believe that wings are best treated with their own recipes and marinades; you'll find those in Chapter 3.

USING A CHARCOAL GRILL

All charcoal grills have two grates; the lower grate holds the charcoal and the upper grate holds the food. Charcoal briquettes or hardwood charcoal rest on the lower grate, and once they are lit you can move them around to create the heat pattern that is best for each recipe.

The temperature of the fire is controlled by opening and closing the top and bottom vents. The more these vents are open, the hotter the fire will be, and the more they are closed the cooler the fire. Here are some tips for all charcoal grilling:

- **Use enough charcoal.** This is perhaps the most common foible of charcoal grilling. Make sure the fire is 4 inches larger in diameter than the food to be cooked over it. The higher the charcoal is banked, the hotter the fire will be. If you want to cook over a very hot fire, build the coals to within 3 inches of the grate on which the food will cook.

- **Make sure the charcoal is ready.** The visual sign that the briquettes or hardwood charcoal is ready is that all are lightly covered with gray ash. This means that the charcoal is fully lit and hot.

- **Clean out the ashes regularly.** The heat of a charcoal fire can be diminished if the bottom vents are clogged with ashes. Remove both grates, close the bottom vents, and scoop out the ashes. Remember to open the vents before lighting the next batch of charcoal.

USING A GAS GRILL

There is no question that a gas grill is more convenient than cooking with charcoal. Lighting a gas grill is like lighting the oven broiler, and gas grills offer unparalleled convenience. Many people believe, however, that what is lost is some of the flavor and aroma transferred to food when cooking on a charcoal grill.

Gas grills use natural or LP gas for heat and flames, so the fire is efficient. Here is how to light most of them, although always consult the manufacturer's instructions: Open the cover, and then open the valve of the gas tank. One at a time, turn the controls to High and ignite the corresponding burner with either a long butane lighter, long matches, or the grill's own electronic ignition. Close the cover and wait 15 to 20 minutes for your grill to reach its highest heat.

Stopping a gas grill is just as easy as lighting one. Turn off each burner, and close off the gas valve. Then turn one of the burners on High for 15 seconds to bleed any gas remaining in the line, turn that burner off, and close the cover.

The most important thing about cooking with gas is making sure your tank is at least 1/3 full when you start. An easy way to do this is to pour a cup of boiling water on the side of the gas tank. The portion of the tank that remains cool is full; the portion that heats from the water is empty. Here are some considerations for safety as well as achieving the best flavor:

- Always keep the lid down except if expressly told to leave it open in a recipe. Gas burns cleanly so no residue accumulates on the interior of the lid from high-heat cooking.

- Remove the warming rack, assuming the grill has one, before lighting the grill. Unless you actually plan to use it, the warming rack gets in the way of turning food at the back of the grate, and can burn your hand as you try.

- Do not skimp on the preheating time. Give it a full 15 minutes, and longer in cold weather.

- Store propane tanks in a well-ventilated space. Even empty, they should *never* be placed in a garage or in a basement. And always keep them upright.

USING WOOD CHIPS FOR FLAVOR

Wood chips made from aromatic woods like hickory, mesquite, and cherry add immeasurably to the flavor of grilled foods, as well as giving the skin of poultry a rich mahogany color. While Americans use wood chips, grillers around the world have other flavorful additions such as woody herb sprigs like rosemary or grape vines. In addition you can gain flavor from garlic cloves and pieces of citrus peel.

For charcoal grills the secret is to soak the chips in water for at least 30 minutes. When the coals just begin to form white ash, but are still somewhat red, drain the chips and scatter them over the charcoal.

Even though they won't produce as pronounced a flavor, you can also use wood chips on a gas grill. Use about 2 cups dry wood chips. Place them in the center of a large (12 x 18-inch) piece of heavy-duty aluminum foil. Bring up the foil on all sides and roll the ends together to seal the pouch. Poke several small holes in the top of the packet. Once the grill is hot, place the wood chip pouch under the grate across the burner shields. Smoke will eventually emerge from the holes.

FIRE CONFIGURATIONS FOR GRILLING

Each recipe in this chapter contains information about the appropriate temperature and configuration of the grill for the success of the recipe. The vast majority of recipes are cooked on a medium-hot grill with food placed directly above the fire; the second most popular configuration is a dual-temperature fire, and then there are a few recipes specifying indirect heat.

This section guides you through what each of these mean:

- **Direct Grilling.** This was how all grilling was accomplished prior to the invention of the covered kettle grill and the gas grill. The coals are lit and then evenly spread three to four levels deep on the lower grate. Gas grills should always be preheated on High, and then adjusted to suit the recipe.

- **Dual-Temperature Grilling.** By spreading the coals so that they are three or four deep on one side of the grill and one or two layers deep on the other side, you can sear food and then transfer it to the cooler side to complete the cooking. For a gas grill, preheat the grill on High, and then reduce half the burners to Medium.

- **Indirect Grilling.** The coals are pushed to the periphery of the grill and the food is place in the center over an aluminum drip pan rather than over direct heat. The grill is always kept covered, and the top and bottom vents are partially closed. If you have a gas grill with more than one burner it is possible to cook over indirect heat. The grills best suited to indirect cooking are those with right and left rather than front and back burners. For most foods it is best to have one burner set on High and the other on either Low or Medium, and you can move food from one side to the other as needed. For indirect cooking the food will only be receiving heat on one side, so it's necessary to keep changing the position of the food.

DETERMINING THE TEMPERATURE OF A GRILL

While many grills have a built-in thermometer, they are measuring the temperature in the air at the top or side of the cover rather than on the grid where the food will be cooked. The best way to judge the intensity of the heat is with the palm of your hand.

After the coals have a light coating of ash or the gas burners have been preheated, place your hand, palm side down, about 4 or 5 inches above the cooking rack, and count slowly. Here are your readings to determine the temperature of the grill:

- Hot grill: 2 seconds

- Medium-hot grill: 3–4 seconds

- Medium grill: 5–6 seconds

- Medium-low grill: 7 seconds

Grilling is a high-heat cooking method, so if you can hold your hand over the coals for more than 7 seconds it means you should be adding more coals or preheating the gas burners longer.

FASTER WHEN FLATTENED

Pressing butterflied chickens under bricks as they grill is a part of traditional Tuscan cooking that has been gaining in popularity for the past few years, and with good reason. Butterflying the birds in conjunction with weighting them produces moister chickens with perfectly crisp skin in less time than it takes to cook a whole bird by any other method.

While the gourmet gadget industry has been busy coming up with high-priced items to replicate what can be done with a few bricks wrapped in foil—an expenditure of a few dollars that can also be used to hold the paper napkins down if it's windy—there is an item you probably have in the kitchen that is also effective. That's a cast iron frying pan. I prefer bricks because you can move them around on the grill, but if you have a cast iron pan, you're ready to try this approach.

RAIN CHECK

So your worst nightmare has happened. You've got a batch of chicken marinated, a bunch of hungry people waiting to eat it, and the heavens open up. Grilling just isn't in the cards for that day.

Don't fret, and don't reach for the phone to call for the pizza. You can bake the chicken in the oven. It won't have the same luscious aroma, but it will be good anyway. There are two ways to cook it:

- For whole pieces with bones and skin, bake them in a 400°F oven in shallow baking pans for a total of 40–45 minutes, or until an instant-read thermometer registers 165°F when inserted into a thigh.

- For boneless, skinless breasts and thighs, the fastest way to cook is on the stovetop on a ridged grill pan, preferably one that covers two burners. Cook the chicken for a total of 12–15 minutes, or until an instant-read thermometer registers 165°F when inserted into the center of the pieces.

Pressed Chicken Tapenade

All through Provence dishes of an olive spread, *tapenade*, are served with cocktails. Its salty, garlicky flavor is excellent as a chicken marinade. Serve this with a tossed salad in a vinaigrette dressing and some crusty grilled bread.

Yield: 6–8 servings | **Active time:** 20 minutes | **Start to finish:** 4 hours, including 3 hours for marinating

> 2 (3–3½-pound) whole chickens
> ½ red onion, peeled and diced
> 2 garlic cloves, peeled
> ½ cup pitted oil-cured black olives
> ½ cup chopped fresh parsley
> 2 tablespoons herbes de Provence
> 1 cup dry white wine
> ¼ cup olive oil
> Salt and freshly ground black pepper to taste

1. Rinse chickens and pat dry with paper towels, and remove giblets, if necessary. Butterfly chickens according to the instructions given on page 19. Save wing tips, backbone, and giblets for making Chicken Stock (recipe on page 30); freeze livers separately.

2. Combine onion, garlic, olives, parsley, herbes de Provence, wine, and olive oil in a food processor fitted with the steel blade or in a blender. Puree until smooth. Season to taste with salt and pepper. Pour mixture into a jumbo resealable plastic bag or divide mixture into 2 (1-gallon) resealable plastic bags, and add chickens. Marinate chickens, refrigerated, for a minimum of 3 hours or up to 12 hours, turning the bag occasionally.

3. Prepare a medium-hot grill according to the instructions given on page 177. Wrap 4 bricks in aluminum foil.

4. Remove chickens from marinade and discard marinade. Place chickens on the grill skin side down. Place 2 bricks on top of each chicken. Grill chicken, covered, for 10 minutes. Remove bricks, and turn chickens over. Replace bricks, and cook for an additional 12–15 minutes, or until an instant-read thermometer registers 165°F when inserted into the thigh. Allow chickens to rest for 5 minutes, then cut into serving pieces, and serve immediately.

Note: The chicken can be grilled up to 2 days in advance and refrigerated, tightly covered. Serve it cold, or reheat it in a 350°F oven, uncovered, for 12–15 minutes, or until hot.

Variation:
- Rather than a whole chicken you can make this dish with the individual parts of your choice. Consult a similar recipe to determine the cooking time.

Herbes de Provence is a combination of aromatic seasonings, with rosemary, lavender, thyme, basil, and oregano prominently featured. If you don't have the blend on hand, feel free to make your own from these choices.

Pressed Lemon Herb Chicken

Whole chickens take very well to seasonings stuffed under their skin because there's a lot of surface area. In this case, it's butter flavored with herbs and aromatic lemon zest that also gives the meat more moisture. A green salad and a loaf of garlic bread are good coordinates.

Yield: 6–8 servings | **Active time:** 20 minutes | **Start to finish:** 50 minutes

> 2 (3–3½-pound) whole chickens
> 1 stick (¼ pound) unsalted butter, softened
> 3 tablespoons chopped fresh parsley
> 1 tablespoon dried rosemary, crumbled
> 1½ teaspoons dried thyme
> 1 tablespoon grated lemon zest
> Salt and freshly ground black pepper to taste
> ½ lemon, seeded and very thinly sliced

1. Rinse chickens and pat dry with paper towels, and remove giblets, if necessary. Butterfly chickens according to the instructions given on page 19. Save wing tips, backbone, and giblets for making Chicken Stock (recipe on page 30); freeze livers separately.
2. Prepare a medium-hot grill according to the instructions given on page 177. Wrap 4 bricks with aluminum foil.
3. Combine butter, parsley, rosemary, thyme, lemon zest, salt, and pepper in a mixing bowl, and mix well. Stuff mixture under the skin of each chicken, being careful not to tear the skin. Lay lemon slices on top of butter.
4. Place chickens on the grill skin side down. Place 2 bricks on top of each chicken. Grill chicken, covered, for 10 minutes. Remove bricks, and turn chickens over. Replace bricks, and cook for an additional 12–15 minutes, or until an instant-read thermometer registers 165°F when inserted into the thigh. Allow chickens to rest for 5 minutes, then cut into serving pieces, and serve immediately.

Note: The chicken can be grilled up to 2 days in advance and refrigerated, tightly covered. Serve it cold, or reheat it in a 350°F oven, uncovered, for 12–15 minutes, or until hot.

Variation:
- Substitute any of the compound butter formulations on page 21 for the butter in this recipe.

Grilled "Fusion" Chicken

A lot has been written in recent years about Fusion cooking, which is basically a blending of Asian and Western cuisines. This basting sauce, made with American ketchup and Chinese chile paste, has all the distinguishing features of this exciting style of cooking.

Yield: 4–6 servings | **Active time:** 15 minutes | **Start to finish:** 40 minutes

    4–8 chicken pieces of your choice (breasts cut crosswise in half,
        thighs, legs) with skin and bones
    Salt and freshly ground black pepper to taste
    1 cup ketchup
    1 cup orange juice
    3 scallions, white parts and 4 inches of green tops, rinsed,
        trimmed, and finely chopped
    3 garlic cloves, peeled and minced
    $1/3$ cup chopped fresh cilantro
    3 tablespoons Chinese chile paste with garlic*
    2 tablespoons soy sauce
    2 tablespoons firmly packed dark brown sugar
    2 tablespoons curry powder

1. Prepare a medium-hot grill according to the instructions given on page 177.
2. Rinse chicken and pat dry with paper towels. Sprinkle chicken with salt and pepper.
3. Combine ketchup, orange juice, scallions, garlic, cilantro, chile paste, soy sauce, brown sugar, curry powder, salt, and pepper in a small saucepan. Bring to a boil over medium heat, stirring frequently. Divide sauce into 2 bowls.
4. Grill chicken, covered, starting with skin side down, for 8–10 minutes per side, or until dark meat registers 165°F on an instant-read thermometer. Brush chicken with sauce for last 4 minutes of grilling per side. Remove chicken from the grill, and serve immediately, passing bowl of sauce not used for basting separately.

Note: The chicken can be grilled up to 1 day in advance and refrigerated, tightly covered. Serve it cold, or reheat it in a 350°F oven for 12–15 minutes, or until hot.

*Available in the Asian aisle of most supermarkets and in specialty markets.

Pressed Thai Chicken

Almost every village in Thailand has its version of *gai yang*, which is a flavorful marinated roast chicken dish. This version includes such fresh flavors as lemongrass, cilantro, and ginger; the sauce is the marinade reduced with creamy coconut milk.

Yield: 6–8 servings | **Active time:** 25 minutes | **Start to finish:** 4½ hours, including 4 hours for marinating

> 2 (3–3½-pound) whole chickens
> 4 stalks fresh lemongrass
> 1 bunch cilantro, rinsed with stems discarded
> 1 small onion, peeled and diced
> 6 garlic cloves, peeled
> 1 (2-inch) piece fresh ginger, peeled and sliced
> ¼ cup firmly packed light brown sugar
> 2 tablespoons curry powder
> ¼ cup Asian fish sauce (*nam pla*)*
> 1 (14.5-ounce) can light coconut milk, divided
> Salt and freshly ground black pepper to taste

1. Rinse chickens and pat dry with paper towels, and remove giblets, if necessary. Butterfly chickens according to the instructions given on page 19. Save wing tips, backbone, and giblets for making Chicken Stock (recipe on page 30); freeze livers separately.
2. Remove woody stalks from lemongrass, trim root end, and discard tough outer leaves; slice bulbs. Combine lemongrass, cilantro, onion, garlic, ginger, brown sugar, curry powder, fish sauce, 1 cup coconut milk, salt, and pepper in a food processor fitted with the steel blade or in a blender. Puree until smooth. Pour mixture into a jumbo resealable plastic bag or divide mixture into 2 (1-gallon) resealable plastic bags, and add chickens. Marinate chickens, refrigerated, for a minimum of 3 hours or up to 12 hours, turning the bag occasionally.
3. Prepare a medium-hot grill according to the instructions given on page 177. Wrap 4 bricks in aluminum foil.
4. Remove chickens from marinade, and transfer marinade to a small saucepan.

*Available in the Asian aisle of most supermarkets and in specialty markets.

5. Place chickens on the grill skin side down. Place 2 bricks on top of each chicken. Grill chicken, covered, for 10 minutes. Remove bricks, and turn chickens over. Replace bricks, and cook for an additional 12–15 minutes, or until an instant-read thermometer registers 165°F when inserted into the thigh. Allow chickens to rest for 5 minutes, then cut into serving pieces, and serve immediately.

6. While chickens grill, add remaining coconut milk to marinade, and bring to a boil over medium heat, stirring occasionally. Reduce the heat to low, and simmer sauce for 10 minutes. Season sauce to taste with salt and pepper. Strain sauce into serving bowl, and keep warm.

Note: The chicken can be grilled up to 2 days in advance and refrigerated, tightly covered. Serve it cold, or reheat it in a 350°F oven, uncovered, for 12–15 minutes, or until hot.

Variation:

- Rather than a whole chicken you can make this dish with the individual parts of your choice. Consult a similar recipe to determine the cooking time.

Basic Beer Can Chicken

There is almost a cult following for this method of cooking a whole chicken by indirect heat, and until I tried it a few years ago, I was skeptical. But it does produce a chicken with outstanding tenderness and moisture. It still looks very odd to see the chicken on the grill perched on a beer can!

Yield: 3–4 servings | **Active time:** 10 minutes | **Start to finish:** 2 hours

> 2 cups hickory or mesquite chips
> (3–3½-pound) whole chicken
> 3 tablespoons Creole Rub (recipe on page 25) or purchased Cajun seasoning, divided
> Salt to taste (omit if using purchased Cajun seasoning that contains salt)
> 1 (12-ounce) can beer

1. Light a charcoal or gas grill, and arrange it for indirect cooking as described on page 177. If using a charcoal grill, soak hickory chips in water for 30 minutes. If using a gas grill, create a packet for wood chips as described on page 176.

2. Rinse chicken and pat dry with paper towels, and remove giblets, if necessary. Save wing tips and giblets for making Chicken Stock (recipe on page 30); freeze livers separately. Season Creole Rub with salt to taste. Rub 1 tablespoon inside cavity of chicken, and rub 1 tablespoon over skin of chicken.

3. Pop top on beer can, and pour off top 1 inch of beer. Use the pointed side of a bottle opener to punch 6 holes in the top of the beer can. Spoon remaining 1 tablespoon seasoning mixture through holes into beer.

4. Place an aluminum foil pan in the center of the grill grate, and add wood chips to coals. Replace top grate. Holding chicken vertically, with the opening to the body cavity down, insert beer can into cavity. Stand chicken up in the center of the top grate over the drip pan, pulling out the legs to form a stable tripod with the beer can.

5. Grill chicken for 1½–2 hours, or until dark meat registers 165°F on an instant-read thermometer. If using a charcoal grill, add 10–15 fresh coals per side to the fire after 1 hour. Using tongs, lift chicken onto a platter, holding a spatula under the beer can. Allow chicken to rest for 10 minutes, then remove it from the beer can, and carve. Serve immediately.

Note: The chicken can be grilled up to 1 day in advance and refrigerated, tightly covered. Serve it cold, or reheat it in a 350°F oven for 12–15 minutes, or until hot.

Variations:
- Substitute any of the spice rubs in Chapter 2 for the Creole Rub.
- Use an empty beer or soft drink can, and substitute white wine for the beer.

Beer can holders are now sold for less than $1 in many stores. If you like making chicken this way it's worth the investment because it adds stability to the chicken on the grill.

Mushroom-Stuffed Chicken

Delicate sautéed mushrooms enhanced with herbs become a flavorful mixture to stuff under the skin of chicken pieces. It adds as much flavor as marinating without the time needed to complete the process.

Yield: 4-6 servings | **Active time:** 20 minutes | **Start to finish:** 40 minutes

> 4-8 chicken pieces of your choice (breasts cut crosswise in half or thighs) with skin and bones
> 3 tablespoons unsalted butter
> 2 tablespoons olive oil
> 1 shallot, peeled and chopped
> 3 garlic cloves, peeled and minced
> 1/2 pound mushrooms, wiped with a damp paper towel, trimmed, and chopped
> 3 tablespoons dry sherry
> 2 tablespoons chopped fresh parsley
> 1/2 teaspoon dried thyme
> 1/2 cup Italian bread crumbs
> Salt and freshly ground black pepper to taste

1. Prepare a medium-hot grill according to the instructions given on page 177. Rinse chicken and pat dry with paper towels.
2. Heat butter and oil in a large skillet over medium-high heat. Add shallot and garlic, and cook for 1 minute. Add mushrooms, and cook for 5-7 minutes, or until mushrooms soften and liquid has almost evaporated. Add sherry, parsley, and thyme, raise the heat to high, and cook for 1 minute, stirring constantly. Remove the skillet from the heat, and stir in bread crumbs. Season stuffing to taste with salt and pepper.
3. Insert a few tablespoons stuffing under the skin of each chicken piece, and sprinkle chicken with salt and pepper.
4. Grill chicken, covered, starting with skin side up, for 8-10 minutes per side, or until dark meat registers 165°F on an instant-read thermometer. Remove chicken from the grill, and serve immediately.

Note: The chicken can be grilled up to 1 day in advance and refrigerated, tightly covered. Serve it cold, or reheat it in a 350°F oven for 12-15 minutes, or until hot.

Sweet and Sour Grilled Apricot Chicken

Sweet and sour is a time-honored culinary tradition from Bangkok to Boston, and this basting sauce with fresh ginger, apricot preserves, and horseradish makes this fast recipe a real winner. Serve it with some fried rice and stir-fried vegetables.

Yield: 4–6 servings | **Active time:** 15 minutes | **Start to finish:** 40 minutes

> 4–8 chicken pieces of your choice (breasts cut crosswise in half, thighs, legs) with skin and bones
> Salt and freshly ground black pepper to taste
> 3/4 cup apricot preserves
> 2 tablespoons soy sauce
> 2 tablespoons grated fresh ginger
> 1 tablespoon cider vinegar
> 1 tablespoon prepared white horseradish

1. Prepare a medium-hot grill according to the instructions given on page 177.
2. Rinse chicken and pat dry with paper towels. Sprinkle chicken with salt and pepper.
3. Combine apricot preserves, soy sauce, ginger, cider vinegar, and horseradish in a small saucepan. Bring to a boil over medium heat, stirring frequently. Divide sauce into 2 bowls.
4. Grill chicken, covered, starting with skin side down, for 8–10 minutes per side, or until dark meat registers 165°F on an instant-read thermometer. Brush chicken with sauce for last 4 minutes of grilling per side. Remove chicken from the grill, and serve immediately, passing bowl of sauce not used for basting separately.

Note: The chicken can be grilled up to 1 day in advance and refrigerated, tightly covered. Serve it cold, or reheat it in a 350°F oven for 12–15 minutes, or until hot.

Variations:
- Substitute orange marmalade or peach preserves for the apricot preserves.
- Add 2–3 tablespoons rum or tequila to the sauce ingredients.

Grilled Jamaican Jerk Chicken

This is not a recipe for delicate eaters! This is an authentic Caribbean recipe made with lots of fresh, hot chiles and assertive spices. But if you're a fan, then this is the dish for you.

Yield: 4–6 servings | **Active time:** 20 minutes | **Start to finish:** 5 hours, including 4 hours for marinating

> 4–8 chicken pieces of your choice (breasts cut crosswise in half, thighs, legs) with skin and bones
> 1/4 cup lime juice
> 1/4 cup soy sauce
> 1/4 cup olive oil
> 5 scallions, white parts and 3 inches of green tops, rinsed, trimmed, and cut into 1-inch lengths
> 4 garlic cloves, peeled
> 3–4 jalapeño or serrano chiles, seeds and ribs removed
> 2 tablespoons firmly packed dark brown sugar
> 1 1/2 teaspoons ground allspice
> 1 teaspoon dried thyme
> 1/2 teaspoon ground cinnamon
> 1/2 teaspoon grated nutmeg
> Salt and freshly ground black pepper to taste

1. Rinse chicken and pat dry with paper towels. Combine lime juice, soy sauce, olive oil, scallions, garlic, chiles, brown sugar, allspice, thyme, cinnamon, nutmeg, salt, and pepper in a blender or in a food processor fitted with the steel blade. Puree until smooth, and transfer marinade to a heavy resealable plastic bag. Add chicken pieces, and marinate chicken, refrigerated, for a minimum of 4 hours and up to 12 hours, turning the bag occasionally.
2. Prepare a medium-hot grill according to the instructions given on page 177.
3. Remove chicken from marinade and discard marinade. Grill chicken, covered, starting with skin side down, for 8–10 minutes per side, or until dark meat registers 165°F on an instant-read thermometer. Remove chicken from the grill, and serve immediately.

**Note: The chicken can be grilled up to 1 day in advance and refriger-
ated, tightly covered. Serve it cold, or reheat it in a 350°F oven for
12–15 minutes, or until hot.**

Variation:

- While hot chiles are part of the authentic formulation for this
  dish, feel free to cut back on the number or omit them entirely
  if you're not a fan. The spices are prominent enough to give you
  great flavor without the "heat."

While true Jamaican marinade is made with habañero or Scotch
bonnet chiles, those are more difficult to find in supermarkets
than the old standbys of jalapeño or serrano. If you can find the
authentic chiles, use only half of the number specified in this
recipe.

Chicken and Vegetable Fajitas

Fajitas, authentically Mexican but now adopted as part of the Tex-Mex tradition, are easy to make on the grill and always a treat. Serve these with some tortilla chips and you are ready to go!

Yield: 4–6 servings | **Active time:** 25 minutes | **Start to finish:** 45 minutes, including 30 minutes for marinating

1¼ pounds boneless, skinless chicken breast halves
1 cup finely chopped fresh cilantro
⅓ cup lime juice
2 garlic cloves, peeled and minced
1 tablespoon ground cumin
1 tablespoon chili powder
Salt and freshly ground black pepper to taste
⅔ cup olive oil
2 green bell peppers, seeds and ribs removed, and quartered
2 sweet onions, such as Vidalia or Bermuda, peeled and cut into
  ½-inch slices
8–12 (8-inch) flour or whole-wheat tortillas
Toppings: Salsa, guacamole, sour cream (optional)

1. Prepare a hot grill according to the instructions given on page 177.
2. Trim chicken breasts of all visible fat, and pound to an even thickness of ½ inch between 2 sheets of plastic wrap. Combine cilantro, lime juice, garlic, cumin, chili powder, salt, and pepper in a heavy resealable plastic bag, and mix well. Add olive oil, and mix well again. Pour off ½ of mixture, and set aside. Add chicken breasts to remaining marinade, and turn well to coat food evenly. Marinate chicken for 30 minutes at room temperature, turning the bag occasionally.
3. While chicken marinates, grill peppers and onions for a total of 10–12 minutes, or until tender, turning once. Remove vegetables from the grill, and when cool enough to handle, cut into thin strips.
4. Remove chicken from marinade, and discard marinade. Grill chicken for 2–3 minutes per side, uncovered, or until chicken is cooked through and no longer pink. Grill tortillas for 30–45 seconds per side, or until grill marks show.

5. To serve, cut chicken crosswise into thin strips, and add to vegetable mixture. Drizzle mixture with some of remaining marinade. Place a portion of mixture on the bottom edge of 1 tortilla. Fold over one side, and roll tortilla firmly but gently to enclose filling. Serve immediately, passing salsa, guacamole, or sour cream separately, if using.

Note: The marinade can be made up to 2 days in advance and refrigerated, tightly covered.

Variation:
- Add 1–2 jalapeño or serrano chiles, seeds and ribs removed, and finely chopped, to the marinade for a spicy dish.

Watch tortillas carefully when you're grilling them. The window between supple, warmed tortillas and tortillas that are too crispy to roll is just a few seconds.

Grilled Chicken Hash

One of the famed dishes in New York is the chicken hash served at the venerable 21 Club, which started life as a speakeasy during Prohibition. Grilling the lean chicken breasts gives them far more flavor than roasting, and you can also use this recipe as a way to utilize any leftover grilled chicken you might have lurking around.

Yield: 6-8 servings | **Active time:** 25 minutes | **Start to finish:** 1 hour

1¼ pounds boneless, skinless chicken breast halves
⅓ cup olive oil, divided
3 garlic cloves, peeled and minced
1 tablespoon herbes de Provence
Salt and freshly ground black pepper to taste
4 tablespoons (½ stick) unsalted butter
2 large sweet onions, such as Vidalia or Bermuda, peeled and diced
1 teaspoon granulated sugar
1½ pounds small redskin potatoes, scrubbed and quartered

1. Prepare a hot grill according to the instructions given on page 177.
2. Trim chicken breasts of all visible fat, and pound to an even thickness of ½ inch between 2 sheets of plastic wrap. Place 3 tablespoons olive oil in a mixing bowl, and add garlic, herbes de Provence, salt, and pepper. Mix well. Add chicken breasts and stir to coat evenly with mixture.
3. Grill chicken for 2–3 minutes per side, uncovered, or until chicken is cooked through and no longer pink. Cut into ½-inch dice, and set aside.
4. Heat butter and remaining olive oil in a large skillet over low heat. Add onions, toss to coat with fat, and cover the pan. Cook over low heat for 10 minutes, stirring occasionally. Uncover the pan, raise the heat to medium, sprinkle with salt and stir in sugar. Cook for 20–30 minutes, stirring frequently, until onions are medium brown. If onions stick to the pan, stir to incorporate the browned juices into the onions.

5. While onions cook, place potatoes in a saucepan and cover with cold water. Salt water and bring potatoes to a boil over high heat. Boil for 12–15 minutes, or until very tender when tested with a knife. Drain potatoes and mash roughly with a potato masher. Add chicken and onions to potatoes and mix well. Season to taste with salt and pepper.
6. Preheat the oven to 450°F. Spread hash into a greased 9 x 13-inch baking pan, and bake for 15 minutes, or until the top is lightly brown. Serve immediately.

Note: The hash can be prepared 2 days in advance and refrigerated, tightly covered. Reheat it, covered with aluminum foil, for 10 minutes, then remove the foil and bake for an additional 15 minutes.

Variation:
- Add 1 small green bell pepper, seeds and ribs removed, and diced, to the skillet when the onions begin to cook uncovered.

I adore redskin potatoes and use them whenever possible. Their thin skins never need peeling, and they add color to dishes too. The alternative that can be treated in the same way is Yukon gold potatoes.

Honey Mustard Chicken

Sweet honey and sharp mustard have been a winning American combination for centuries. This chicken marinade adds an Asian accent with aromatic sesame oil and spices. But it's still a basically American flavor, so I suggest coleslaw and cornbread to go with it.

Yield: 4-6 servings | **Active time:** 20 minutes | **Start to finish:** 5 hours, including 4 hours for marinating

> 4-8 chicken pieces of your choice (breasts cut crosswise in half, thighs, legs) with skin and bones
> ½ cup apple juice
> ¼ cup Dijon mustard
> ¼ cup honey
> 2 tablespoons Asian sesame oil*
> 2 garlic cloves, peeled and minced
> 1 teaspoon Chinese five-spice powder*
> Salt and freshly ground black pepper to taste

1. Rinse chickens and pat dry with paper towels. Combine apple juice, mustard, honey, sesame oil, garlic, five-spice powder, salt, and pepper in a heavy resealable plastic bag.
2. Add chicken pieces, and marinate, refrigerated, for a minimum of 4 hours and up to 12 hours, turning the bag occasionally.
3. Remove chicken from marinade and discard marinade. Grill chicken, covered, starting with skin side up, for 8-10 minutes per side, or until dark meat registers 165°F on an instant-read thermometer. Remove chicken from the grill, and serve immediately.

Note: The chicken can be grilled up to 1 day in advance and refrigerated, tightly covered. Serve it cold, or reheat it in a 350°F oven for 12-15 minutes, or until hot.

Variation:
- Substitute ⅓ cup pure maple syrup for the honey.

*Available in the Asian aisle of most supermarkets and in specialty markets.

Chapter 9:
The Second Time Around: Dishes Made with Precooked Chicken

It takes merely minutes to get dinner on the table with the recipes in this chapter. In the same way that used cars are now dubbed "pre-owned vehicles," my term for leftovers is "precooked chicken (or turkey)."

The recipes in this chapter—which run the gamut from treasured American favorites to all sorts of foreign fare—are also a great way to use up the color of chicken meat that your family may not like on its own. While in most families that's the dark meat, in my sister's family no one touches the breast meat—so to this chapter she turns for the white meat.

While most of the recipes are written for chicken, feel free to substitute turkey on any occasion; it will work equally well. One difference you'll notice in the recipes is that some call for diced meat while others call for shredded meat. How I prepare the meat for the dish depends on its sauce and presentation. For example, for a dish like the Chicken and Cheese Enchiladas on page 200, I wanted to keep the filling smooth for rolling in the tortillas, so the meat is shredded. On the other hand, the meat for the Old-Fashioned American Chicken Pot Pie on page 206 is diced; it works better with the sauce and other ingredients.

The best way to shred chicken or turkey is either with your fingers or with two forks, pulling it apart into small bundles.

Fettucine Alfredo with Chicken

While commercial Alfredo sauces are thick and gloppy, the authentic dish is light and luscious; it's just cream enriched with Parmesan. Serve this with a tossed salad in a vinaigrette dressing.

Yield: 4-6 servings | **Active time:** 10 minutes | **Start to finish:** 20 minutes

> ⅔ pound fettucine
> 4 tablespoons (½ stick) unsalted butter, divided
> ¾ cup heavy cream
> 2-3 cups diced cooked chicken
> ⅔ cup freshly grated Parmesan cheese
> Salt and freshly ground black pepper to taste
> 3 tablespoons chopped fresh parsley

1. Bring a large pot of salted water to a boil over high heat. Add fettucine, and cook according to package directions until al dente. Drain, reserving ½ cup of the pasta cooking water, and toss pasta with 1 tablespoon butter. Return to the pot to stay warm.

2. Combine remaining butter and cream in a saucepan over medium-high heat, and bring to a simmer, stirring occasionally. Add chicken, and simmer for 2 minutes. Add Parmesan, and season to taste with salt and pepper. Pour mixture over fettucine, and add some of reserved pasta water if mixture seems dry. Serve immediately, sprinkling parsley on each serving.

Note: The dish can be prepared up to 4 hours in advance and kept at room temperature. Reheat it over low heat, covered, stirring occasionally.

Variation:

- While it's not authentic, you can add 1-2 teaspoons Italian seasoning to the dish to give it more flavor.

> Reserving some of the water in which the pasta cooked is an old trick of authentic Italian cooking. It's done when the sauce is rather minimal, and adding some of it can enhance the sauce without making the dish taste watery.

Chicken Fried Rice

Fried rice, when made with egg and this number of healthful vegetables, is your whole meal. And it's one that's on the table in mere minutes.

Yield: 4-6 servings | **Active time:** 20 minutes | **Start to finish:** 20 minutes

  2 tablespoons Asian sesame oil*
  6 scallions, white parts and 4 inches of green tops, rinsed, trimmed, and thinly sliced
  1 tablespoon grated fresh ginger
  2 garlic cloves, peeled and minced
  1 cup chopped green cabbage
  2 tablespoons vegetable oil
  3 large eggs, lightly beaten
  4 cups cooked white or brown rice, cold
  2 cups diced cooked chicken
  ½ cup frozen peas, thawed
  3 tablespoons oyster sauce*
  2 tablespoons soy sauce
  1 cup fresh bean sprouts, rinsed
  Salt and freshly ground black pepper to taste

1. Heat sesame oil in a wok or large skillet over high heat, swirling to coat the pan. Add scallions, ginger, garlic, and cabbage, and stir-fry for 2 minutes, stirring constantly. Scrape mixture onto a plate.
2. Heat vegetable oil over medium-high heat. Add eggs, and scramble lightly until halfway set. Add rice, chicken, and peas, and cook for 2 minutes. Return vegetables to the pan, and add oyster sauce, soy sauce, and bean sprouts. Cook for 2 minutes, or until bean sprouts wilt. Season to taste with salt and pepper, and serve immediately.

Note: Up to adding the bean sprouts, the dish can be cooked up to 4 hours in advance and kept at room temperature.

Variation:
• For lo mein, substitute 3 cups cooked spaghetti for the rice.

*Available in the Asian aisle of most supermarkets and in specialty markets.

Chicken and Cheese Enchiladas

Enchiladas are a Mexican specialty, and the only constants are that they are hot dishes made with corn tortillas, and they contain some sort of cheese. In this version the flavorful filling is made with cream cheese and then the sauce is enhanced with cream.

Yield: 6-8 servings | **Active time:** 20 minutes | **Start to finish:** 50 minutes

> 2 tablespoons olive oil
> 1 large onion, peeled and chopped
> 3 garlic cloves, peeled and minced
> 1 jalapeño or serrano chile, seeds and ribs removed, and finely chopped
> 2 tablespoons chili powder
> 1 tablespoon ground cumin
> 1 teaspoon dried oregano
> 1 (4-ounce) can diced mild green chiles, drained
> 3 cups shredded cooked chicken
> 1 (3-ounce) package cream cheese, softened
> 2 cups grated Monterey Jack cheese, divided
> 3 tablespoons unsalted butter
> 3 tablespoons all-purpose flour
> 1 cup Chicken Stock (recipe on page 30) or purchased stock
> 1 cup half-and-half
> Salt and freshly ground black pepper to taste
> 12-16 (6-inch) corn tortillas
> Vegetable oil spray

1. Preheat the oven to 400°F, and grease a 10 x 14-inch baking pan.
2. Heat oil in a small skillet over medium-high heat. Add onion, garlic, and chile. Cook, stirring frequently, for 3 minutes, or until onion is translucent. Add chili powder, cumin, and oregano. Cook, stirring constantly, for 1 minute. Add canned chiles, and set aside.
3. Combine chicken, cream cheese, and 1 cup Monterey Jack cheese in a mixing bowl. Season to taste with salt and pepper, and set aside.

4. Heat butter in a saucepan over low heat. Stir in flour, and cook, stirring constantly, for 2 minutes. Whisk in stock, and bring to a boil over medium-high heat, whisking constantly. Add half-and-half, and simmer 2 minutes. Stir in cooked vegetables, and season to taste with salt and pepper.

5. Heat a large nonstick skillet over medium heat. Spray tortillas lightly with vegetable oil spray, and cook for 10 seconds per side, turning gently with tongs. Tortillas should be pliable, but not crisp.

6. Place $1/3$ of sauce in the bottom of the prepared pan. Divide chicken mixture into tortillas, and roll each gently. Arrange enchiladas seam side down in the pan. Pour remaining sauce over top, and cover pan with aluminum foil. Bake for 10 minutes, uncover pan, sprinkle with remaining cheese, and bake for 15–20 minutes, or until bubbly and browned. Allow to sit for 5 minutes before serving.

Note: The dish can be prepared up to baking 1 day in advance and refrigerated, tightly covered. Add 10 minutes to covered bake time if filling is chilled.

Variation:

- Substitute 1–2 chipotle peppers in adobo sauce, finely chopped, for the canned green chiles for a spicier dish.

Mexican Turkey "Lasagna"

Corn tortillas are used in place of pasta to separate the layers of this dish, which contains ricotta, as well as cooked turkey, in a lively tomato sauce. Serve it with a tossed salad.

Yield: 6–8 servings | **Active time:** 15 minutes | **Start to finish:** 50 minutes

3 tablespoons olive oil
1 large onion, peeled and diced
2 garlic cloves, peeled and minced
1 tablespoon chili powder
1 teaspoon ground cumin
1 teaspoon dried oregano
1 (14.5-ounce) can diced tomatoes, drained
1 (8-ounce) can tomato sauce
1 (15-ounce) can kidney beans, drained and rinsed
3 cups shredded cooked turkey
Salt and freshly ground black pepper to taste
1½ cups whole milk ricotta cheese
2 large eggs, lightly beaten
1 (4-ounce) can diced mild green chiles, drained
3 tablespoons chopped fresh cilantro
12 (6-inch) corn tortillas
1½ cups grated Monterey Jack cheese, divided

1. Preheat the oven to 375°F, and grease a 9 x 13-inch baking pan.
2. Heat oil in a large skillet over medium-high heat. Add onion and garlic, and cook, stirring frequently, for 3 minutes, or until onion is translucent. Stir in chili powder, cumin, and oregano. Cook, stirring constantly, for 1 minute. Add tomatoes, tomato sauce, beans, and turkey. Bring to a boil, and simmer 2 minutes. Season to taste with salt and pepper, and set aside.
3. Combine ricotta, eggs, chiles, and cilantro in a mixing bowl. Season to taste with salt and pepper, and stir well.
4. Place ½ of turkey mixture in the bottom of the prepared pan. Top with 6 tortillas, overlapping to cover filling. Spread cheese mixture on top, and sprinkle with ½ cup Monterey Jack cheese. Layer remaining tortillas, then spread remaining turkey mixture and sprinkle with remaining cheese.

5. Cover the pan with aluminum foil, and bake for 15 minutes. Uncover the pan, and bake for an additional 20 minutes, or until bubbly and cheese melts. Allow to sit for 5 minutes, then serve.

Note: The dish can be prepared up to baking 1 day in advance and refrigerated, tightly covered. Add 10 minutes to the covered bake time if filling is chilled.

Variation:
- Substitute jalapeño Jack cheese for the Monterey Jack for a spicier dish.

I use corn tortillas and brown rice pasta whenever I'm cooking for friends suffering from gluten-intolerance who can't have anything made with wheat. Both are readily available and easy to use.

Jambalaya

Saffron is the world's most expensive food ounce for ounce, but the fact that some is included in rice mixes makes this dish fall into our budgetary zone. This recipe blends all the vegetables and seasonings of a traditional Louisiana jambalaya, and all it needs is a tossed salad.

Yield: 4-6 servings | **Active time:** 15 minutes | **Start to finish:** 40 minutes

> 3 tablespoons olive oil
> 1 large onion, peeled and diced
> 3 garlic cloves, peeled and minced
> 2 celery ribs, rinsed, trimmed, and sliced
> ½ green bell pepper, seeds and ribs removed, and diced
> 2½ cups Chicken Stock (recipe on page 30) or purchased stock
> 3 tablespoons chopped fresh parsley
> 1 teaspoon dried thyme
> 1 bay leaf
> 2 (5-ounce) packages saffron rice, such as Carolina brand
> 2-3 cups diced cooked chicken
> 1 cup frozen peas, thawed
> Salt and freshly ground black pepper to taste

1. Heat oil in a large, deep skillet over medium-high heat. Add onion, garlic, celery, and green bell pepper. Cook, stirring frequently, for 3 minutes, or until onion is translucent.
2. Add stock, parsley, thyme, bay leaf, and rice to the skillet, and bring to a boil. Cover the pan, reduce the heat to low, and cook for 15–17 minutes, or until rice is almost tender.
3. Stir chicken and peas into the skillet, recover the skillet, and cook for 2-3 minutes, or until hot and remaining liquid is absorbed. Remove and discard bay leaf, season to taste with salt and pepper, and serve immediately.

Note: The dish can be cooked up to 2 days in advance and refrigerated, tightly covered. Reheat in a 350°F oven, covered, for 20–25 minutes, or until hot.

Variation:

- Substitute 1 cup sliced spicy turkey sausage for 1 cup of the chicken. Cook the sausage along with the vegetables and rice.

Jambalaya was created in the bayous of Louisiana in the late seventeenth century. It is a first cousin to Spanish paella and can be made with anything from poultry to seafood.

Old-Fashioned American Chicken Pot Pie

Many people have a negative reaction to the concept of chicken pot pie because of all those tasteless ones inflicted on them from the freezer case. But a *real* Chicken Pot Pie, filled with vegetables in a flavorful sauce beneath a flaky crust, is a work of art. It has all the vegetables you need for a healthy meal right in the pie.

Yield: 4-6 servings | **Active time:** 20 minutes | **Start to finish:** 55 minutes

> 5 tablespoons unsalted butter, divided
> 1 medium onion, peeled and diced
> ½ pound mushrooms, wiped with a damp paper towel, trimmed, and sliced
> 1 cup Chicken Stock (recipe on page 30) or purchased stock
> 1 large carrot, peeled and thinly sliced
> 2 celery ribs, rinsed, trimmed, and thinly sliced
> 1 (10-ounce) russet potato, peeled and cut into ½-inch dice
> 2 tablespoons chopped fresh parsley
> ½ teaspoon dried thyme
> 1 bay leaf
> 1 cup frozen peas, thawed
> 3 tablespoons all-purpose flour
> 1 cup half-and-half
> Salt and freshly ground black pepper to taste
> 3 cups diced cooked chicken
> 8½ ounces (½ of a 17-ounce package) puff pastry, thawed
> 1 large egg
> 1 tablespoon whole milk

1. Preheat the oven to 375°F, and grease a 9 x 13-inch baking pan.

2. Heat 2 tablespoons butter in a medium skillet over medium-high heat. Add onion and mushrooms, and cook, stirring frequently, for 5 minutes, or until mushrooms soften. Add stock, carrot, celery, potato, parsley, thyme, and bay leaf to skillet. Bring to a boil, reduce the heat to low, and simmer, covered, for 8–10 minutes, or until potato is tender. Add peas to pan, and cook 2 minutes. Strain mixture, reserving stock. Remove and discard bay leaf, and transfer vegetables to the prepared pan.

3. Heat remaining butter in saucepan over low heat. Stir in flour, and stir constantly for 2 minutes. Whisk in reserved stock, and bring to a boil over medium-high heat, whisking constantly. Add half-and-half, and simmer 2 minutes. Season to taste with salt and pepper. Add chicken to pan with vegetables, and stir in sauce.

4. Roll puff pastry into an 11 x 15-inch rectangle. Beat egg lightly with milk. Brush egg mixture around outside edge of pan. Place pastry on top of pan, and crimp the edges, pressing to seal the pastry to the sides of the pan. Brush top of the pan with egg mixture, and cut 6 vents, each 1 inch long, to allow steam to escape.

5. Bake pie for 35 minutes, or until pastry is golden brown. Serve immediately.

Note: The filling can be made 1 day in advance and refrigerated, tightly wrapped. Reheat it in a microwave oven or in a saucepan over low heat, stirring frequently, before baking the pie.

Variations:
- Substitute cut green beans for the peas.

The purpose of an egg wash is to give pastry a browned and shiny crust. But it's important to brush the crust before cutting the steam vents. The egg wash can clog the vents.

Creamed Chicken and Broccoli

This dish is an updated version of Chicken Divan, a popular dinner party entree when I was learning how to cook in the 1960s. It's really just broccoli and chicken in a cream sauce, but it's layered to look pretty.

Yield: 4–6 servings | **Active time:** 15 minutes | **Start to finish:** 35 minutes

> 2 cups Chicken Stock (recipe on page 30) or purchased stock
> 1 pound fresh broccoli, cut into florets with stems peeled and cut into ½-inch slices
> 4 tablespoons (½ stick) unsalted butter
> 3 tablespoons all-purpose flour
> ½ cup heavy cream
> 1 teaspoon dried tarragon
> ½ cup freshly grated Parmesan cheese
> Salt and freshly ground black pepper to taste
> 1 pound thinly sliced cooked chicken
> ½ cup grated Swiss cheese

1. Preheat the oven to 475°F, and grease a 9 x 13-inch baking pan.
2. Place stock in a small saucepan, and bring to a boil over high heat. Reduce the heat to medium, and reduce stock by ⅓. Set aside. Bring a pot of salted water to a boil over high heat. Add broccoli, and cook for 4–6 minutes, or until crisp-tender. Drain, and arrange broccoli in the baking dish.
3. Melt butter in a small saucepan over medium heat. Stir in flour, reduce the heat to low, and cook for 2 minutes, stirring constantly. Whisk in reduced stock, cream, and tarragon, and bring to a boil. Simmer sauce for 2 minutes, or until slightly thickened. Stir in Parmesan cheese, and season to taste with salt and pepper.
4. Pour ½ of sauce over broccoli, and top sauce with chicken. Top chicken with remaining sauce, and sprinkle with Swiss cheese. Bake for 12–15 minutes, or until bubbly and cheese browns. Allow to sit for 5 minutes, then serve immediately.

Note: The dish can be prepared for baking up to 2 days in advance and refrigerated, tightly covered. If chilled, bake it, covered with foil, at 350°F for 20 minutes. Then increase the oven temperature to 450°F, uncover the pan, and bake for an additional 10 minutes.

Variations:
- Substitute cauliflower or asparagus (when they're on sale) for the broccoli.
- Substitute cheddar cheese for both the Parmesan and Swiss cheeses.

If you're using purchased stock for this dish, even if it's billed as low-sodium, you won't have to add additional salt.

Biscuit-Topped Chicken Pie

Biscuits are to the American South what a baguette is to France; it wouldn't be a day without them. In this case, they're flavored with cheddar cheese, and used to top a pot pie made with lots of vegetables in a creamy sauce.

Yield: 4-6 servings | **Active time:** 20 minutes | **Start to finish:** 50 minutes

CHICKEN

4 tablespoons ($\frac{1}{2}$ stick) unsalted butter, divided
1 small onion, peeled and chopped
1 cup Chicken Stock (recipe on page 30) or purchased stock
1 large carrot, peeled and thinly sliced
2 celery ribs, rinsed, trimmed, and thinly sliced
1 large russet potato, peeled and cut into $\frac{1}{2}$-inch dice
2 tablespoons chopped fresh parsley
1 teaspoon dried thyme
1 bay leaf
1 cup frozen peas, thawed
3 tablespoons all-purpose flour
1 cup half-and-half
3 cups diced cooked chicken

BISCUITS

$1\frac{1}{2}$ cups all-purpose flour
2 teaspoons baking powder
$\frac{1}{2}$ teaspoon baking soda
Salt and freshly ground black pepper to taste
2 tablespoons cold unsalted butter, cut into bits
1 cup grated sharp cheddar cheese
1 cup sour cream

1. Preheat oven to 400°F, and grease a 9 x 13-inch baking pan.
2. Heat 2 tablespoons butter in a medium skillet over medium-high heat. Add onion, and cook, stirring frequently, for 3 minutes, or until onion is translucent. Add stock, carrot, celery, potato, parsley, thyme, and bay leaf to the skillet. Bring to a boil, reduce heat to low, and

simmer, partially covered, for 8–10 minutes, or until potato is tender. Add peas to the skillet, and cook 1 minute. Strain mixture, reserving stock. Remove and discard bay leaf, and transfer vegetables to the prepared baking pan.

3. Heat remaining butter in a saucepan over low heat. Stir in flour, and cook, stirring constantly, for 2 minutes. Whisk in reserved stock, and bring to a boil over medium-high heat, whisking constantly. Add half-and-half, and simmer 2 minutes. Season to taste with salt and pepper. Add chicken to the baking pan with vegetables, and stir in sauce.

4. While vegetables simmer, prepare biscuits. Sift flour, baking powder, baking soda, salt, and pepper together into a mixing bowl. Cut in butter using a pastry blender, two knives, or your fingertips until mixture resembles coarse meal. Add cheddar and sour cream, and stir until it forms a soft but not sticky dough. Knead dough gently on a lightly floured surface, roll or pat it out 1/2 inch thick, and cut out 8–12 rounds with a floured cookie cutter. Arrange biscuits on top of filling, and bake for 30–40 minutes, or until biscuits are brown and filling is bubbling. Allow to stand for 5 minutes, then serve.

Note: The chicken mixture can be prepared up to 2 days in advance and refrigerated, tightly covered. Reheat mixture in a saucepan or in the microwave oven before topping with biscuits, and do not make biscuit dough until just prior to serving.

Variations:
- Substitute Swiss cheese for the cheddar cheese.
- For a Southwestern pot pie, substitute cilantro for the parsley and substitute 2 tablespoons chili powder for the thyme. Add 1 (4-ounce) can chopped mild green chiles, drained, to the filling, and substitute jalapeño Jack cheese for the cheddar.

Skillet Chicken and Dumplings

Dumplings are basically biscuits that are steamed rather than baked, which makes this a great dish for warm weather because you don't have to turn on the oven and add heat to the kitchen. The creamy filling is flavored with herbs, and the dumplings are light and fluffy.

Yield: 4–6 servings | **Active time:** 20 minutes | **Start to finish:** 40 minutes

CHICKEN

4 tablespoons (½ stick) unsalted butter, divided
1 large onion, peeled and chopped
2 garlic cloves, peeled and minced
2 carrots, peeled and thinly sliced
2 celery ribs, rinsed, trimmed, and thinly sliced
¼ cup dry white wine
3 tablespoons all-purpose flour
1 cup Chicken Stock (recipe on page 30) or purchased stock
1 cup half-and-half
2 tablespoons chopped fresh parsley
2 teaspoons dried rosemary, crumbled
1 teaspoon rubbed dried sage
½ teaspoon dried thyme
Salt and freshly ground black pepper to taste
3 cups bite-size pieces cooked chicken
1 cup frozen cut green beans, thawed

DUMPLINGS

1 cup all-purpose flour
1½ teaspoons baking powder
Pinch of salt
½ teaspoon dried thyme
½ teaspoon dried rosemary
3 tablespoons unsalted butter
⅓ cup whole milk

1. For chicken, melt 2 tablespoons butter in a large covered skillet over medium-high heat. Add onion, garlic, carrots, and celery, and cook, stirring frequently, for 3 minutes, or until onion is translucent. Add wine, and cook for 3 minutes, stirring occasionally, or until wine is almost evaporated. Set aside.

2. Heat remaining butter in saucepan over low heat. Stir in flour, and cook, stirring constantly, for 2 minutes. Whisk in stock, and bring to a boil over medium-high heat, whisking constantly. Add sauce to skillet, and cook vegetables for 5 minutes. Stir in half-and-half, parsley, rosemary, sage, and thyme. Simmer 2 minutes, season to taste with salt and pepper, and stir in chicken.

3. While vegetable mixture simmers, prepare dumpling dough. Combine flour, baking powder, salt, thyme, and rosemary in mixing bowl. Cut in butter using a pastry blender, two knives, or your fingertips until mixture resembles coarse crumbs. Add milk, and stir to blend. Knead dough lightly on lightly floured counter, then cut into 12 parts.

4. Stir green beans into chicken mixture, and place dough on top of chicken. Cover the skillet, and cook over medium-low heat for 15–20 minutes, or until dumplings are puffed and cooked through. Do not uncover the pan while dumplings are steaming. Serve immediately.

Note: The chicken mixture can be prepared up to 2 days in advance and refrigerated, tightly covered. Reheat mixture in the skillet before topping with dumplings, and do not make dumpling dough until just prior to serving.

Variation:
- For Cajun flavor, substitute Cajun seasoning for the salt and pepper in both the filling and topping.

Chicken Croquettes

Croquettes of all types have been used as a way to stretch leftovers for centuries; they are basically a thick white sauce into which cooked food is folded, formed into patties, and fried. I adore them, and they are very easy to make.

Yield: 4–6 servings | **Active time:** 20 minutes | **Start to finish:** 1½ hours, including 1 hour to chill mixture

CROQUETTES

4 tablespoons (½ stick) unsalted butter

1 small onion, peeled and finely chopped

1 cup all-purpose flour, divided

⅔ cup whole milk

⅔ cup Chicken Stock (recipe on page 30) or purchased stock

3 cups finely chopped cooked chicken

2 tablespoons chopped fresh parsley

1 tablespoon Cajun seasoning

2 large eggs, lightly beaten

2 tablespoons water

1 cup plain bread crumbs

2 cups vegetable oil for frying

SAUCE

3 tablespoons unsalted butter

3 tablespoons all-purpose flour

2 cups hot whole milk

¾ cup grated Swiss cheese

Salt and freshly ground black pepper to taste

1. Heat butter in a saucepan over medium heat. Add onion and cook, stirring frequently, for 2 minutes. Add ⅓ cup flour, reduce the heat to low, and cook for 2 minutes, stirring constantly. Whisk in milk and stock, and bring to a boil over medium heat, whisking constantly. Reduce the heat to low, and simmer sauce for 2 minutes. Remove the pan from the heat.

2. Stir chicken, parsley, and Cajun seasoning into sauce, and transfer mixture to a 9 x 13-inch baking pan. Spread mixture evenly, and refrigerate for 30 minutes, or until cold, loosely covered with plastic wrap.

3. Place remaining flour on a sheet of plastic wrap, combine eggs and water in a shallow bowl, and place bread crumbs on another sheet of plastic wrap. With wet hands, form chilled chicken mixture into 2-inch balls, and flatten balls into patties. Dust patties with flour, dip into egg mixture, and dip into bread crumbs, pressing to ensure crumbs adhere. Refrigerate patties for 30 minutes.

4. While patties chill, make sauce. Melt butter in a saucepan over low heat. Stir in flour, and cook, stirring constantly, for 2 minutes, or until mixture bubbles. Slowly but steadily pour milk into the pan, whisking constantly, over medium heat until sauce comes to a boil. Simmer 2–3 minutes, thinning with more liquid if necessary to reach the right consistency. Add cheese, and stir until cheese melts. Season to taste with salt and pepper, and keep warm.

5. Heat oil in a deep-sided skillet over medium-high heat to 375°F. Add patties, being careful not to crowd the pan. Cook for a total of 3–5 minutes, or until browned. Remove croquettes from the pan with a slotted spoon, and drain well on paper towels. Serve immediately, passing sauce separately.

Note: The croquettes can be prepared for frying up to 1 day in advance and refrigerated, tightly covered. They can also be fried in advance; reheat them in a 375°F oven for 10–12 minutes, or until hot and crusty again.

Variation:
- Substitute Italian seasoning, salt, and pepper for the Cajun seasoning. Substitute ½ cup grated whole-milk mozzarella and ¼ cup freshly grated Parmesan cheese for the Swiss cheese.

Italian Creamed Chicken and Vegetable Casserole

This casserole is similar to a pasta primavera, but it's baked in the oven so the pasta really absorbs all the flavors in the sauce. Serve it with a tossed salad.

Yield: 4–6 servings | **Active time:** 20 minutes | **Start to finish:** 55 minutes

½ pound penne or gemelli pasta
3 tablespoons unsalted butter
2 tablespoons olive oil
1 medium onion, peeled and diced
2 garlic cloves, peeled and minced
1 small zucchini, rinsed, trimmed, and sliced
1 small yellow squash, rinsed, trimmed, and sliced
3 tablespoons all-purpose flour
1 cup Chicken Stock (recipe on page 30) or purchased stock
2 ripe plum tomatoes, rinsed, cored, seeded, and diced
2 tablespoons chopped fresh parsley
1 teaspoon Italian seasoning
1 cup heavy cream
2–3 cups diced cooked chicken
⅔ cup freshly grated Parmesan cheese, divided
Salt and freshly ground black pepper to taste
⅔ cup Italian bread crumbs

1. Preheat the oven to 400°F, and grease a 9 x 13-inch baking pan. Bring a large pot of salted water to a boil over high heat. Cook pasta according to package directions until al dente. Drain, and place pasta in the prepared pan.
2. Heat butter and oil in a heavy, large skillet over medium-high heat. Add onion and garlic, and cook, stirring frequently, for 3 minutes, or until onion is translucent. Add zucchini and yellow squash, and cook, stirring frequently, for 5 minutes, or until vegetables soften.
3. Stir in flour, and cook for 2 minutes, stirring constantly. Stir in stock, and bring a boil. Add tomatoes, parsley, and Italian seasoning, and cook for 5 minutes. Add cream, and cook for an additional 5 minutes, stirring occasionally. Stir in chicken and ½ cup cheese, and season to taste with salt and pepper. Pour sauce over pasta, and stir well.

4. Combine bread crumbs with remaining Parmesan, and sprinkle mixture on top of casserole.

5. Bake casserole for 20 minutes, or until bubbly and top is brown. Allow to sit for 5 minutes, then serve.

Note: The casserole can be prepared for baking up to 2 days in advance and refrigerated, tightly covered. If chilled, bake for 10 minutes covered with foil; then remove the foil and bake for an additional 25 minutes.

Variation:
- Substitute herbes de Provence for the Italian seasoning, and substitute Swiss cheese for the Parmesan cheese.

Greek Chicken with Tomatoes, Orzo, and Feta

Orzo is a rice-shaped pasta that's used extensively in Greek cooking, as are aromatic dill and sharp feta cheese. They're all here in this easy and quick casserole, melded together with a tomato sauce.

Yield: 4-6 servings | **Active time:** 20 minutes | **Start to finish:** 35 minutes

2 cups orzo
3 tablespoons olive oil
1 large onion, peeled and diced
3 garlic cloves, peeled and minced
1 (14.5-ounce) can tomatoes, undrained
1 (8-ounce) can tomato sauce
1/4 cup chopped fresh dill
2 teaspoons dried basil
2-3 cups shredded cooked chicken
Salt and freshly ground black pepper to taste
1 cup crumbled feta cheese

1. Preheat oven to 400°F, and grease a 9 x 13-inch baking pan. Bring a large pot of salted water to a boil over high heat. Add orzo, and boil for 7-9 minutes, or until orzo is double in size but still slightly hard; the amount of time depends on the brand of orzo. Drain, and set aside.

2. While orzo cooks, heat oil in a medium skillet over medium-high heat. Add onion and garlic, and cook, stirring frequently, for 3 minutes, or until onion is translucent. Add tomatoes, tomato sauce, dill, and basil to the skillet. Bring to a boil, reduce the heat to low, and simmer 5-7 minutes, or until onion is tender. Add orzo and chicken to the skillet, season to taste with salt and pepper, and stir well.

3. Scrape mixture into prepared pan, and sprinkle feta on top. Cover the pan with foil, and bake for 10 minutes. Uncover the pan, and bake for an additional 5 minutes, or until cheese is melted. Serve immediately.

Note: The dish can be prepared for baking up to 2 days in advance and refrigerated, tightly covered. If chilled, bake it, covered with foil, at 375°F for 20 minutes. Then increase the oven temperature to 400°F, uncover the pan, and bake for an additional 10 minutes.

Variation:
- Substitute fresh oregano for the dill.

Small pasta shapes absorb moisture and finish cooking when added to any dish that will be baked; that's why they should be slightly undercooked. Larger shapes need to be fully cooked, however, before adding.

North African Chicken

Olives, garbanzo beans, and aromatic spices are characteristic ingredients used in the cuisines of African countries bordering on the Mediterranean Sea. Serve this aromatic dish with a tossed salad.

Yield: 4–6 servings | **Active time:** 15 minutes | **Start to finish:** 40 minutes

    3 tablespoons olive oil
    1 large onion, peeled and diced
    1 carrot, peeled and sliced
    ½ green bell pepper, seeds and ribs removed, and diced
    3 garlic cloves, peeled and minced
    1 tablespoon ground cumin
    1 tablespoon paprika
    2 teaspoons ground coriander
    ½ teaspoon ground cinnamon
    2 cups Chicken Stock (recipe on page 30) or purchased stock
    1 (15-ounce) can garbanzo beans, drained and rinsed
    ½ cup sliced pimiento-stuffed green olives
    ¼ cup chopped fresh cilantro, divided
    3 tablespoons lemon juice
    2 tablespoons honey
    ½–1 teaspoon hot red pepper sauce, or to taste
    2–3 cups shredded cooked chicken
    1 cup frozen peas, thawed
    Salt and freshly ground black pepper to taste
    4–6 cups cooked couscous, hot

1. Heat olive oil in a large, heavy skillet over medium-high heat. Add onion, carrot, green pepper, and garlic, and cook, stirring frequently, for 3 minutes, or until onion is translucent. Add cumin, paprika, coriander, and cinnamon, and cook, stirring constantly, for 1 minute.
2. Add stock, beans, olives, 1 tablespoon cilantro, lemon juice, honey, and hot red pepper sauce to the skillet. Bring to a boil, then reduce the heat to low, and simmer, uncovered, for 15 minutes, stirring occasionally.

3. Add chicken and peas to the skillet, and simmer for 5 minutes. Season to taste with salt and pepper. To serve, mound couscous into low soup bowls and ladle chicken on top, sprinkling each serving with remaining cilantro.

Note: The dish can be prepared up to 2 days in advance and refrigerated, tightly covered. to serve, reheat it, covered, over low heat, stirring occasionally.

Variation:
- Substitute cut green beans for the peas.

Couscous is a food that is less expensive to buy in bulk bins at the health food store than packaged in the supermarket. The general formula for cooking it is 1⅓ cups boiling water or boiling stock and 1 tablespoon olive oil to each 1 cup of couscous. Stir the couscous into the liquid, cover the pan, turn off the heat, and allow it to sit for 5 minutes. Then fluff it with a meat fork.

Chinese Frittata

Don't even think about that mushy Egg Foo Yung you were fed as a child in a Chinese-American restaurant. This is a light frittata, flavorful from the seasonings, and topped with a quick and easy sauce.

Yield: 4-6 servings | **Active time:** 15 minutes | **Start to finish:** 25 minutes

FRITTATA

8 large eggs
2 tablespoons Chicken Stock (recipe on page 30) or purchased stock
2 tablespoons soy sauce
Freshly ground black pepper to taste
2 tablespoons Asian sesame oil*
1 tablespoon vegetable oil
6 scallions, white parts and 4 inches of green tops, rinsed, trimmed, and sliced
2 garlic cloves, peeled and minced
1 cup bean sprouts, rinsed
1½ cups shredded cooked chicken
½ cup chopped water chestnuts

SAUCE

¾ cup Chicken Stock (recipe on page 30) or purchased stock
2 tablespoons soy sauce
2 tablespoons oyster sauce*
1 tablespoon hoisin sauce*
1 tablespoon rice vinegar
2 teaspoons cornstarch

1. Preheat the oven to 425°F. Whisk eggs with chicken stock, soy sauce, and pepper, and set aside.

*Available in the Asian aisle of most supermarkets and in specialty markets.

2. Heat sesame oil and vegetable oil in a large, ovenproof skillet over medium-high heat. Add scallions and garlic, and cook for 1 minute. Add bean sprouts, chicken, and water chestnuts, and cook for 1 minute.

3. Reduce the heat to medium, add egg mixture, and cook for 4 minutes, or until the bottom of cake is lightly brown. Transfer the skillet to the oven, and bake for 10–15 minutes, or until top is browned.

4. While frittata bakes, make sauce. Combine stock, soy sauce, oyster sauce, hoisin sauce, vinegar, and cornstarch in a small saucepan, and whisk well. Bring to a boil over medium-high heat, stirring frequently. Reduce the heat to low, and simmer sauce for 2 minutes, or until slightly thickened. Set aside.

5. Run a spatula around the sides of the skillet and under the bottom of the cake to release it. Slide cake gently onto a serving platter, and cut it into wedges. Serve immediately, passing sauce separately.

Note: The sauce can be prepared up to 2 days in advance and refrigerated, tightly covered. Reheat it over low heat. The vegetables can be cooked up to 6 hours in advance and kept at room temperature. Reheat them over medium heat before adding the eggs.

Variation:
- Add 1 tablespoon Chinese chile paste with garlic to the sauce for a spicy dish.

Chapter 10:

Salad Daze: Entree Salads with Cold Veggies and Sometimes Hot Chicken

Entree salads are a delicious way to ensure you're getting all nine daily servings of fruits and vegetables into your diet. And they can be on the table in a matter of minutes. So entree salads satisfy both our need to eat more frugally and our need to eat more healthfully.

It used to be that salads were relegated to the warm summer months, but that's no longer the case. While chef salads and the now ubiquitous grilled chicken Caesar salad have been around for decades, a trend gaining favor now is the warm salad. Not a misnomer, the warm, freshly cooked chicken tops cold vegetables (with the occasional fruit thrown in) and then all components are napped with a light dressing.

Entree salads are also a great way to stretch leftover roast or grilled chicken that's not enough to serve on its own. If using a precooked protein, it's possible to prep the ingredients and make the salad dressing earlier in the day and refrigerate the various items in plastic bags or bowls; you'll need one for the "wet" ingredients like onions or beans, and another for the "dry" salad greens.

Feel free to substitute precooked chicken for almost all the recipes calling for grilled chicken in this chapter, too.

DRESSINGS DEMYSTIFIED

Beware of the center aisles in the supermarket! Those rows and rows of condiments, salad dressings, barbecue sauces, and marinades are like a slow leak on your wallet. If you look at the cost per pound or quart of those foods it's always much more expensive than their component ingredients.

That's why all of these simple salads are accompanied by equally simple dressings—all of which you make yourself. Salad dressing is what's called in cooking schools a "temporary emulsion." Or, in other words, oil and water don't mix. So it makes not a bit of difference if you carefully whisk oil into your dressing or throw everything together in a jar with a tight-fitting lid, and shake away. The only reason why I advocate two steps in most of these dressing recipes is that granular ingredients like salt and sugar dissolve in liquids but not in oil. So the oil goes in second.

While I developed these dressings to moisten specific salads, if you like them, consider the dressing recipes a "two-fer"; use them for your tossed salads on other occasions.

Chicken Salad with Pecans and Dried Cranberries

Crunchy nuts and succulent dried cranberries are a great combination for this salad, tossed with a sharp mustard vinaigrette and topped with some crumbles of creamy goat cheese.

Yield: 4–6 servings | **Active time:** 15 minutes | **Start to finish:** 15 minutes

>   ½ cup chopped pecans
>   ¼ cup cider vinegar
>   2 tablespoons Dijon mustard
>   2 tablespoons pure maple syrup
>   1 shallot, peeled and chopped
>   2 garlic cloves, peeled and minced
>   Salt and freshly ground black pepper to taste
>   ½ cup olive oil
>   4–6 cups mixed salad greens, rinsed and dried
>   2–3 cups diced cooked chicken
>   ½ cup dried cranberries
>   ¾ cup crumbled goat cheese

1. Preheat the oven to 350°F, and line a baking sheet with aluminum foil. Bake pecans for 5–7 minutes, or until browned. Remove pecans from the oven, and set aside.
2. While pecans bake, combine vinegar, mustard, maple syrup, shallot, garlic, salt, and pepper in a jar with a tight-fitting lid. Shake well, add olive oil, and shake well again. Set aside.
3. Combine pecans, greens, chicken, and cranberries in a mixing bowl. Toss with ½ of dressing, and serve immediately, mounding salad on individual plates or on a serving platter. Sprinkle goat cheese on top of salad, and pass remaining dressing separately.

Note: The dressing can be made up to 2 days in advance and refrigerated, tightly covered. Allow it to sit at room temperature for 30 minutes before serving, if chilled.

Variations:
- Substitute feta for the goat cheese.
- Substitute chopped dried apricots or raisins (dark or golden) for the dried cranberries.

Curried Chicken Salad with Garbanzo Beans

The beans add a nutty quality to this flavorful salad of chicken, fruits, and vegetables. *Nan*, Indian bread, is now found in most supermarkets, and it makes an excellent addition to this meal.

Yield: 4–6 servings | **Active time:** 20 minutes | **Start to finish:** 20 minutes

> 2–3 cups diced cooked chicken
> 3 celery ribs, rinsed, trimmed, and cut into $1/2$-inch dice
> 1 cup canned garbanzo beans, drained and rinsed
> 1 sweet eating apple, rinsed, cored, and cut into $1/2$-inch dice
> $1/3$ cup chopped dried apricots
> 1 cup plain nonfat yogurt
> $1/4$ cup mango chutney, such as Major Grey's
> 1 tablespoon cider vinegar
> 2 teaspoons curry powder
> 1 teaspoon ground cumin
> Salt and hot red pepper sauce to taste
> 2–3 cups shredded iceberg lettuce
> 2 tablespoons chopped fresh cilantro

1. Combine chicken, celery, garbanzo beans, apple, and dried apricots in a mixing bowl.
2. Combine yogurt, chutney, vinegar, curry powder, cumin, salt, and hot red pepper sauce in a food processor fitted with the steel blade or in a blender. Puree until smooth.
3. Pour dressing over salad, and stir well to combine. Serve immediately, mounding salad on top of lettuce on individual plates or on a serving platter, and sprinkling each serving with cilantro.

Note: The salad can be prepared up to 1 day in advance and refrigerated, tightly covered. Do not add the apple until just prior to serving.

Variation:
- Substitute dried cranberries, dried cherries, or raisins for the dried apricots.

Southern Fried Chicken Salad with Honey-Mustard Dressing

Nuggets of crispy pan-fried chicken on a salad drizzled with an old-fashioned honey and mustard dressing is one that appeals to all generations, and is a great way to induce children to eat more vegetables. Serve it with cornbread or biscuits.

Yield: 4-6 servings | **Active time:** 30 minutes | **Start to finish:** 30 minutes

SALAD

1 pound boneless, skinless chicken breast halves
Salt and freshly ground black pepper to taste
1/2 cup all-purpose flour
3 large eggs
1/4 cup whole milk
1 1/2 cups plain bread crumbs
6-9 cups bite-size pieces salad greens of your choice, rinsed and dried
2 carrots, peeled and cut into thin strips
1 green bell pepper, seeds and ribs removed, and cut into thin slices
1 small red onion, peeled, halved lengthwise, and cut into thin rings
2 cups vegetable oil for frying

DRESSING

3 tablespoons honey
3 tablespoons Dijon mustard
1/3 cup cider vinegar
Salt and freshly ground black pepper to taste
1/2 cup olive oil

1. Rinse chicken and pat dry with paper towels. Trim chicken of all visible fat, and cut chicken into 1-inch nuggets. Sprinkle nuggets with salt and pepper. Place flour on a sheet of plastic wrap, beat eggs with milk in a shallow bowl, and place bread crumbs on another sheet of plastic wrap. Dip chicken pieces in flour, shaking to remove any excess, then dip in egg mixture, and then in bread crumbs.

2. Arrange greens, carrots, green pepper, and onion on individual plates or on a serving platter. Combine honey, mustard, vinegar, salt, and pepper in a jar with a tight-fitting lid. Shake well, add olive oil, and shake well again. Set aside.

3. Heat vegetable oil in a deep-sided saucepan over medium-high heat to a temperature of 375°F. Add chicken pieces, being careful not to crowd the pan, and fry for 5 minutes, or until golden brown and chicken is cooked through and no longer pink; this may have to be done in batches. Remove chicken from the pan with a slotted spoon and drain well on paper towels.

4. To serve, arrange chicken pieces on top of the salad, and drizzle dressing over all.

Note: Chicken and dressing can be prepared 1 day in advance and refrigerated, tightly covered. Reheat chicken, uncovered, in a 375°F oven for 8–10 minutes, or until hot and crisp. Allow dressing to sit at room temperature for at least 30 minutes if chilled.

Variation:

- Substitute panko bread crumbs, crushed cornflakes, or crushed popped rice cereal for the bread crumbs.

Chicken and Potato Salad

Both chicken and potatoes are delicious when dressed with a mayonnaise dressing laced with mustard, and they're even better together. In addition to the usual vegetables, some chopped sweet pickle adds crunch and flavor.

Yield: 4–6 servings | **Active time:** 20 minutes | **Start to finish:** 1½ hours, including 45 minutes to chill

1 pound redskin potatoes, scrubbed and cut into 1-inch cubes

¼ cup distilled white vinegar

3 tablespoons granulated sugar

Salt and freshly ground black pepper to taste

¾ cup mayonnaise

3 tablespoons Dijon mustard

2–3 cups diced cooked chicken

½ sweet onion, such as Bermuda or Vidalia, peeled and diced

1 green bell pepper, seeds and ribs removed, and diced

2 celery ribs, rinsed, trimmed, and diced

3 hard-cooked eggs, peeled and diced

½ cup chopped bread-and-butter pickle

2–3 cups shredded iceberg lettuce, rinsed and dried

1. Place potatoes in a saucepan and cover with cold salted water. Bring to a boil over high heat, and cook for 10–12 minutes, or until potatoes are tender when pierced with the tip of a knife. Drain potatoes, and place them in a 9 x 13-inch baking pan.

2. While potatoes cook, combine vinegar, sugar, salt, and pepper in a bowl, and stir well to dissolve sugar. Pour mixture over hot potato cubes, and let potatoes cool for 30 minutes.

3. Combine mayonnaise and mustard in a small bowl, and whisk well. Add chicken, onion, green bell pepper, celery, eggs, and pickle to the dish with potatoes. Pour dressing over salad, and stir well to combine. Chill for 15 minutes, refrigerated, and then serve, mounding salad on top of lettuce on individual plates or on a serving platter.

Note: The salad can be prepared up to 1 day in advance and refrigerated, tightly covered.

Variation:

- Substitute sweet potatoes or yams for the white potatoes.

Chicken Salad with Blue Cheese, Grapes, and Walnuts

This salad is a variation on the Waldorf salad of my youth. Grapes take the place of apples, and the creamy dressing sparkles with the addition of heady blue cheese. Serve it with some hot rolls.

Yield: 4-6 servings | **Active time:** 20 minutes | **Start to finish:** 20 minutes

- ½ cup chopped walnuts
- ½ cup mayonnaise
- ½ cup crumbled blue cheese
- ¼ cup sour cream
- 2 tablespoons cider vinegar
- 2 tablespoons chopped fresh parsley
- 2 scallions, white parts and 3 inches of green tops, rinsed, trimmed, and chopped
- Salt and freshly ground black pepper to taste
- 2-3 cups diced cooked chicken
- 1½ cups seedless grapes, halved
- 2 celery ribs, rinsed, trimmed, and diced
- 2-3 cups shredded iceberg lettuce

1. Preheat the oven to 350°F, and line a baking sheet with aluminum foil. Bake walnuts for 5-7 minutes, or until browned. Remove walnuts from the oven, and set aside.
2. Combine mayonnaise, blue cheese, sour cream, vinegar, parsley, scallions, salt, and pepper in a mixing bowl, and whisk well.
3. Combine chicken, grapes, celery, walnuts, and dressing in a mixing bowl, and stir well. Serve immediately, mounding salad on top of lettuce on individual plates or on a serving platter.

Note: The salad can be prepared up to 1 day in advance and refrigerated, tightly covered.

Variations:
- Substitute pecans or almonds for the walnuts.
- Substitute diced apple for the grapes.

Grilled Chicken Caesar Salad

Caesar salad has nothing to do with Rome. It was the invention of Caesar Cardini, who owned a restaurant in Tijuana, Mexico. The salad caught on with his Hollywood patrons and became popularized at such Los Angeles bastions as Chasen's. In my recipe the chicken is marinated in the dressing, which boosts its flavor.

Yield: 4–6 servings | **Active time:** 25 minutes | **Start to finish:** 35 minutes

> 1 pound boneless, skinless chicken breast halves
> 1 large egg
> 1 (2-ounce) tube anchovy paste
> 5 garlic cloves, peeled and minced
> ¼ cup lemon juice
> 2 tablespoons Dijon mustard
> ½ cup olive oil, divided
> Freshly ground black pepper to taste
> 6–8 (½-inch-thick) slices French or Italian bread
> 6–8 cups bite-size pieces romaine lettuce, rinsed and dried
> ½ cup freshly grated Parmesan cheese
> 4–6 anchovy fillets (optional)

1. Light a charcoal or gas grill, or preheat the oven broiler.
2. Rinse chicken and pat dry with paper towels. Trim chicken breasts of all visible fat, and pound to an even thickness of ½ inch between 2 sheets of plastic wrap. Place chicken breasts in a mixing bowl.
3. To prepare dressing, bring a small saucepan of water to a boil over high heat. Add egg and boil for 1 minute. Remove egg from water with a slotted spoon and break it into a jar with a tight-fitting lid, scraping the inside of the shell. Add anchovy paste, garlic, lemon juice, and mustard, and shake well. Add ⅓ cup olive oil, and shake well again. Season to taste with pepper.
4. Reserve ½ of dressing, and mix remaining dressing into bowl with chicken breasts. Use reserved oil to brush both sides of bread.
5. Grill or broil chicken for 2–3 minutes per side, or until chicken is cooked through and no longer pink. Grill or broil bread for 1–2 minutes per side, or until toasted. Remove chicken from the grill, and cut into thin slices against the grain. Remove bread from the grill, and cut into ½-inch croutons.

6. To serve, combine croutons, lettuce, and Parmesan in a mixing bowl, and toss with enough dressing to coat lightly. Mound mixture onto a serving platter or individual plates, and top with chicken slices. Serve immediately, topped with anchovy fillets, if using. Pass extra dressing separately.

Note: The dressing can be made up to 1 day in advance and refrigerated, tightly covered. Bring to room temperature before using.

Variation:
- Substitute olive bread, herb bread, or cheese bread for the French bread for the croutons.

While I adore the salty, robust flavor anchovy paste gives foods, I realize that there are distinct camps about these tiny fish. They are primarily used for salt, so if you hate the fishy flavor, just replace the paste with salt.

Mexican Grilled Chicken Salad

I based this recipe on the concept of the popular Mexican fajita; the chicken is grilled and then joined with grilled onions and slices of pepper in a spicy dressing. Crushed tortilla chips add additional texture to the salad.

Yield: 4–6 servings | **Active time:** 20 minutes | **Start to finish:** 1 hour

1 pound boneless, skinless chicken breast halves
3 tablespoons orange juice
3 tablespoons lime juice
1 tablespoon cider vinegar
2 tablespoons chopped fresh cilantro
2 garlic cloves, peeled and minced
1 small jalapeño or serrano chile, seeds and ribs removed, and finely chopped
Salt and freshly ground black pepper to taste
1/2 cup olive oil
2 tablespoons chili powder
1 tablespoon ground cumin
1 large green bell pepper, seeds and ribs removed, and quartered lengthwise
1 large red onion, peeled and cut into 1/2-inch slices
4–6 cups bite-size pieces romaine lettuce, rinsed and dried
2 large tomatoes, rinsed, cored, seeded, and diced
2 cups broken tortilla chips

1. Light a charcoal or gas grill, or preheat the oven broiler.
2. Rinse chicken and pat dry with paper towels. Trim chicken breasts of all visible fat, and pound to an even thickness of 1/2 inch between 2 sheets of plastic wrap. Place chicken breasts in a heavy resealable plastic bag.
3. Combine orange juice, lime juice, vinegar, cilantro, garlic, chile, salt, and pepper in a jar with a tight-fitting lid, and shake well. Add olive oil, and shake well again. Pour 1/2 of dressing into the bag with chicken, and add chili powder and cumin. Mix well. Marinate at room temperature for 20 minutes, turning the bag occasionally.

4. Remove chicken from marinade and discard marinade. Grill or broil chicken for 2–3 minutes per side, uncovered, or until chicken is cooked through and no longer pink. Remove chicken from the grill, and cut into thin slices against the grain. Brush vegetables with dressing. Grill pepper sections and onion slices for 4–5 minutes per side. Cut peppers into strips, and separate onion slices into rings.

5. Combine lettuce and tomato in a large mixing bowl. Toss salad with $\frac{1}{2}$ of remaining dressing. Mound mixture onto a serving platter or individual plates, and top with chicken, pepper, and onion slices. Sprinkle broken tortilla chips over all, and serve immediately, passing extra dressing separately.

Note: The dressing can be made up to 1 day in advance and refrigerated, tightly covered. Bring to room temperature before using.

Variation:

- Omit the chile for a milder dish.

Guacamole Chicken Salad

This chicken salad has all the ingredients of a traditional Mexican guacamole, including creamy and buttery avocado.

Yield: 4-6 servings | **Active time:** 20 minutes | **Start to finish:** 20 minutes

> 1 ripe avocado, peeled and diced
> ³/₄ cup plain nonfat yogurt or sour cream
> ¹/₄ cup lime juice
> 3 garlic cloves, peeled
> 1 jalapeño or serrano chile, seeds and ribs removed
> Salt and freshly ground black pepper to taste
> 2-3 cups shredded cooked chicken
> 2-3 ripe plum tomatoes, rinsed, cored, seeded, and diced
> ¹/₂ cucumber, peeled, seeded, and diced
> ¹/₂ small red onion, peeled and diced
> ¹/₄ cup chopped fresh cilantro
> 2-3 cups shredded iceberg lettuce

1. Combine avocado, yogurt, lime juice, garlic, chile, salt, and pepper in a food processor fitted with the steel blade or in a blender. Puree until smooth.
2. Combine chicken, tomatoes, cucumber, onion, and cilantro in a mixing bowl. Pour dressing over salad, and stir well to combine. Serve immediately, mounding salad on top of lettuce on individual plates or on a serving platter.

Note: The salad can be prepared up to 1 day in advance and refrigerated, tightly covered. Push a sheet of plastic wrap directly into the surface of the salad to prevent discoloration.

Variation:
- Substitute 1-2 chipotle peppers in adobo sauce for the fresh chile; it will give the salad a smoky nuance.

Avocadoes are expensive, so you certainly don't want to waste one. If you cut one open and it's not ripe, rub the exposed surfaces with mayonnaise, push the halves back together, and allow it to continue ripening at room temperature.

Tabbouleh Chicken Salad with Feta

Tabbouleh, pronounced *ta-BOOL-a*, is the potato salad of the Middle East; it's served as an accompaniment to almost everything and as an entree if augmented with protein. The characteristic ingredients are bulgur, parsley, and lemon juice. From that base it's open to interpretation.

Yield: 4–6 servings | **Active time:** 15 minutes | **Start to finish:** 45 minutes, including 15 minutes for chilling

 $^3/_4$ pound bulgur wheat
 $^1/_2$ cup lemon juice
 $2^1/_3$ cups very hot water
 Salt and freshly ground black pepper to taste
 2–3 cups diced cooked chicken
 1 cucumber, rinsed, seeded, and chopped
 4 ripe plum tomatoes, rinsed, cored, seeded, and chopped
 1 small red onion, peeled and minced
 2 garlic cloves, peeled and minced
 1 cup chopped fresh parsley
 $^1/_2$ cup olive oil
 2–3 cups shredded iceberg lettuce, rinsed and dried
 $^1/_2$ cup crumbled feta cheese

1. Place bulgur in a large mixing bowl and add lemon juice and hot water. Let stand, covered, for 30 minutes, or until bulgur is tender. Drain off any excess liquid, and season to taste with salt and pepper.
2. Add chicken, cucumbers, tomatoes, onion, garlic, and parsley to bulgur, and toss to combine. Add olive oil, a few tablespoons at a time, to make salad moist but not runny. Season to taste with salt and pepper.
3. Refrigerate salad for at least 15 minutes before serving. Serve immediately, mounding salad on top of lettuce on individual plates or on a serving platter. Sprinkle each serving with feta.

Note: The tabbouleh can be made up to 1 day in advance and refrigerated, tightly covered.

Variation:

- Substitute $^1/_4$ cup chopped fresh mint for $^1/_4$ of the chopped parsley.

Satay-Style Chicken Salad

Satays are served with a peanut sauce, and such a sauce becomes the dressing for this salad. The salad also includes lots of vegetables as well as chopped peanuts for crunch. Serve it with a chilled rice salad.

Yield: 4–6 servings | **Active time:** 20 minutes | **Start to finish:** 20 minutes

- $2/3$ cup chunky peanut butter
- 2 tablespoons firmly packed dark brown sugar
- $1/4$ cup boiling water
- 3 scallions, white parts and 4 inches of green tops, rinsed, trimmed, and chopped
- 2 garlic cloves, peeled and minced
- 2 tablespoons soy sauce
- 2 tablespoons rice vinegar
- 2 tablespoons Asian sesame oil*
- 1 tablespoon grated ginger
- 1 tablespoon Chinese chile paste with garlic*
- 2–3 cups shredded cooked chicken
- 2–3 cups shredded Napa cabbage
- 2 celery ribs, rinsed, trimmed, and thinly sliced on the diagonal
- $1/2$ green bell pepper, seeds and ribs removed, and thinly sliced
- $1/2$ small red onion, peeled and thinly sliced
- $1/2$ cup chopped salted peanuts
- $1/4$ cup chopped fresh cilantro

1. Combine peanut butter, brown sugar, and water in a mixing bowl, and whisk well. Add scallions, garlic, soy sauce, vinegar, sesame oil, ginger, and chile paste, and whisk again. Set aside.
2. Combine chicken, cabbage, celery, green pepper, and onion in a mixing bowl. Pour dressing over salad, and stir well to combine. Serve immediately, sprinkling each serving with peanuts and cilantro.

Note: The salad can be made up to 1 day in advance and refrigerated, tightly covered.

*Available in the Asian aisle of most supermarkets and in specialty markets.

Variations:
- Omit the chile paste for a milder dish.
- Add 2 cups cooked and chilled white rice or pasta.

When you're using "sturdy" vegetables like cabbage, celery, and bell peppers, you can make a salad much further in advance than when using "tender" vegetables like tomato and scallions.

Provençal Grilled Chicken Salad

You are lighting the grill to cook the vegetables as well as the chicken for this flavorful salad that is then arranged with crisp raw vegetables as well. The dressing is a classic French vinaigrette, or you can substitute any of your favorite dressings.

Yield: 4–6 servings | **Active time:** 25 minutes | **Start to finish:** 35 minutes

1 pound boneless, skinless chicken breast halves
⅓ cup red wine vinegar
½ small onion, peeled and chopped
2 garlic cloves, peeled and minced
1 tablespoon Dijon mustard
2 teaspoons granulated sugar
2 teaspoons herbes de Provence
Salt and freshly ground black pepper to taste
1 cup olive oil
2 small zucchini, rinsed, trimmed, and quartered lengthwise
½ (1-pound) eggplant, rinsed, trimmed, and cut into ½-inch slices
1 green bell pepper, seeds and ribs removed, and cut into 1-inch strips
4–6 cups bite-size pieces romaine lettuce, rinsed and dried
½ small red onion, peeled, halved, and thinly sliced
1 cup cherry tomatoes, rinsed, stemmed, and halved

1. Light a charcoal or gas grill, or preheat the oven broiler.
2. Rinse chicken and pat dry with paper towels. Trim chicken breasts of all visible fat, and pound to an even thickness of ½ inch between 2 sheets of plastic wrap. Place chicken breasts in a mixing bowl.
3. To prepare dressing, combine vinegar, onion, garlic, mustard, sugar, herbes de Provence, salt, and pepper in a jar with a tight-fitting lid, and shake well. Add olive oil, and shake well again. Divide dressing into 2 containers.
4. Brush dressing on zucchini, eggplant, and bell pepper, and then mix remaining dressing from 1 bowl into the mixing bowl with chicken breasts.

5. Grill or broil chicken and vegetables for 2–3 minutes per side, uncovered, or until chicken is cooked through and no longer pink and vegetables are crisp-tender. Remove chicken from the grill, and cut into thin slices against the grain. Remove vegetables from the grill, and cut into bite-size pieces.

6. To serve, combine lettuce, red onion, and cherry tomatoes in a mixing bowl, and toss with enough of remaining dressing to coat lightly. Mound mixture onto a serving platter or individual plates, and top with chicken slices and vegetables. Serve immediately, passing extra dressing separately.

Note: The dressing can be made up to 1 day in advance and refrigerated, tightly covered. Bring to room temperature before using.

Variation:

- Substitute mushrooms for the eggplant and yellow squash for the zucchini.

Chicken and Pasta Salad Niçoise

Traditional French *salade Niçoise* is a composed salad made with tuna, but the same ingredients create a fantastic chicken salad, too. And the pasta makes it a whole meal.

Yield: 4–6 servings | **Active time:** 15 minutes | **Start to finish:** 25 minutes

½ pound green beans, rinsed, trimmed, and cut into 1-inch lengths
⅔ pound small pasta shells or gemelli
¼ cup lemon juice
1 tablespoon anchovy paste
1 tablespoon Dijon mustard
1 tablespoon chopped fresh parsley
1 teaspoon herbes de Provence
2 garlic cloves, peeled and minced
Salt and freshly ground black pepper to taste
½ cup olive oil
2–3 cups diced cooked chicken
½ green bell pepper, seeds and ribs removed, and chopped
½ small red onion, peeled and chopped
3 ripe plum tomatoes, rinsed, cored, seeded, and chopped
⅓ cup oil-cured black olives
2–3 cups bite-size pieces salad greens, rinsed and dried
2 hard-cooked eggs, cut into wedges (optional)

1. Bring a pot of salted water to a boil, and have a bowl of ice water handy. Boil green beans for 2–3 minutes, or until crisp-tender. Remove beans from the water with a slotted spoon, and plunge them into the ice water to stop the cooking action. Drain when chilled, and place beans in a large mixing bowl.
2. Add pasta to the boiling water and cook according to package directions until al dente. Drain and run under cold water until cold. Add pasta to the mixing bowl.
3. While pasta cooks, combine lemon juice, anchovy paste, mustard, parsley, herbes de Provence, garlic, salt, and pepper in a jar with a tight-fitting lid, and shake well. Add olive oil, and shake well again.

4. Add dressing to the mixing bowl, and allow to sit for 5 minutes so pasta absorbs flavor. Add chicken, green bell pepper, onion, tomatoes, and olives, and toss. To serve, arrange lettuce on individual plates or on a serving platter, and top with salad. Serve immediately, garnished with egg wedges, if using.

Note: The salad can be prepared up to 1 day in advance and refrigerated, tightly covered. Allow it to sit at room temperature for 30 minutes prior to serving.

Variation:

- If you're not a fan, omit the anchovy paste, but then add salt to taste to the dressing.

Running pasta under cold water after draining speeds up the completion of all pasta salads. It's not as effective to soak it in cold water because the pasta can become soggy.

Moroccan Chicken and Couscous Salad

Couscous is a tiny granular pasta that "cooks" just by being mixed into boiling water. In this healthful salad, the traditional North African spice mix of cumin and coriander flavors the light dressing.

Yield: 4–6 servings | **Active time:** 15 minutes | **Start to finish:** 45 minutes, including 15 minutes to chill

    3 cups water
    2 cups couscous
    ½ cup chopped raisins
    ½ cup orange juice
    2 tablespoons balsamic vinegar or red wine vinegar
    2 garlic cloves, peeled and minced
    2 teaspoons ground cumin
    1 teaspoon ground coriander
    Salt and freshly ground black pepper to taste
    ⅓ cup olive oil
    2–3 cups diced cooked chicken
    4 scallions, white parts and 3 inches of green tops, rinsed,
        trimmed, and sliced
    2 ripe plum tomatoes, rinsed, cored, seeded, and diced
    1 cup canned garbanzo beans, drained and rinsed
    ⅓ cup chopped kalamata olives
    ¼ cup chopped fresh cilantro
    2–3 cups shredded iceberg lettuce

1. Bring water to a boil in a saucepan over high heat. Stir in couscous and raisins, remove the pan from the heat, and let stand 5 minutes, covered. Fluff couscous with a fork, and transfer it to a 9 x 13-inch baking dish. Refrigerate for 15 minutes, or until cooled.
2. While couscous cools, combine orange juice, vinegar, garlic, cumin, coriander, salt, and pepper in a jar with a tight-fitting lid, and shake well. Add olive oil, and shake well again. Set aside.
3. Add chicken, scallions, tomatoes, garbanzo beans, olives, and cilantro to the pan with couscous. Pour dressing over salad, and stir well to combine. Serve immediately, mounding salad on top of lettuce on individual plates or on a serving platter.

Note: The salad can be prepared up to 1 day in advance and refrigerated, tightly covered.

Variation:

- Substitute chopped dried apricots or dried cranberries for the raisins.

Greek Chicken Salad

Sharp feta cheese and a tart dressing made with lemon juice and oregano are the hallmarks of a Greek salad, and that Mediterranean favorite is transformed into a more filling meal with the addition of cooked chicken.

Yield: 4–6 servings | **Active time:** 20 minutes | **Start to finish:** 20 minutes

> 1/3 cup lemon juice
> 2 tablespoons chopped fresh parsley
> 3 garlic cloves, peeled and minced
> 2 teaspoons dried oregano
> Salt and freshly ground black pepper to taste
> 1/2 cup olive oil
> 6–9 cups bite-size pieces iceberg lettuce, rinsed and dried
> 2 small cucumbers, peeled, seeded, and cut into 1/2-inch dice
> 4 ripe plum tomatoes, rinsed, cored, seeded, and cut into 1/2-inch dice
> 2–3 cups diced cooked chicken
> 1/2 red onion, peeled and cut into 1/2-inch dice
> 1/2 cup sliced kalamata olives
> 1/2 cup crumbled feta cheese

1. Combine lemon juice, parsley, garlic, oregano, salt, and pepper in a jar with a tight-fitting lid, and shake well. Add olive oil, and shake well again.
2. Combine lettuce, cucumber, tomato, chicken, onion, and olives in a large mixing bowl, and toss with enough dressing to moisten ingredients well. Serve immediately, sprinkling feta over each serving and passing extra dressing separately.

Note: The salad ingredients and dressing can be prepared up to 6 hours in advance and refrigerated, tightly covered. Do not dress the salad until just prior to serving.

Variation:
- Substitute goat cheese or blue cheese for the feta cheese.

Gazpacho Chicken Salad

No, this isn't a mistake; I know that gazpacho is a Spanish vegetable soup. But all the ingredients are in this refreshing salad, which is napped with a dressing similar to the other flavors in the soup.

Yield: 4–6 servings | **Active time:** 15 minutes | **Start to finish:** 25 minutes

2–3 cups cooked chicken, cut into ½-inch dice

1 green bell pepper, seeds and ribs removed, and cut into ½-inch dice

2 cucumbers, rinsed, seeded, and cut into ½-inch dice

1 small red onion, peeled and cut into ½-inch dice

3 large ripe tomatoes, rinsed, cored, seeded, and cut into ½-inch dice

⅓ cup chopped fresh cilantro

1 jalapeño or serrano chile, seeds and ribs removed, and finely chopped

3 garlic cloves, peeled and minced

¼ cup balsamic vinegar

Salt and freshly ground black pepper to taste

⅓ cup olive oil

4–6 cups chopped iceberg or romaine lettuce

1. Combine chicken, green pepper, cucumbers, red onion, and tomatoes in a large mixing bowl.
2. Combine cilantro, chile, garlic, vinegar, salt, and pepper in a jar with a tight-fitting lid. Shake well, add olive oil, and shake well again. Pour dressing over salad, and refrigerate 10 minutes.
3. Arrange lettuce on individual plates or a serving platter and mound salad in the center. Serve immediately.

Note: The salad can be prepared 4 hours in advance and refrigerated, tightly covered. Do not add dressing until 10 minutes before serving.

Spanish Chicken Salad with White Beans and Oranges

Oranges are an ingredient commonly found in Spanish cuisine, and their sweet flavor is amplified by the heady aroma of smoked paprika in the dressing.

Yield: 4–6 servings | **Active time:** 15 minutes | **Start to finish:** 30 minutes

> 2–3 cups diced cooked chicken
> 1 (15-ounce) can white cannellini beans, drained and rinsed
> 2 navel oranges, peeled and cut into ½-inch dice
> ½ green bell pepper, seeds and ribs removed, cut into ½-inch dice
> ¼ cup chopped fresh cilantro
> 3 garlic cloves, peeled and minced
> 1 small onion, peeled and finely chopped
> 2 tablespoons smoked Spanish paprika
> 1 teaspoon ground cumin
> ¼ teaspoon ground cinnamon
> ⅓ cup orange juice
> 3 tablespoons lime juice
> 3 tablespoons cider vinegar
> Salt and cayenne to taste
> ⅓ cup olive oil
> 2–3 cups shredded mixed salad greens, rinsed and dried

1. Combine chicken, beans, oranges, green bell pepper, and cilantro in a mixing bowl.

2. Combine garlic, onion, paprika, cumin, cinnamon, orange juice, lime juice, vinegar, salt, and cayenne in a jar with a tight-fitting lid. Shake well, add olive oil, and shake well again.

3. Pour dressing over salad, and stir well to combine. Refrigerate salad for at least 15 minutes before serving. Serve immediately, mounding salad on top of lettuce on individual plates or on a serving platter.

Note: The salad can be made 1 day in advance and refrigerated, tightly covered.

Variation:
- Substitute mango for the oranges.

Smoked Spanish paprika is a relative newcomer to the spice section of the supermarket, and I adore it. The peppers are dried, and then smoked before they're ground into a powder. They give a smoky nuance to dishes that's subtle, not overpowering like chemical "liquid smoke."

Appendix A:
Metric Conversion Tables

The scientifically precise calculations needed for baking are not necessary when cooking conventionally. The tables in this appendix are designed for general cooking. If making conversions for baking, grab your calculator and compute the exact figure.

CONVERTING OUNCES TO GRAMS

The numbers in the following table are approximate. To reach the exact quantity of grams, multiply the number of ounces by 28.35.

Ounces	Grams
1 ounce	30 grams
2 ounces	60 grams
3 ounces	85 grams
4 ounces	115 grams
5 ounces	140 grams
6 ounces	180 grams
7 ounces	200 grams
8 ounces	225 grams
9 ounces	250 grams
10 ounces	285 grams
11 ounces	300 grams
12 ounces	340 grams
13 ounces	370 grams
14 ounces	400 grams
15 ounces	425 grams
16 ounces	450 grams

CONVERTING QUARTS TO LITERS

The numbers in the following table are approximate. To reach the exact amount of liters, multiply the number of quarts by 0.95.

Quarts	Liter
1 cup (¼ quart)	¼ liter
1 pint (½ quart)	½ liter
1 quart	1 liter
2 quarts	2 liters
2½ quarts	2½ liters
3 quarts	2¾ liters
4 quarts	3¾ liters
5 quarts	4¾ liters
6 quarts	5½ liters
7 quarts	6½ liters
8 quarts	7½ liters

CONVERTING POUNDS TO GRAMS AND KILOGRAMS

The numbers in the following table are approximate. To reach the exact quantity of grams, multiply the number of pounds by 453.6.

Pounds	Grams; Kilograms
1 pound	450 grams
1½ pounds	675 grams
2 pounds	900 grams
2½ pounds	1,125 grams; 1¼ kilograms
3 pounds	1,350 grams
3½ pounds	1,500 grams; 1½ kilograms
4 pounds	1,800 grams
4½ pounds	2 kilograms
5 pounds	2¼ kilograms
5½ pounds	2½ kilograms
6 pounds	2¾ kilograms
6½ pounds	3 kilograms
7 pounds	3¼ kilograms
7½ pounds	3½ kilograms
8 pounds	3¾ kilograms

CONVERTING FAHRENHEIT TO CELSIUS

The numbers in the following table are approximate. To reach the exact temperature, subtract 32 from the Fahrenheit reading, multiply the number by 5, and then divide by 9.

Degrees Fahrenheit	Degrees Celsius
170°F	77°C
180°F	82°C
190°F	88°C
200°F	95°C
225°F	110°C
250°F	120°C
300°F	150°C
325°F	165°C
350°F	180°C
375°F	190°C
400°F	205°C
425°F	220°C
450°F	230°C
475°F	245°C
500°F	260°C

CONVERTING INCHES TO CENTIMETERS

The numbers in the following table are approximate. To reach the exact number of centimeters, multiply the number of inches by 2.54.

Inches	Centimeters
½ inch	1.5 centimeters
1 inch	2.5 centimeters
2 inches	5 centimeters
3 inches	8 centimeters
4 inches	10 centimeters
5 inches	13 centimeters
6 inches	15 centimeters
7 inches	18 centimeters
8 inches	20 centimeters
9 inches	23 centimeters
10 inches	25 centimeters
11 inches	28 centimeters
12 inches	30 centimeters

Table of Weights and Measures of Common Ingredients

Food	Quantity	Yield
Apples	1 pound	2$\frac{1}{2}$–3 cups sliced
Avocado	1 pound	1 cup mashed
Bananas	1 medium	1 cup sliced
Bell peppers	1 pound	3-4 cups sliced
Blueberries	1 pound	3$\frac{1}{3}$ cups
Butter	$\frac{1}{4}$ pound (1 stick)	8 tablespoons
Cabbage	1 pound	4 cups packed shredded
Carrots	1 pound	3 cups diced or sliced
Chocolate, morsels	12 ounces	2 cups
Chocolate, bulk	1 ounce	3 tablespoons grated
Cocoa powder	1 ounce	$\frac{1}{4}$ cup
Coconut, flaked	7 ounces	2$\frac{1}{2}$ cups
Cream	$\frac{1}{2}$ pint (1 cup)	2 cups whipped
Cream cheese	8 ounces	1 cup
Flour	1 pound	4 cups
Lemons	1 medium	3 tablespoons juice
Lemons	1 medium	2 teaspoons zest
Milk	1 quart	4 cups
Molasses	12 ounces	1$\frac{1}{2}$ cups
Mushrooms	1 pound	5 cups sliced
Onions	1 medium	$\frac{1}{2}$ cup chopped
Peaches	1 pound	2 cups sliced
Peanuts	5 ounces	1 cup
Pecans	6 ounces	1$\frac{1}{2}$ cups
Pineapple	1 medium	3 cups diced
Potatoes	1 pound	3 cups sliced
Raisins	1 pound	3 cups
Rice	1 pound	2 to 2$\frac{1}{2}$ cups raw
Spinach	1 pound	$\frac{3}{4}$ cup cooked
Squash, summer	1 pound	3$\frac{1}{2}$ cups sliced
Strawberries	1 pint	1$\frac{1}{2}$ cups sliced

Food	Quantity	Yield
Sugar, brown	1 pound	2$\frac{1}{4}$ cups, packed
Sugar, confectioners'	1 pound	4 cups
Sugar, granulated	1 pound	2$\frac{1}{4}$ cups
Tomatoes	1 pound	1$\frac{1}{2}$ cups pulp
Walnuts	4 ounces	1 cup

TABLE OF LIQUID MEASUREMENTS

Dash	=	less than $\frac{1}{8}$ teaspoon
3 teaspoons	=	1 tablespoon
2 tablespoons	=	1 ounce
8 tablespoons	=	$\frac{1}{2}$ cup
2 cups	=	1 pint
1 quart	=	2 pints
1 gallon	=	4 quarts

Index